MW00710586

LAN Management with SNMP and RMON

Gilbert Held

WILEY COMPUTER PUBLISHING

John Wiley & Sons, Inc.
New York • Chichester • Brisbane
• Toronto • Singapore

Publisher: Katherine Schowalter
Editor: Theresa Hudson
Managing Editor: Angela Murphy
Text Design & Composition: Publishers' Design and Production Services, Inc.

Designations used by companies to distinguish their products are often claimed as trademarks. In all instances where John Wiley & Sons, Inc., is aware of a claim, the product names appear in initial capital or all capital letters. Readers, however, should contact the appropriate companies for more complete information regarding trademarks and registration.

This text is printed on acid-free paper.
Copyright © 1996 by John Wiley & Sons, Inc.
All rights reserved. Published simultaneously in Canada.

This publication is designed to provide accurate and authoritative information in regard to the subject matter covered. It is sold with the understanding that the publisher is not engaged in rendering legal, accounting, or other professional service. If legal advice or other expert assistance is required, the services of a competent professional person should be sought.

Reproduction or translation of any part of this work beyond that permitted by section 107 or 108 of the 1976 United States Copyright Act without the permission of the copyright owner is unlawful. Requests for permission or further information should be addressed to the Permissions Department, John Wiley & Sons, Inc.

Library of Congress Cataloging-in-Publication Data:

Held, Gilbert.
    LAN management with SNMP and RMON / Gilbert Held.
      p. cm.
    Includes index.
    ISBN 0-471-14736-2 (pb : alk. paper)
    1. Computer networks—Management. 2. Computer network protocols—Standards. 3. Simple Network Management Protocol (Computer network protocol) I. Title.
TK5105.5H4425   1996
004.6'8—dc20   96-14112

Printed in the United States of America
10 9 8 7 6 5 4 3 2 1

Contents

Preface

Local area networks represent one of the most rapidly evolving fields of communications technology. Similar to other fields of communications technology, the ability to manage LANs requires the use of certain tools as well as the ability to understand how to effectively use such tools. Two of the most important tools that provide a LAN management capability are SNMP and RMON, both of which are the focus of this book.

Although it is important to obtain an appreciation for the methods used to transport SNMP commands, this book was not written as a developer's guide. Instead, the goal of this book is to provide LAN mangers and administrators with practical, informative information concerning the use of SNMP and RMON, as well as commercial software products developed to use those tools.

This book examines the SNMP protocol, the construction of the Management Information Base, and the use of RMON probes. Using this information as a base, it explores the use of several network management tools that are constructed upon the use of SNMP and RMON. As a practical, informative book written for LAN managers and administrators, it not only covers the retrieval of information from SNMP- and RMON-compatible devices, but also examines what the range of values retrievable can mean. Thus, although it is important to understand how to retrieve data elements, it also focuses attention upon an equally important topic—how to interpret the effect of values retrieved.

Since few LANs are isolated islands of communications, and are either interconnected via a wide area network transmission facility to other LANs or support modem dial-in or dial-out capability, it also focuses on device management. In doing so it examines how SNMP can be used to manage such diverse products as bridges, switches, and even a UPS.

As an author I place a considerable value upon reader feedback and I welcome comments you may wish to provide concerning my coverage of topics, new topics you believe should be covered in a revised edition of this book, or other comments you may wish to share. You can write to me through my publisher whose address is printed on the back cover of this book.

ACKNOWLEDGMENTS

Although many readers associate an author only with a book, in actuality its publication represents the culmination of a team effort that deserves acknowledgment.

I would like to thank Terri Hudson and Katherine Schowalter at John Wiley & Sons for backing my writing effort. The ability to illustrate many SNMP and RMON operational examples resulted from the generosity of NetManage, LogTel Computer Communications, and Triticom, as they provided evaluation copies of several software products I used to illustrate key concepts throughout this book.

As an old-fashioned writer who frequently travels, I prefer to use paper and pen to write books and draft illustrations. Once again, I am indebted to Ms. Junnie Heath and Mrs. Linda Hayes for their fine efforts in converting my written notes and hand-drawn illustrations into a manuscript. Last but not least, I am indebted to my family for their cooperation and understanding over the past year, especially during evenings and weekends when I experimented with the construction and operation of several *in-house* LANs to obtain examples appropriate for use in this book.

Introduction to Network Management

1

A LAN represents a special type of network, as it can be both local and, via wide area communications facilities, remote from a management console. Thus, the management of a LAN requires the use of tools and techniques that provide users with the ability to observe and control the flow of information on a local or distant network.

Network management has its roots in the mainframe and minicomputer era, with computer manufacturers and third-party software developers producing proprietary products dating back to the 1960s. Those products were originally developed to manage hierarchically structured networks, in which terminals were connected to controllers, which in turn were connected to mainframes or minicomputers. Although only a limited number of mainframe computer manufacturers survived the 1980s, their proprietary network management systems made it both expensive and difficult to mix and match products from third-party vendors that could be managed from a central console. In fact, in many organizations it is still quite common to visit a network management center whose series of consoles may resemble the interior of the Houston Space Center, with separate systems used to manage leased lines, dial modems, leased line modems, multiplexers, data service units, and other communications devices. Recognizing this interoperability problem resulted in the development of a series of standards that, while applicable to both LANs and WANs have been quick to be adopted by manufacturers of LAN products. Two of those standards are the Simple Network Management Protocol (SNMP) and the Remote Monitoring (RMON) Management Information Base (MIB), which can be considered to represent key tools you can use for LAN management.

This introductory chapter will provide you with a foundation concerning the role of SNMP and RMON to facilitate LAN management, and will first review the rationale for network management, which should indicate the importance of this field to facilitate both operational and planning activities. Then the network management process will be described to include the Open System Interconnect (OSI) framework for network management functional areas and its relationship to LAN management. This discussion will be followed by an overview of tools and systems that facilitate network management to include SNMP and RMON, as well as their relationship via the use of a network management platform to the OSI network management functional areas. Thus, this chapter will make you aware of the role of SNMP and RMON in LAN management, and how these standards facilitate the network management process.

RATIONALE FOR NETWORK MANAGEMENT

There are a number of reasons used to justify the purchase of network management products, with the ability to obtain information concerning the operational status of equipment and communications facilities usually at the top of a justification list.

Alarm Processing

Through the use of an appropriate network management system, with the term *system* used to represent a combination of hardware and software working as an entity, you can set thresholds that when reached generate alarms. The resulting alarms, which can be visual or audible, alert you to certain predefined conditions. For example, a threshold of no activity for a predefined period of time could be set to indicate the occurrence of a break in a cable, and allow you to initiate your investigation of the situation prior to receiving calls from your end-user community.

Other common alarm situations can provide you with an indication of the failure of a bridge, router, gateway, or another network component; or alert you to the fact that a wide area network communications facility used to interconnect geographically separated LANs is inoperative. Such alarms are extremely valuable in that they alert network managers and administrators to abnormal situations that directly or indirectly result in the interruption of service to the end-user community. The effect of this interruption will vary based upon the use of the LAN, but can range from a small inconvenience to a significant economic effect upon the ability of an organization to maintain a competitive edge in a very competitive business environment. Concerning the latter, picture a bank branch office, where tellers and ATM machines lose access to a database of customer accounts; or a travel agency where agents cannot provide potential clients with requested airfare information due to the failure of a gateway. If such situations occur frequently or extend over a relatively long period of time, the steps taken to restore a client/ server computing environment may be too late to maintain the human client.

Network Size and Complexity Management

Other areas of concern in today's communications environment that network management systems are designed to address include the size and complexity of networks, their operating costs and utilization, and the ability to learn enough information to take advantage of the sophistication of many complex network devices. As the need for communications has expanded, the mixture of vendor products used in networks as well as the size, complexity, operating cost, and training required to maintain networks have increased in tandem. Each of these areas can be considered as driving forces for the development of management systems to monitor network equipment and facilities, provide technicians with the ability to implement configuration changes from a central console, and generate alarms when predefined conditions occur.

Personnel Productivity and Cost Control

In addition to making a network more manageable, the use of a network management system makes it possible to manage more devices and transmission facilities with fewer personnel. Thus, a network management system can be viewed as a labor-saving device that enables the performance and capacity of networks to be monitored. A related function is the management of network costs, since as a general rule excellent performance occurs at a low level of utilization, which can result in an excessive expenditure of funds for equipment and facilities only partially used. Thus, another rationale for network management is to balance performance and utilization while attempting to minimize costs.

As local area networks evolved from curiosities to corporate necessities they began to be interconnected, resulting in the use of wide area transmission facilities to link geographically separated networks. Unlike the cable infrastructure of LANs, which represents a fixed installation cost, WAN transmission facilities represent recurring costs that over a period of time can exceed the cost of workstations and servers a WAN facility interconnects. Thus, LAN management does not necessarily stop at the LAN, and may require the ability to obtain information concerning the operational state and level of utilization of wide area network communications equipment and transmission facilities.

Network Planning

Regardless of whether your organization uses WAN transmission facilities, the information obtained from a management system can be vital for the network planning process. By plotting network utilization over a period of time, you may be able to determine if network segmentation or the use of new equipment will be required to alleviate potential performance problems, or if network adjustments are warranted due to a lower than expected level of activity. Thus, a network management system can provide a variety of tools that enable network managers and administrators to perform their job functions in a more expedient manner using up-to-the-minute data that may not otherwise be obtainable. Table 1.1 summarizes the main reasons why networks must be managed, providing the rationale for network management.

NETWORK MANAGEMENT PROCESS

Network management as a process resembles many other common activities in that we are fairly certain about what it is, but would probably be hard pressed to provide a definition. The following definition, while not all-inclusive, provides a base upon which I will expand: Network management is the process of using hardware and software by trained personnel to monitor the status of network equipment and transmission facilities; question end users, vendors, and communications carrier personnel; and implement or recommend actions to alleviate outages and/or improve communications performance, as well as conduct administrative tasks associated with the operation of a network.

As indicated by the previous definition, network management first and foremost requires trained personnel. Here the level of expertise will vary based upon the characteristics of the network being managed, with knowledge of workstation hardware, the network operating system, device drivers, and equipment configuration settings usually representing a minimum

TABLE 1.1   Rationale for Network Management

Determine operational status of equipment and transmission facilities.

Obtain visual/audible notification of the occurrence of threshold conditions.

Better manage large and complex networks.

Cope with network device sophistication.

Facilitate configuration changes.

Make more efficient use of personnel resources.

Balance network performance and capacity.

Contain operating costs.

base of knowledge. Second, network management involves the use of hardware and software to examine the configuration settings and operational state of hardware, software, and transmission facilities. Hardware examined can range from adapter card switch settings to router port configuration settings, while software examined can range from workstation configuration file statements to network operating system parameter settings. Transmission facilities can range in scope from a LAN cable to analog and digital wide area network circuits obtained from communications carriers. Thus, the use of hardware and software can also include the diagnostic testing of communications facilities.

Since most network problems are reactive, being reported by end users, the network manager or network administrator must be people-oriented and able to effectively communicate with the end-user population. Once a problem is recognized and the skills of trained network personnel are applied to expedite a resolution, a variety of personnel contacts may be required. Information may be required from hardware and software vendors, and communications carrier personnel may be asked to initiate one or more tests of wide area network transmission facilities. In addition, after acquiring knowledge concerning an activity or event, network personnel will either implement or recommend actions to fix an existing problem or device.

Concerning communications performance, methods to improve this vital area can include tuning the network operating system, changing the network topology, or even moving to a higher-speed network. Since an improvement to communications performance normally results from a detailed analysis of existing operations as well as the development of a study to examine the operational effect of potential network changes, another key management process is planning. Finally, network managers must consider the security of data. Doing so can result in the use of filters to prevent unauthorized access to a LAN via the Internet, and policies and procedures concerning the use of files downloaded from bulletin-board systems to prevent a virus attack. Thus, the network management process can be much more involved than simply reacting to workstation move and change requests.

OSI Framework for Network Management

Based on the previously presented information, the tasks associated with network management can be subdivided into functional areas. This subdivision was performed by the *International Standards Organization (ISO)* with the development of *Open System Interconnection (OSI)* standards that can be expected to eventually provide a large degree of interoperability with respect to performing network management functions in a network containing multivendor equipment. In developing standards, the ISO defined five network management functional areas or disciplines, as indicated in Table 1.2.

Configuration/Change Management

Configuration or *change management* involves the process of keeping track of the various parameters of devices and facilities that make up a network. Parameters can be set, reset, or simply read and displayed.

For complex networks that have hundreds or thousands of devices and line facilities, a network management system operating under the control of specialized software will more than likely be used to facilitate the control of the network from a single point. Marketed as a network management system, this system will most probably display a geographical representation of the network in addition to providing the user with the ability to read and change device parameters as well as display a variety of line parameters.

Unlike devices whose parameters can be displayed and reset, line facilities are controlled by one or more communications carriers, and the adjustment of those parameters is normally beyond

TABLE 1.2 OSI Framework for Network Management

Configuration/Change Management

Fault/Problem Management

Performance/Growth Management

Security/Access Management

Accounting/Cost Management

the control of the network end-user operator. In this situation, the ability to rapidly display line parameters and obtain knowledge about the status of all line facilities may enable alternative routing procedures to be implemented when an outage of a marginal or failed line facility is reported to a carrier and the circuit is removed from operation for carrier testing. Like life, there are exceptions to almost all typical network-related operations to include carrier facility management. Today you can obtain the installation of a Frame Relay transmission service to interconnect LANs that can be managed through the same management platform used to manage your LAN.

Although a network management system facilitates configuration management, most organizations do not have one ubiquitous system. Instead, many organizations may maintain several systems, some of which control modems obtained from one vendor, while others may control multiplexers or digital service units obtained from other vendors. In addition, other devices may simply be controlled from their front panel display. As vendors continue to incorporate a standardized network management capability into their products, the necessity to maintain multiple management consoles will diminish; however, for most organizations with geographically separated locations and a large mixture of products obtained from different vendors, the ability to have a ubiquitous management platform may reside in the distant future.

No discussion of the performance of configuration management is complete without mentioning its dependence upon a database of parameter settings, and the ability of management platform operations to understand their meanings. This database may consist of information recorded on index cards, typewritten sheets, or files stored on a computer. Regardless of the media used to store information, the database provides a repository of information that can be used to determine alternatives and implement changes in the operation of network components and line facilities, as well as the structure of the network.

Fault/Problem Management

Fault or *problem management* is the process by which the detection, logging and ticketing, isolation, tracking, and eventual resolution of abnormal conditions is accomplished. Since you must know that a problem exists, the first step, and one of the most important, in fault management is to detect an abnormal situation. This can be accomplished in a variety of ways ranging from the setting of thresholds on a network management system, which generate different types of alarm conditions when exceeded, to users calling a technical control center to report problems. Once a problem has been detected, many installations will have a predefined operating procedure whereby the situation is recorded in a log and, if determined to be a legitimate problem, assigned a trouble ticket.

It is important to understand that many problem-related calls to a technical control center are immediately resolved. Such calls may require trained personnel to spend a few minutes to a few hours checking hardware or software settings, or performing other functions that resolve the problem without further action. Other calls or alarms may result in the issuing of a trouble ticket that requires carrier action or the assistance of vendor maintenance personnel. Regardless of the extent of the problem, the initial logging involves an attempt to identify the cause of the abnormal situation and determine appropriate action for its correction.

Problem isolation can include a simple discussion with an end user, diagnostic testing of equipment and carrier facilities, or extensive research. Once the cause is isolated it may be beyond the capability of an end user's organization for correction, such as an unacceptable level of performance on a circuit or a failed bridge or router. Thus, in addition to seeking appropriate assistance, another important step of the fault management process is to track progress of both internal and external personnel in their efforts toward correcting faults. Many times, fault management will require aged trouble tickets to be escalated to receive the attention they deserve. At other times, repetitive calls to a vendor or carrier to track the progress of a trouble ticket may reveal that the ticket was closed. Although we would hope that the carrier or vendor fixed the problem and inadvertently forgot to inform us of the problem resolution, we live in an imperfect world in which a trouble ticket can inadvertently be closed without resolving the problem. Thus, it is very important to track problems, including the status of trouble tickets.

While the resolution of an abnormal condition may appear to be the last task involved in the fault management process, in actuality it may require the performance of a configuration or change management task. For example, if an abnormal condition resulted in the implementation of alternative routing, the resolution of the problem could result in a configuration change in which routing reverts to its normal condition. This illustrates the interrelationship between each of the functional areas of network management.

Performance/Growth Management

Performance or *growth management* involves tasks required to evaluate the utilization of network equipment and facilities and adjust them as required. Tasks performed can range from the visual observation of equipment indicators to the gathering of statistical information into a database that can be used to project utilization trends. Regardless of the method used, the objective of performance and growth management is to ensure that sufficient capacity exists to support end-user communications requirements. Another term commonly used for performance or growth management is *capacity planning*.

One of the more interesting aspects of capacity planning concerns the reaction of end users to capacity problems. If your network has insufficient capacity, end-user complaints will commonly occur whenever response time increases or user sessions are terminated due to excessive collision, an inability to reach the destination in a timely manner, or another network-related problem. Conversely, you will probably never encounter end users complaining that they always receive good response time or never encounter a performance-related problem, and that the network has excessive capacity. This means that excessive capacity will more than likely require recognition by network management personnel, and it is incumbent upon such personnel to examine the potential for both network expansion and contraction.

A variety of tools can be used for the performance or growth management process, including communications carrier bills, network management systems, and the programming of protocol analyzers and other test equipment. Carrier bills may indicate the utilization of dial-in lines, WATS facilities, or packet network activity. Network management systems may provide information concerning the utilization of individual or segmented LANs, dial-in modem usage, and the operation of bridges, routers, gateways, and other network devices. Through the use of protocol analyzers, you may be able to generate statistical or performance data, such as the utilization level of a network and circuits connected to different network components.

Security/Access Management

Security or *access management* is that set of tasks that ensure that only authorized personnel can use the network. Tasks and functions associated with security management can include the authentication of users, encryption of data links and the management and distribution of encryption keys, maintenance and examination of security logs, as well as the performance of audits and traces to ensure that only authorized users use network facilities and resources.

Allied to security and access management are such tasks and functions as virus prevention measures, continuity of operation procedures, and the planning for and implementation when necessary of disaster recovery methods. Although a network manager or administrator cannot perform guard duty to ensure personnel do not transmit suspicious files to others over the network, managers can and should publicize methods to test unknown software, as well as procedures to follow concerning the distribution of public-domain software obtained from bulletin-board access.

Accounting/Cost Management

In addition to the assurance of birth, death, and taxes, you can also expect the old adage—*there is no free lunch*—to be essentially true. One of the processes of network management thus involves obtaining the right information at the right time, which provides a basis for establishing charges for the utilization of network resources. Tasks associated with accounting or cost management include the issuing of orders and the reconciliation and recording of invoices, the computation of depreciation and amortization charges and the assignment of personnel costs to network operations, the development of algorithms to prorate charges to users, and the periodic review of billing methods to ensure the fair and equitable assignment of costs based upon network usage.

The accounting management process may require the efforts of a team of specialists at large organizations. For small and medium-size organizations, the effort involved in accounting management may still be substantial, especially when compared to the necessity to perform other network management functions. Many organizations thus centrally fund the cost of communications, or add a surcharge to the cost of using their data processing facilities. While this will certainly reduce the tasks associated with accounting management, other cost management functions, including budgeting, examining the effect of tariff changes upon the structure of network circuits, and verifying the correctness of vendor and carrier bills, must still continue. Accounting and cost management functions thus remain an important part of the network management process regardless of whether the cost of the network is directly charged back to network users.

Other Network Management Functions

Although the OSI framework for network management is comprehensive, it is not all-inclusive. Two key functional areas that are only partially covered within the OSI framework—and are important enough to justify their identification as separate entities—are *asset management* and *planning* or *support management*.

Asset Management

Asset management is that set of tasks associated with the development and retrieval of records of equipment, facilities, and personnel. Equipment records can include one or more databases of software and hardware settings of devices used in the network, usage statistics, manufacturer data and telephone numbers to call for maintenance, and similar information. Equipment records may reside on a network management system, may supplement information obtained from a network management system, or may be completely independent of a network management system.

Facility records may simply include circuit numbers and

carrier points of contact, or they can contain such additional information as the parameters of a Frame Relay service or the level of conditioning of analog leased lines as well as the results of previous tasks. If the latter is included, end users may be able to note trends that indicate deterioration in circuit quality parameters, which if unchecked could result in a communications outage. The analysis of circuit record data may thus enable end users to contact their communications carrier to request assistance prior to a degradation in service, resulting in the failure of a circuit inhibiting communications. Although trend analysis can be extremely useful for asset management purposes, it is equally and perhaps more useful for planning and support management. Thus, a discussion of trend analysis will be deferred until the next section in this chapter, which focuses on planning and support management.

Unfortunately, personnel are often excluded from the asset-management process even though they are your most valuable assets. Under the asset management process you should develop records that indicate employee work experience, education, and training. You can use information concerning an individual's work experience, education, and training—supplemented by your personal knowledge of persons—to assign projects. Similarly, information concerning prior education and training can be used in conjunction with organizational requirements to implement individual development plans that allocate training and travel funds to enable employees to receive appropriate training.

Records of equipment, facilities, and personnel may be recorded on index cards, typed on paper placed in folders, or stored in magnetic files as part of a database management system. Even when stored as files, it is more than likely that those files will reside on separate computers, as it is very doubtful that one ubiquitous network management system will provide a central repository for all of the information required for the performance of the asset management process.

Planning/Support Management

Planning and *support management* includes those tasks that enable network managers and administrators to provide support for current users, as well as plan for the future. Support for current users can be viewed as a superset of previously described network management functional areas. In fact, support as well as planning consistently draws upon other network management functional areas. Examples of support management functions can include adjusting network facilities to accommodate changes in the use of such facilities, ordering equipment and facilities to support new or expanded applications, and meeting with end users to determine their degree of satisfaction or dissatisfaction with current communications methods.

Perhaps the key to effective planning and support management is *trend analysis*. Within the context of LANs and WANs, trend analysis provides information necessary for determining utilization trends on both local and wide area networks. By plotting the results of network utilization over a period of time, you might avoid a variety of network saturation problems by obtaining the ability to initiate proactive operations. For example, by noting an increase in LAN utilization, you might decide to order equipment required to segment the network. Similarly, a WAN utilization report might result in the upgrade of an existing leased line to a higher operating rate to avoid a potential WAN bottleneck situation.

Closely related to support management is the planning management process. During the planning process you may meet with end users to determine both their requirements as well as their satisfaction or dissatisfaction with existing communications. In addition, the planning process can involve the collection of data from other functional network management areas, which enables you to develop models to assist in the design of a new network structure or the optimization of an existing network structure. Finally, if the planning process results in a recommendation for a change in the structure of a network, upon approval those changes must be implemented. Thus, the planning process must include steps required to implement configuration or change management tasks.

Figure 1.1 summarizes the network management functional areas and tasks associated with each area. Readers should note that a valid case can be made for the inclusion of many tasks under two or more functional areas. You should thus view the tasks associated with the functional areas, as shown in Figure 1.1,

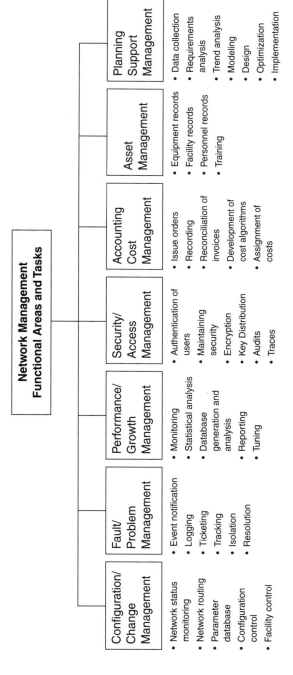

FIGURE 1.1 Network management functional areas and tasks.

as a guide to the primary areas in which certain tasks are performed and not as an all-inclusive example of where tasks are performed.

TOOLS AND SYSTEMS

Tools in the form of specialized communications equipment are indispensable for the performance of many network management tasks. In general, network management tools can be divided into three primary categories: *diagnostic tools*, *monitoring tools*, and *computer-based management systems*.

Diagnostic Tools

Diagnostic tools, including time domain reflectometers (TDRs), breakout boxes, pattern generators, bit-error rate testers, and similar equipment, are primarily used for detecting problems with equipment or line facilities. This type of equipment is manufactured as stand-alone devices, as well as provided on a functional basis through hardware or software modules incorporated into monitoring equipment. The key to the operation of diagnostic tools is the generation of a known sequence of data commonly referred to as a *test pattern*. Through the examination of the response or lack of response to the test pattern, cable opens and shorts as well as the operational state of equipment and circuits can be determined. Another type of diagnostic tool is an alarm that is generated when a predefined condition or threshold is reached. Through the generation of an alarm, you can be notified of a potential or actual equipment or line problem, providing you with a diagnostic tool capability. Thus, the use of diagnostic tools to include alarms facilitates the isolation of network problems.

Monitoring Tools

Monitoring tools provide users with the ability to observe the operation and performance of communications equipment and line facilities. Examples of monitoring tools include RMON probes, protocol analyzers, test equipment, equipment indicators, and breakout boxes. Note that most monitoring tools are capable of being used as diagnostic tools. For example, an RMON probe includes the capability to sample a network at a predefined interval. Those samples are compared to predefined alarm thresholds that when reached result in the generation of a specific type of alarm.

Computer-Based Management Systems

Computer-based management systems run the gamut from personal computers used to manage the operation of specific types of local and remotely located LANs, to modems or multiplexers, to mainframe computers upon which Enterprise network management systems operate. Most, if not all, such computer-based management systems store operational information concerning the usage of network facilities and equipment onto one or more databases that can be queried or manipulated. Through the use of specialized software or an interface to popular spreadsheet programs, a statistical analysis of equipment and facility usage can be performed to predict traffic growth and determine bottlenecks for use as a basis for the reconfiguration of network resources. Other databases when used with different software or software modules may enable you to track trouble calls, issue trouble tickets, and scan a database for entries concerning similar problems whose alleviation may serve as a guide to the resolution of a current problem.

Another class of computer-based management systems that are important tools for the network management process includes *project planning*, *network tariff analysis*, and *network design programs*. Project planning programs can include software that produces PERT and GANTT charts. Network tariff analysis programs that facilitate the selection of appropriate cost-effective WAN facilities require the use of database information that is frequently updated to compare the cost of obtaining facilities from different communications carriers. Thus, many organizations subscribe to a service in which they access tariff analysis software operating on a commercial service, and use that software on a usage-fee basis. In comparison, most other computer-based management software used in the network management process is purchased to operate upon computational facilities owned or leased by the organization. Similarly, unless your organization has an extensive network in which segments must frequently be reanalyzed, network design programs may be used via remote access to a third party's computer system in place of its purchase for operation on computational facilities owned or leased by the organization.

Based upon the preceding, a few general observations concerning computer-based management systems can be made. First, we can segregate their general use into operational and planning functions. Secondly, as a general observation, we can note that essentially all computer-based management systems involved in network operational aspects—such as managing bridges, routers, and gateways as well as controlling modems or multiplexers—are internal to the organization. In comparison, many organizations use the services of third-party vendors to access computer-based management systems to use network planning software.

STANDARDS

As we approach a new century, several trends in the areas of data processing and communications are becoming more pronounced. In the area of data processing, mainframe computers are rapidly being replaced or supplemented by departmental computers based upon powerful microprocessors; while departmental computers for the most part have been replaced by personal computers tied together by local area networks. In the area of communications, images as well as voice and data are being integrated into one corporate network, resulting in the requirement for network management to control a new series of devices, such as PBXs and video conferencing equipment, in addition to conventional LAN and WAN data networking products.

To compound the problems of network managers and administrators, the resulting corporate network can be expected to interconnect computers and communications equipment from a variety of vendors that have incompatible architectures and whose network management systems can be expected to vary considerably with respect to functionality, capability, and interoperability with one another. Although this evolution in the areas of computing and communications has created serious problems for network managers, it has also resulted in the realization of the necessity for network management standards. This in turn resulted in the requirements of end users for the interoperability of network management systems becoming a driving force for vendors to commit themselves to support network management standards as those standards evolve.

A few years ago an international standard called *Common Management Information Services and Protocols (CMIP)*, which defines the format for exchanging data between network management systems as well as for managing network devices and line facilities, was expected to emerge as the *de facto* method to control multivendor equipped Enterprise networks. Instead, a standard with its origination dating back to 1988 has emerged as the *de facto* method for managing multivendor equipped Enterprise networks. That standard is the *Simple Network Management Protocol (SNMP)* to include its *Remote Monitoring (RMON) Management Information Base (MIB)*. The remainder of this section will present a brief overview of SNMP and RMON.

SNMP

To a large extent the development of SNMP parallels the evolution of the *Transmission Control Protocol/Internet Protocol (TCP/IP)* protocol suite. TCP/IP has its origins in the packet switching network sponsored by the U.S. Department of Defense Advanced Research Projects Agency during the late 1960s and early 1970s. Eventually TCP/IP was adopted as a U.S. Department of Defense networking standard, and the ARPA network research resulted in the development of the global set of networks based upon the TCP/IP protocol suite known as the Internet.

A desire to monitor the performance of protocol gateways linking individual networks to the Internet resulted in the development of the *Simple Gateway Monitoring Protocol (SGMP)*, which can be viewed as the predecessor of SNMP. The need for changes and improvements to SGMP resulted in the *Internet*

Activities Board (IAB), which in 1992 was renamed the *Internet Architecture Board*, recommending the development of an expanded Internet network management standard in a *Request For Comment (RFC)*. Under the auspices of the IAB, the *Internet Engineering Task Force (IETF)* became responsible for designing, testing, and implementing the new Internet network management standard. The result of the efforts of a group of IETF researchers and engineers was the publication of three RFCs in August, 1988, which formed the basis of the Simple Network Management Protocol (SNMP).

Table 1.3 lists the initial RFCs which formed the basis for SNMP. It should be noted that RFCs are not static documents, as they go through several stages of review and refinement prior to being adopted as standards by the Internet community. Once standardized, over time they will commonly be superseded by other RFCs. Refer to Appendix A for a comprehensive list of SNMP-related RFCs.

Basic Architecture

An SNMP-based network management system consists of three components—a *manager, agent,* and a *database*—referred to as a Management Information Base (MIB). Although SNMP is a protocol that governs the transfer of information between its three entities, it also defines a client/server relationship. Here the client program is the manager, while the agent that executes on a remote device can be considered to represent a server; then the database controlled by the SNMP agent represents the SNMP MIB. Figure 1.2 illustrates the general relationship between the three SNMP components.

TABLE 1.3 Original RFCs Defining SNMP

RFC 1065	Structure and Identification of Management Information for TCP/IP-based internets.
RFC 1066	Management Information Base for Network Management of TCP/IP-based internets.
RFC 1067	A Simple Network Management Protocol.

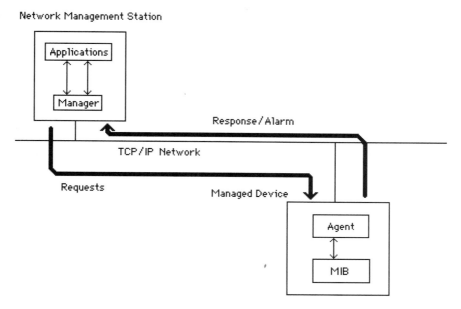

Network Management Station

FIGURE 1.2 The general relationship between SNMP components.

Manager The manager is a program that operates on one or more host computers. Depending upon its configuration, each manager can be used to manage a different subnet, or multiple managers can be used to manage the same subnet or a common network. The actual interaction between an end user and the manager is obtained through the use of one or more application programs that, together with the manager, turn the hardware platform into a *Network Management Station (NMS)*. Today in the era of *Graphic User Interface (GUI)* programs almost all application programs provide a point-and-click window environment that interoperates with the manager to generate graphs and charts, providing visual summaries of network activities.

Through the manager, requests are transmitted to one or more managed devices. Originally SNMP was developed to be used on TCP/IP networks, and those networks continue to provide the transport for the vast majority of SNMP-based network management products. However, SNMP can also be transported via NetWare IPX and other transport mechanisms.

Agents Each managed device includes software or firmware in the form of code that interprets SNMP requests and responds to those requests. The software or firmware is referred to as an agent. Although a device must include an agent to be directly managed, non-SNMP-compatible devices can also be managed if they support a proprietary management protocol. To accomplish this you must obtain a *proxy agent.* The proxy agent can be viewed as a protocol converter as it translates SNMP requests into the proprietary management protocol of the non-SNMP device.

Although SNMP is primarily a poll-response protocol with requests generated by the manager, resulting in agent responses, the agent also has the ability to initiate an *unsolicited response*, which is an alarm condition resulting from the agent monitoring a predefined activity and noting that a predefined threshold was reached. Under SNMP that alarm transmission is referred to as a *trap*.

Management Information Base Each managed device can have a variety of configuration, status, and statistical information that defines its functionality and operational capability. This information can include hardware switch settings, variable values stored as data in-memory tables, records or fields in records stored in files, and similar variables or data elements. Collectively those data elements are referred to as the Management Information Base (MIB) of the managed device. Individually, each variable data element is referred to as a *managed object* and consists of a name, one or more attributes, and a set of operations that can be performed on the object. Thus, the MIB defines the type of information that can be retrieved from a managed device and the device settings you can control from a management system.

RMON

One of the problems associated with SNMP is the fact that its request-response (poll-select) operation, while having a relatively minor effect on the utilization of the bandwidth of a LAN, can result in the significant degradation of lower operating rate

WAN bandwidth when monitoring geographically separated networks. Recognizing this problem the Remote Network Monitoring Working Group of the IETF developed the Remote Monitoring (RMON) network management standard.

RMON represents an extension of the network manager's operation to distant networks. At those networks, intelligent devices known as *probes* or *RMON agents* monitor the data flowing on the remote network, organizing it into information the manager can easily access and interpret, with SNMP used as the transport mechanism between the manager and agent. Figure 1.3 illustrates the relationship between a network management station on one LAN used to manage a distant network through the use of an RMON agent or probe. Since the remote probe monitors and organizes data traffic occurring on the distant network, this considerably reduces the amount of information that would otherwise be required to be transmitted to the network management station for analysis. As the WAN circuit

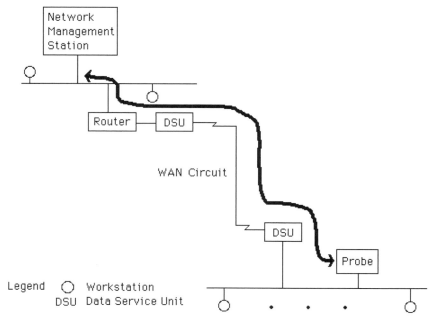

FIGURE 1.3 Extending network management to a remote location via an RMON probe.

used to connect the geographically separated networks normally operates at a fraction of the operating rate of a LAN, the use of an RMON probe also reduces the potential for the saturation of the bandwidth of the WAN circuit, which could occur if each device on the remote network had to be individually polled.

Each RMON agent or probe includes an MIB that defines the attributes of the objects being monitored. The first RMON MIB, RFC 1271, was published in November 1991, and was limited to Ethernet LANs. RFC 1513, which was published in September, 1993, extended RMON to Token-Ring networks, and extensions to other types of networks to include ATM were under consideration when this book was prepared. Refer to Appendix A for a list of SNMP-relevant RFCs.

Although SNMP and RMON MIBs define the attributes of objects that are monitored, the actual value and use of information is highly dependent upon the application program that controls the manager. Some application programs may support a full complement of the network management functional areas and tasks previously described in this chapter, while other applications may be limited to supporting a subset of those functional areas and tasks. Thus, it is extremely important to evaluate the capability and functionality of the application as well as its support of SNMP and RMON.

To illustrate an example of a GUI-based manager accessing an agent, consider the screen display shown in Figure 1.4. In this example of the use of a GUI-based manager, Network General's Foundation Manager is shown accessing a remote Token-Ring RMON probe. The actual screen shown in Figure 1.4 illustrates the results obtained from selecting three icons—the display of three windows. Two windows display predefined statistics in the form of bar graphs, while the third window illustrates information concerning predefined alarm conditions.

The first statistics window, which is illustrated in the upper left portion of Figure 1.4, displays information concerning the percentage of Token-Ring network usage and traffic information in the form of data bytes/second, data frames/second, MAC frames/second, broadcast frames/second, and soft errors/second. The second statistics screen, which is displayed along the bottom of the screen, provides a distribution of traffic based upon

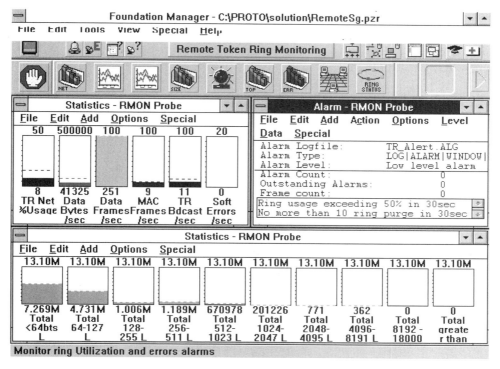

FIGURE 1.4 A Network General Foundation Manager screen displaying statistical and alarm information for a previously selected Token-Ring RMON probe.

frame length. Thus, simply clicking on icons on some GUI-based SNMP managers can result in the display of information in a graphical format from which abnormalities may be easy to observe. Later, this book will discuss the use of RMON probes in detail to include the meaning associated with different values retrieved from Ethernet and Token-Ring MIBs.

2

SNMP Protocol

The conclusion of the previous chapter provided an overview of the basic components of SNMP and their relationship to one another. Although it was noted that the manager and agent communicate with one another in essentially a client-server environment, focus was not put upon the specific mechanism by which they communicate. This chapter will do so, examining the commands supported by SNMP as well as the mechanism by which those commands are transported. In doing so, this chapter will discuss the operation of the originally developed SNMP as well as SNMP Version 2, which was developed to address some of the inadequacies of its predecessor.

SNMP COMMANDS

Under SNMP Version 1, five types of commands or verbs, transported in a formatted message referred to as *Protocol Data Units* (*PDUs*), are defined. Since a detailed description of the syntax and composition of each PDU depends upon knowledge of a subset of the *Abstract Syntax Notation.1* (*ASN.1*) language, a detailed examination of PDUs will be deferred until later in this book. This will enable a general overview of the SNMP protocol to be presented prior to providing a review of the ASN.1 language, which is important to understanding the structure and operations of PDUs and MIBs.

Table 2.1 lists each SNMP command, as well as provides a short description of the operation of each command. Figure 2.1 illustrates the basic data flow of each command with respect to the manager and agent.

GetRequest

The *GetRequest* command is issued by the network manager to an agent. This command can be used to read a single MIB variable or a list of MIB variables from the destination agent. The GetRequest, as well as all other SNMP commands, requires the address of a manager or agent. Since SNMP is transported by IP, an IP address must be associated with each SNMP command.

GetNextRequest

The *GetNextRequest* command is similar to the GetRequest command; however, upon receipt by the agent the next entry in the MIB will be retrieved. Under SNMP a variable stored at a device is referred to as an *individual instance of a managed object*. Thus, the GetNextRequest command results in the agent attempting to retrieve the next larger value than the requested managed object instance.

TABLE 2.1 SNMP Version 1 Commands

Command	Operational Result
GetRequest	Requests the values of one or more Management Information Base (MIB) variables.
GetNextRequest	Enables MIB variables to be read sequentially, one variable at a time.
SetRequest	Permits one or more MIB values to be updated.
GetResponse	Used to respond to a GetRequest, GetNextRequest, or SetRequest.
Trap	Indicates the occurrence of a predefined condition.

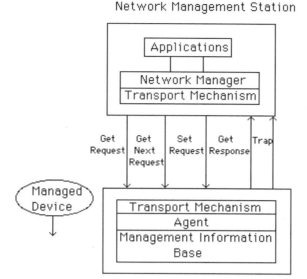

FIGURE 2.1 SNMP version 1 command flow.

By issuing a sequence of GetNextRequest commands with incrementing values for the managed object instance, the network manager obtains the capability to *walk* through an agent's MIB. One common use of the GetRequest command is to read the first value in a row, while a series of GetNextRequest commands are then used to read sequentially through the row, with the incrementation of the values for the requested managed object instance used to control which entries in the MIB are retrieved.

SetRequest

The *SetRequest* command is similar to the GetRequest and GetNextRequest commands in that all three are issued by a network manager to a defined agent. Unlike the GetRequest and GetNextRequest commands that seek to extract information from an MIB, the SetRequest command is used to request the agent to set the value of a managed object instance or instances contained in the command. Whether the command is successful depends upon several factors to include the existence of the managed object, and whether it has an access mode of write-only or read-write. For example, a read-only mode would result in the failure of a SetRequest command, since the value of the managed object instance or instances could not be changed.

GetResponse

As indicated in Figure 2.1, the flow of the *GetResponse* command is from the agent to the network manager. Thus, this command provides the mechanism by which an agent responds to GetRequest, GetNextRequest, and SetRequest commands.

Information returned by the GetResponse command as a GetResponse PDU consists of several fields that enable the response to be correlated to a previously received command, note whether the received command was successfully processed, and, if successfully processed, return a list of instances of the managed objects that were operated upon by the received command together with their current values. Thus, the latter provides a mechanism to verify that a command issued to an agent was successfully executed, as well as to determine the current value of one or more affected variables in the MIB.

Trap

Unlike the previously described commands that are generated in response to a manager or agent request, the *Trap* command is unsolicited. Through the use of this command an agent can take the initiative to inform the manager of the occurrence of a predefined condition, such as a Cold Start or Warm Start of equipment or a Link Down or Link Up condition.

SNMP VERSION 2

One of the problems associated with SNMP Version 1 was its lack of built-in security. This means that it could be relatively easy for the unintentional or intentional use of the SetRequest command to corrupt the configuration parameters of a managed device, which in turn could seriously impair network operations. Due to this problem some communications hardware and software developers elected to disable the ability of an agent within their SNMP implementation to process SetRequest commands. The introduction of SNMP Version 2 (SNMPv2) alleviated this problem through the addition of encryption and authentication. Encryption is used to protect the contents of messages, while authentication is used to verify the originator of a message.

SNMPv2 dates to the fall of 1992, when the IETF formed two working groups to define enhancements to SNMPv1. One working group focused upon defining security functions, while the other working group focused its efforts upon defining enhancements to the SNMP protocol. The efforts of those two groups resulted in SNMPv2, which will hopefully arrive by the time you read this book.

In addition to the previously described security features, SNMPv2 incorporates a manager-to-manager capability and two new PDUs. The manager-to-manager capability permits SNMP to support distributed network management in which one network management station can report management information to another management station. In comparison, SNMPv1 is restricted to supporting a manager-to-manager model.

To support effective manager-to-manager interactions, SNMPv2 added Alarm and Event groups to the SNMP MIB. The Alarm group permits thresholds to be established, which when crossed will result in the initiation of alarm messages. The Event group specifies when a trap should be issued based upon one or more MIB element values.

The PDUs added to SNMPv2 are GetBulkRequest and InformRequest. Those PDUs supplement the five commands developed under SNMPv1, which were slightly improved with respect to their operations and operational capability under SNMPv2. In addition, the GetResponse command was renamed Response, which to many persons appears to be a much more appropriate name.

GetBulkRequest

The *GetBulkRequest* command functions similarly to the Get-NextRequest command with one key exception. Unlike the Get-NextRequest command, which requires the amount of data to be retrieved to be specified, the GetBulkRequest tells the agent to return as much data as possible that can fit into a response message commencing with the next larger value than the requested managed object instance. Not only does the GetBulkRequest make more efficient use of the transmission facility, but its use can also reduce or eliminate certain error conditions that can occur if a GetRequest command is used. For example, if a GetRequest command requests too much data the GetResponse PDU will return a *too big* error message without returning any data.

InformRequest

The *InformRequest* command provides SNMPv2 with the ability to support a hierarchy of network management stations. As previously discussed, the use of this command enables one management station to communicate with another management station, a feature conspicuous by its absence under SNMPv1.

Under SNMPv1 you can establish a series of management stations, with each station used to control one or more independently managed network segments. Since there is no standardized mechanism that enables each management station to communicate with other management stations, the construction of an Enterprise management station was based upon a proprietary design. The need for a proprietary system was eliminated under SNMPv2, as the InformRequest command standardizes communications between management stations.

Figure 2.2 illustrates the use of InformRequest to construct an Enterprise Management System. In this example, a two-level hierarchy of network management stations was created, with an Enterprise network manager at the top of the hierarchy. Through the use of the InformRequest command, the local network managers, which are local with respect to the networks being managed but can be geographically distant with respect to the Enterprise Management system or other local network managers, can communicate with one another.

Under SNMPv2, alarm conditions can be established when thresholds are reached that generate an event. The resulting event can be used to initiate the transmission of an InformRe-

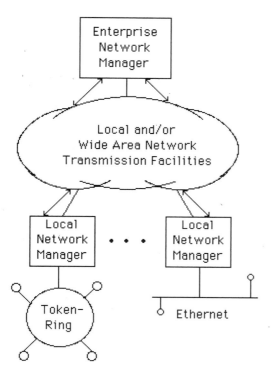

FIGURE 2.2 Through the use of the InformRequest command, communications between network managers becomes possible, permitting the construction of a multitier Enterprise network manager.

quest command that informs another management station of the occurrence of the predefined condition. Thus, through the establishment of a multilevel hierarchy of management stations, one or more stations can be informed of important conditions occurring at distant locations. In fact, with appropriate application software, information can be transferred on a timed basis, so the sun never sets on the operational status of a truly global network. That is, one Enterprise network manager station could be continuously staffed while other network management stations are programmed to report information to the Enterprise manager only during those periods of time when they are unattended.

TRANSPORT MECHANISMS

The exchange of information between a manager and agent or two managers requires the use of a transport mechanism or method. Currently defined SNMP transport mechanisms include the *TCP/IP User Datagram Protocol (UDP)*, *Ethernet frames*, *Novell's Internet Packet Exchange (IPX)* protocol, and *Apple Computer's AppleTalk*, with UDP by far the primary method used to transport SNMP. This section will therefore focus upon TCP/IP and UDP.

Figure 2.3 provides a general comparison of TCP/IP to the International Standards Organization (ISO) Open Systems Interconnection (OSI) Reference Model. This well-known model, which is shown in the left portion of Figure 2.3, subdivided communications related tasks and functions into seven independent

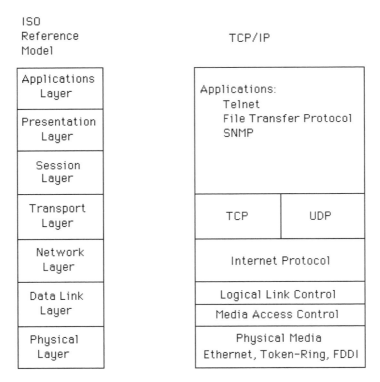

FIGURE 2.3 Comparing TCP/IP to the ISO seven-layer reference model.

layers. Doing so facilitates the interoperability of communications hardware and software, as developers have to consider only the functions of adjacent layers when developing a product to operate at a specific layer. Although TCP/IP predates the OSI Reference Model, it represents a layered protocol that is best explained by comparing and contrasting it to the previously referenced model.

OSI Layers

An understanding of the OSI layers is best obtained by first examining a possible network structure that illustrates the components of a typical network. Figure 2.4 illustrates a network structure that is typical only in the sense that it will be used for a discussion of the components upon which networks are constructed.

The circles in Figure 2.4 represent nodes that are points where data enters or exits a network or is switched between two paths. Nodes are connected to other nodes via communications paths within the network where the communications paths can

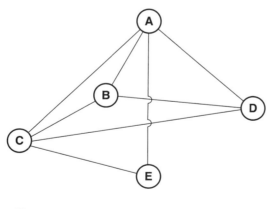

= Node
Lines represent paths

FIGURE 2.4 Network components. The path between a source and destination node established on a temporary basis is called a logical connection.

be established on any type of communications media, such as cable, microwave, or radio.

From a physical perspective, a node can be based upon the use of one of several types of computers, including a personal computer, minicomputer or mainframe computer, or specialized computer, such as a front-end processor. Connections to network nodes into a network can occur via the use of personal computers directly connected to other computers, terminals connected to a node via the use of one or more intermediate communications devices, or via paths linking one network to another network.

The routes between two nodes, such as C–E–A, C–D–A, C–A, and C–B–A, which could be used to route data between nodes A and C, are information paths. Due to the variability in the flow of information through a network, the shortest path between nodes may not be available for use, or may represent a nonefficient path with respect to other paths constructed through intermediate nodes between a source and destination node. A temporary connection established to link two nodes whose route is based upon such parameters as current network activity is known as a logical connection. This logical connection represents the use of physical facilities to include paths and node switching capability on a temporary basis.

The major functions of each of the seven OSI layers are described in the following seven subsections.

Layer 1—Physical Layer

At the lowest or most basic level, the *physical layer* (layer 1) is a set of rules that specify the cable connections and the electrical rules necessary to transfer data between devices. Typically, the physical link corresponds to established interface standards— such as RS-232 for attaching a computer to a modem, or an RJ connector used for attaching a 10BASE-T Ethernet card to a hub port.

Layer 2—Data Link Layer

The next layer, known as the *data link layer* (layer 2), denotes how a device gains access to the medium specified in the physical layer; it also defines data formats, including the framing of data within transmitted messages, error control procedures, and other link-control activities. From defining data formats to include procedures to correct transmission errors, this layer becomes responsible for the reliable delivery of information. WAN data link control protocols, such as *binary synchronous communications* (*BSC*) and *high-level data link control* (*HDLC*), reside in this layer.

On LANs the data link layer was subdivided into media access control (MAC) and logical link control (LLC) sublayers, as illustrated in the right portion of Figure 2.3. The MAC layer governs the method by which a station gains access to the LAN media. For example, the *Ethernet Carrier Sense Multiple Access with Collision Detection* (*CSMA/CD*) access technique represents the MAC sublayer for an Ethernet LAN.

The LLC sublayer governs the method by which information is transferred between workstations. The two basic LLC methods are *connectionless* and *connection*. A connectionless or best-effort method results in a station transmitting data to a destination without first having to establish a connection, and continuing transmission unless stopped by a higher layer, such as an application that disengages the attempt after noting a lack of response from the destination station. The rationale for connectionless transmission is the extremely low error rate of LANs, which essentially negates the necessity to acknowledge the correctness of each transmission. Although connectionless communications is commonly employed on LANs, it is also used on WANs with higher layers, then becoming responsible for the accurate delivery of information. One exception to the use of connectionless transmission at the LLC sublayer is LLC2, a method used for transporting information on several LANs but primarily used to carry mainframe session data via local area networks. Mainframe session data transportation is time-dependent and requires a connection to be established between the mainframe and a LAN workstation prior to the exchange of acknowledged data.

Layer 3—Network Layer

The *network layer* (layer 3) is responsible for arranging a logical connection between a source and destination on the network, including the selection and management of a route for the flow of information between source and destination based upon the available data paths in the network. Services provided by this layer are associated with the movement of data through a network, including addressing, routing, switching, sequencing, and flow-control procedures. In a complex network the source and destination may not be directly connected by a single path, but instead require a path to be established that consists of many subpaths. Thus, routing data through the network onto the correct paths is an important feature of this layer.

Several protocols have been defined for layer 3, including X.25 packet switching protocol and X.75 gateway protocol. X.25 governs the flow of information through a packet network, while X.75 governs the flow of information between packet networks. In a TCP/IP environment the Internet Protocol (IP) represents a network layer protocol.

Layer 4—Transport Layer

The *transport layer* (layer 4) is responsible for guaranteeing that the transfer of information occurs correctly after a route has been established through the network by the network level protocol. Thus, the primary function of this layer is to control the communications session between network nodes once a path has been established by the network control layer. Error control, sequence checking, and other end-to-end reliability factors are the primary concern of this layer. Both the User Datagram Protocol (UDP) and the Transmission Control Protocol (TCP) represent transport layer protocols.

Layer 5—Session Layer

The *session layer* (layer 5) provides a set of rules for establishing and terminating data streams between nodes in a network. The services that this session layer can provide include establishing and terminating node connections, message flow control, dialogue control, and end-to-end data control.

Layer 6—Presentation Layer

The *presentation layer* (layer 6) services are concerned with data transformation, formatting, and syntax. One of the primary functions performed by the presentation layer is the conversion of transmitted data into a display format appropriate for a receiving device. Data encryption/decryption and data compression and decompression are examples of the data transformation that could be handled by this layer.

Layer 7—Application Layer

Finally, the *application layer* (layer 7) acts as a window through which the application gains access to all of the services provided by the model. Examples of functions performed at this level include file transfers, resource sharing and database access. While the first four layers are fairly well defined, the top three layers may vary considerably, depending upon the network used. In a TCP/IP environment SNMP, *File Transfer Protocol* (*FTP*) and *Telnet* represent applications that perform session, presentation, and application layer functions associated with the ISO reference model.

Figure 2.5 illustrates the OSI model in schematic format, showing the various levels of the model with respect to a terminal or personal computer accessing an application on a host computer system.

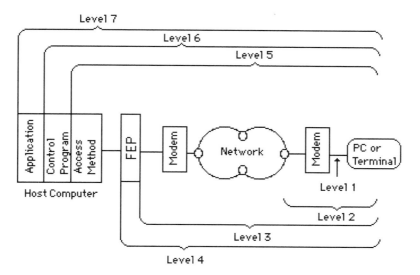

FIGURE 2.5 OSI model schematic.

Data Flow

As data flows within an ISO network, each layer appends appropriate heading information to frames of information flowing within the network while removing the heading information added by a lower layer. In this manner, layer (n) interacts with layer (n–1) as data flows through an ISO network.

Figure 2.6 illustrates the appending and removal of frame header information as data flows through a network constructed according to the ISO reference model. Since each higher level removes the header appended by a lower level, the frame traversing the network arrives in its original form at its destination.

As the reader will surmise from the previous illustrations, the ISO reference model is designed to simplify the construction of data networks. This simplification is due to the eventual standardization of methods and procedures to append appropriate heading information to frames flowing through a network, permitting data to be routed to its appropriate destination following a uniform procedure.

TCP/IP

The Transmission Control Protocol/Internet Protocol (TCP/IP) represents two specific protocols within a protocol suite commonly referenced by its acronym, TCP/IP. This protocol suite has

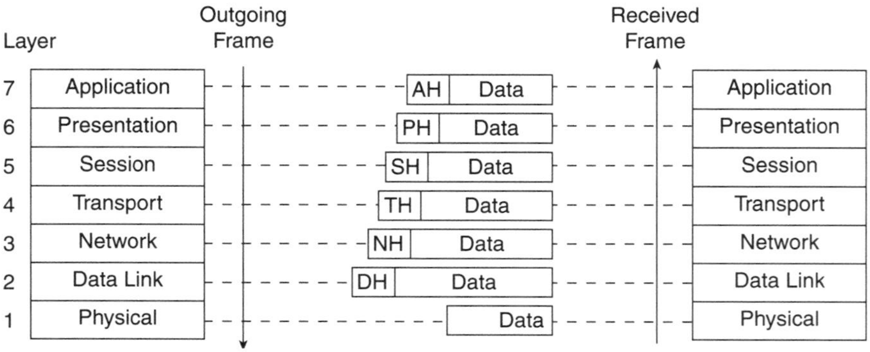

FIGURE 2.6 Data flow within an ISO reference model network.

its roots in the development of the *Department of Defense Advanced Research Projects Agency (ARPA)* network, called *ARPAnet*, a research network that was among the first to provide a reliable method of data interchange among computers manufactured by different vendors.

There are two methods supported by the TCP/IP protocol suite for the routing of data between network nodes, a layer-3 function. Those methods include the establishment of a virtual circuit and the use of datagrams.

Virtual Circuit Transmission

In a *virtual circuit transmission* environment, network nodes establish a fixed path between originating and destination locations. To accomplish this, network nodes must maintain a table of addresses and destination routes to permit a path to be established and, once established, to enable information to flow on the previously established path. The fixed path established for the duration of the transmission session is referred to as a *virtual circuit*. Once the session is completed the previously established path is *torn down*.

Although the establishment of a virtual circuit does not enable the use of an alternate route if a break in the path of the circuit occurs, it provides two advantages that facilitate its operation. First, information always flows on the same path, which precludes a data sequencing problem from occurring. Second, since only one transmission path is used, the possibility of duplicate frames or packets of data occurring is reduced, providing an easier mechanism for the management of the flow of data.

Datagram Transmission

A second mechanism used for the transmission of data at the network layer avoids the use of a fixed path. Referred to as *datagram transmission*, frames are broken into units of data, known as *datagrams*, which are broadcast onto every port other than the receiving port of each node in a network. Although this technique results in duplicate traffic occurring on some paths, it can considerably simplify network routing. In addition, since there are no fixed paths between nodes, no recovery method is required to reestablish a path if a line or intermediate node should fail.

The Internet Protocol (IP) is a network layer protocol that supports a datagram gateway service between subnetworks, enabling hosts on one network to communicate with hosts on another network. To accomplish this, IP will fragment large datagrams so that they can be transferred over networks that support small, maximum packet sizes, as well as perform the reassembly of those datagrams.

One of the problems associated with datagram transmission is the fact that, depending upon network topology, duplicate datagrams can arrive at a destination location. For example, consider Figure 2.7, which illustrates the transmission to LAN C of a datagram from the router connected to LAN A. One copy of the datagram is transmitted on path A-C, while a second copy of the datagram arrives on LAN C via the paths A-B and B-C.

Since a layer-3 protocol is responsible for the routing of information, the removal of duplicate datagrams becomes a layer-4 or end-to-end responsibility. At layer 4 the TCP/IP proto-

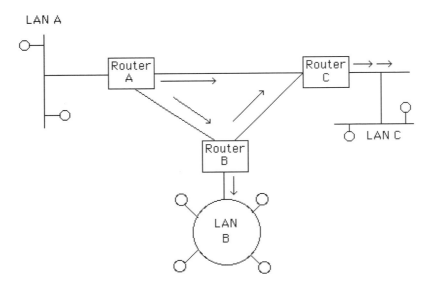

A datagram leaving LAN A will be routed onto paths A–B and A–C. This results in two copies of the datagram arriving at router C.

FIGURE 2.7 Depending upon network topology, datagram transmission can result in duplicate packets arriving at certain network nodes.

col suite supports two transport protocols: the *Transport Control Protocol (TCP)* and the *User Datagram Protocol (UDP)*. TCP provides a reliable, connection-oriented service that supports end-to-end transmission reliability. To accomplish this, TCP supports error detection and correction as well as flow control to regulate the flow of datagrams. In comparison, UDP provides an unreliable, connectionless transport service. This requires the higher layer application to be responsible for ensuring that messages are properly delivered. SNMP runs on top of UDP, which means that a session does not have to be established for network management information to be transmitted. Thus, the use of UDP provides a degree of flexibility for the transmission of network management information.

IP Operation

Figure 2.8 illustrates the fields of an IP datagram, and the octet length of each field. Note that the first 20 octets represent an IP header followed by user data.

The version field consists of 4 bits and identifies the format of the IP header. Currently, version 4 is the latest version of IP. The header length is also 4 bits in length and denotes the length of the header in 32-bit words. The minimum value of this field is 5.

The type of service field indicates the quality of service desired for the datagram. Values for this field can be used to specify precedence, delay, throughput, and reliability.

The total length field consists of two octets that denote the length of the datagram. The value in this field specifies the length of the header plus user data.

The identification field contains a 16-bit value assigned by the originator of the datagram. If the datagram must be fragmented to flow on another network, and the flags field permits fragmentation, two or more fragments consisting of a portion of the user data from the original datagram will be created. Since each fragment contains a portion of user data, the fragment offset field is used to identify the position of the fragment, in units of 8 octets, in the original datagram.

The Time to Live field was designed to indicate in seconds the time the datagram can flow on the internet. Each time the datagram passes through the internet layer on any network

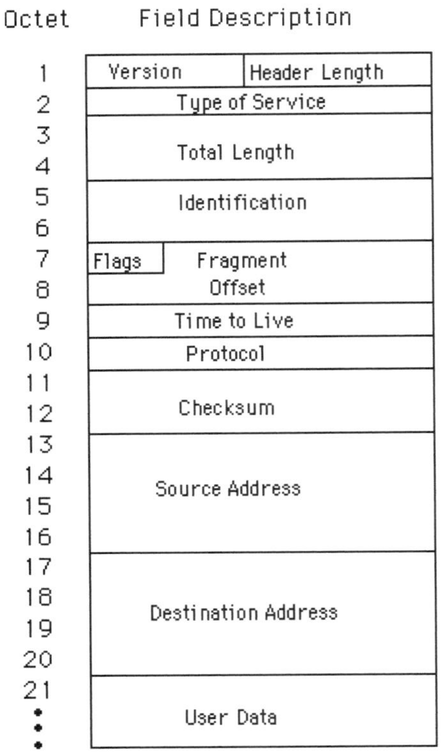

Octet   Field Description

Octet	Field Description
1	Version · Header Length
2	Type of Service
3, 4	Total Length
5, 6	Identification
7, 8	Flags · Fragment Offset
9	Time to Live
10	Protocol
11, 12	Checksum
13, 14, 15, 16	Source Address
17, 18, 19, 20	Destination Address
21 ⋮	User Data

FIGURE 2.8 The IP header.

device, the value of this field is decremented, being discarded when a value of zero is reached. In most implementations, the Time to Live field is a hop-count field, with decrementation performed by each router.

The Protocol field simply identifies the upper layer protocol using IP, such at TCP or UDP.

The 2-byte header Checksum field contains a 1's complement arithmetic sum, which is computed over the header of the IP datagram. When the datagram is originally transmitted, as well as each time it is forwarded, the checksum is recalculated.

Both the source and destination addresses consist of 32 bits that represent the IP address of the originator and recipient, respectively. Since IP addressing is an important concept to understand, let us temporarily defer a discussion of UDP until IP addressing, address formats, and subnetting are examined, important topics to note that facilitate the management of devices.

IP Addressing An IP address is 32 bits in length. The actual address is generated by combining a network identifier assigned by the *Internet Network Information Center* (*InterNIC*) and a local host computer address. To understand how this address is generated requires an examination of the method by which IP addresses are constructed or classified, and how they are expressed through the use of decimal numbers.

Currently IP addressing can be divided into five unique network classes, of which two are reserved for special purposes and will not be discussed. Figure 2.9 illustrates the IP address formats currently in use, with the address class distinguished by the setting of the first, first pair, or first 3 bits in the address.

In examining the IP address formats illustrated in Figure 2.9, note that each address is subdivided into a network and a host identifier portion. The network portion of the IP address

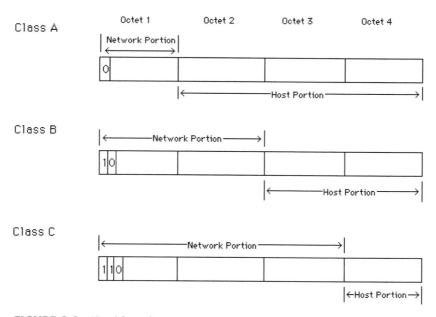

FIGURE 2.9 IP address formats.

indicates its network class, as the network portion includes the bit or bits used to classify the address. The network portion of the address is assigned by the InterNIC, and its size governs the number of networks assignable as well as the number of hosts addressable on each network. Each IP address is expressed as four decimal numbers ranging from 0 to 255, with each number separated by a dot. Hence, an IP address is commonly referred to as a *dotted decimal number*.

Class A   A *Class A* network uses 7 bits in the first octet to distinguish one address from another. Thus, Class A networks have network numbers from 1 to 127. The first octet is assigned by the InterNIC, while the remaining octets are assigned by Class A network administrators. Since there are relatively few Class A networks in comparison to Class B and Class C networks, and Class A networks support the largest number of hosts, they are assigned primarily to large organizations and countries.

Class B   A *Class B* IP address is denoted by the bit sequence 10 in the first two bit positions of its address. The first two octets of a Class B address are assigned by the InterNIC, resulting in two octets network administrators can assign. Thus, network administrators whose organizations receive a Class B address can use that address to identify up to 65,636 hosts on their networks.

Class C   A *Class C* address can be considered to represent the reverse of a Class A address, favoring the network portion instead of the host portion of the address. The first three octets of a Class C address are used to identify a network address and are assigned by the InterNIC, leaving one octet for the network administrator to assign. This limits a Class C address to a maximum of 256 hosts. Due to this limitation some organizations that do not justify a Class B address may have to obtain multiple Class C addresses to satisfy the requirements of the organization.

Subnetting an IP Address   The assignment of an address by the InterNIC to an organization provides the organization with a distinct identifier. While that identifier is suitable for one physical network, from a practical perspective many organizations operate two or more physical networks to obtain more manageable networks, reduce Ethernet collision domains, or avoid exceeding LAN physical constraints. Rather than request an additional address from the InterNIC, which may not be granted due to the scarcity of IP addresses, organizations can subdivide their assigned IP addresses through a process referred to as *subnetting.* An important benefit of subnetting is that to the outside world, the organization maintains a common network IP address. This permits, for example, a single router to be used for a corporate connection to the Internet while two or more subnets could be connected to the Internet via the router.

Subnetting represents a division of the host portion of an IP address into subnet and host entities. To the outside world, information transmitted to the organization is addressed to the network portion of the address, while the host portion appears to represent a distinct host address. At the destination site the subnet field within the host portion of the address is used to identify a predefined physical network. Then, the remaining portion of the host portion is used to identify a host on the physical network.

Figure 2.10 illustrates the subnetting of a Class C network address. Note that the subnet portion of the address can be one or more bit positions, with the length dependent upon the number of physical networks the organization has. For example, an organization with two networks at one location could assign 1 bit to the derived subnet portion of the IP address, resulting in 7 bits being used for the host portion of the address. In this exam-

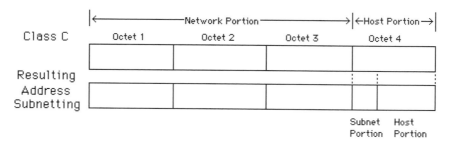

FIGURE 2.10 IP address subnetting.

ple, each network could support up to 127 identifiable hosts. Before discussing how subnetting is accomplished, let's focus upon the routing of information on an IP network to provide us with information necessary to understand the functionality of a process known as *IP subnet masking*, which is the process that supports multiple networks via a common IP network address.

Routing The transfer of information between two devices is based upon an examination of the network portion of the IP address. If the destination address has the same network portion, then the destination device must be on the same network. Thus, a router receiving a datagram with matching source and destination network addresses will not transmit the datagram off the local network. If the destination address contains a network identifier that is different from the existing network, the destination address must reside on a different network. Thus, in this situation the router would forward the datagram off the local network.

Using a Subnet Mask Since the subnet portion of an IP address represents an extension of the network address, a mechanism is required to inform each workstation as well as routers about this extension. The mechanism used to accomplish this is a *subnet mask*.

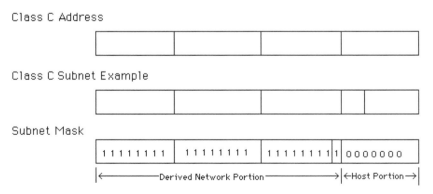

FIGURE 2.11 Creating a subnet mask.

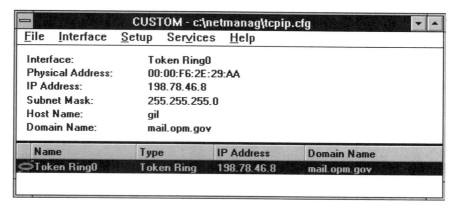

FIGURE 2.12 Viewing the current address settings via Chameleon's Custom application.

A subnet mask is a 32-bit number for which the network identifier and subnet portions are set to 1s, while the host portion is set to 0s. The logical ANDing of the subnet mask with an IP address results in the generation of the physical network address.

Figure 2.11 illustrates the construction of a subnet mask for the previously subnetted Class C address in which one bit position of the host portion of the IP address was used for the subnet portion of the address. By ANDing the 25 set bits in the subnet mask with each 32-bit IP address, an extended IP network portion is derived. This derived network is used internally as a mechanism to determine whether a datagram should remain on the internal network.

Figures 2.12 and 2.13 illustrate the initial setting and modification of a subnet mask, using the popular NetManage Chameleon TCP/IP application suite. Figure 2.12 illustrates the Chameleon Custom application window, which identifies current settings and provides the ability to modify those settings. In Figure 2.12 a subnet mask of 255.255.255.0 is shown, corresponding to setting every bit in the first three octets of a 32-bit mask. Figure 2.13 illustrates the display of a dialog box labeled Subnet Mask, which is displayed by selecting a Subnet Mask entry from the Setup menu. In this example, setting the first bit

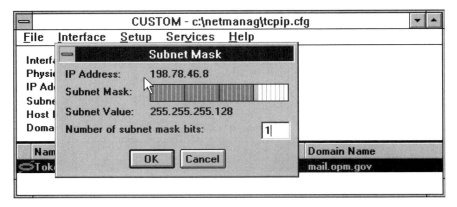

FIGURE 2.13 Changing the subnet mask.

in the fourth octet is shown, resulting in the value of the subnet mask changing to 255.255.255.128.

UDP

The *User Datagram Protocol (UDP)* is a layer-4 transport service used by SNMP. UDP is a connectionless service, which means that the higher layer application is responsible for the reliable delivery of the transported message.

Figure 2.14 illustrates the composition of the UDP header. The Source and Destination port fields are each 16 bits in length and identify the port number of the sending and receiving process, respectively. Here each port number process identifies an application running at the corresponding IP address in the IP header, and is also commonly referred to as a *well-known port*. The use of a port number provides a mechanism of identifying network services, as they denote communications points where particular services can be accessed. For example, a value of 161 in a port field is used in UDP to identify SNMP.

The length field indicates the length of the UDP packets in octets to include the header and user data. The checksum, which is a 1's complement arithmetic sum, is computed over a pseudoheader and the entire UDP packet. The pseudoheader is created by the conceptual prefix of 12 octets to the header previously illustrated in Figure 2.14. The first eight octets are used

```
Octet        Field

  1       ┌─────────────────────┐
  2       │     Source Port     │
  3       ├─────────────────────┤
  4       │  Destination Port   │
  5       ├─────────────────────┤
  6       │   Datagram Length   │
  7       ├─────────────────────┤
  8       │  Datagram Checksum  │
  9       ├─────────────────────┤
          │     User Data       │
          └─────────────────────┘
```

FIGURE 2.14   The UDP header.

by source and destination IP addresses obtained from the IP packet. This is followed by a zero-filled octet and an octet that identifies the protocol. The last two octets in the pseudoheader denote the length of the UDP packet. By computing the UDP checksum over the pseudoheader and user data, a degree of additional data integrity is obtained.

3

Understanding the MIB

The Management Information Base (MIB) can be viewed as a database whose structure and elements are both standardized. The process by which the MIB is standardized was originally defined in RFC 1065, which was published in August 1988 and updated by a rerelease of that RFC as RFC 1155 in May 1990. Although the official title of both RFCs is Structure and Identification of Management Information for TCP/IP-Based Internets, they are commonly referenced as the *Structure of Management Information (SMI)*. SMI denotes such information as how MIB variables in an MIB are related to one another, how variables are formatted, and similar information necessary for obtaining the standardization of the MIB. To accomplish this, RFC 1065 uses a subset of the *International Standards Organization Abstract Syntax Notation One (ASN.1)* language. Thus, the ability to understand the SNMP MIB process requires an understanding of the Structure of Management Information, which in turn requires some knowledge of the ISO's ASN.1 language.

Although the primary focus of this chapter is upon the Management Information Base, the ability to understand the MIB is considerably improved by understanding the Structure of Management Information. Similarly, an understanding of the Structure of Management Information is improved by obtaining an understanding of the formal descriptions of the structure, which are given using Abstract Syntax Notation One language. Thus, we will first focus upon ASN.1 prior to examining the Structure of Management Information. We will then proceed to the primary topic of this chapter, reviewing the formal notations based upon ASN.1, which defines the structure and composition of the MIB. In concluding, this chapter will cover a topic mentioned but deferred until after explaining the three primary topics of this chapter. This concluding topic is an explanation of the construction of the SNMP message, whose explanation requires a degree of knowledge of ASN.1 as well as the MIB. Since the SNMP message provides the communications capability between a manager and agent, as well as transports MIB information, its coverage at the end of this chapter is a fitting conclusion to obtaining an overview of the MIB.

ASN.1

Abstract Syntax Notation One (ASN.1) represents an Open Systems Interconnection (OSI) method of specifying abstract objects, providing a mechanism that can be used to define a variety of data structures, including the syntaxes of different protocols. Through the use of ASN.1, a designer may specify a data structure without considering its actual implementation. Although this might at first glance appear unusual, the separation of design and implementation tasks—as well as the standardization of those tasks—provides several key advantages when used in the development of communications systems to include SNMP. First, the standardization of the design of a data structure makes it considerably easier for software developers to modify a previously developed design, since the implementation process is separated from the design process. Second, since the implementation process converts the data structure into a bit stream for transportation by a protocol, the standardization of an implementation method makes the data structure protocol independent.

The implementation method for ASN.1 is known as *Basic Encoding Rules (BER)*, which describes how ASN.1 datatypes are converted into a string of bits. Since there is more than one way by which some ASN.1 datatypes can be encoded, another set of rules, known as the *Distinguished Encoding Rules (DER)*, provides a unique encoding to each ASN.1 datatype. DER actually represents a subset of Basic Encoding Rules, and both BER and DER were introduced with ASN.1.

Overview

Under ASN.1, a type references a set of values and can have a finite or infinite number of values. Then, a value within an ASN.1 type becomes an element of the type's set.

Although ASN.1 defines a rich set of datatypes, only a subset of those datatypes is defined for use under SMI.

Datatype And Value Definitions

Under ASN.1, *datatype* definitions are constructed using the Backus-Naur form, in which a pair of colons (::) followed by an equal sign (=) provides a definition symbol (::=). Thus, an ASN.1 datatype definition follows the following format:

```
Name of Type ::= definition
```

By convention the name of a new datatype always begins with an uppercase letter, while the definition can consist of uppercase and lowercase letters, numbers, and a hyphen. Each type assignment must begin on a new line, and the three components of the type assignment must be separated from one another by one or more spaces, tabs, line feeds, or other special characters. For example, suppose you want to define a type, TrafficVolume, which consists of an ordered list of packets received and packets transmitted. Through the use of the SEQUENCE structured type, which is described later in this section, you could define the previously mentioned type as follows:

```
TrafficVolume ::= SEQUENCE
    {
        inpackets INTEGER,
        outpackets INTEGER
    }
```

In the previous example the braces contain the ordered list, while INTEGER represents a type whose values are the set of all positive and negative whole numbers and zero. Thus the type, TrafficVolume, represents an ordered list of two integers, one associated with the variable inpackets and the other with the variable outpackets.

Under ASN.1 you can also define an instance or *value* of a datatype by using the following assignment format:

```
nameOfValue NameOfType ::= Value
```

In the preceding assignment format, the variable (nameOf-Value) is first named and associated with its type (NameOfType) prior to having a value associated with the variable. Returning to our previous defined type, TrafficVolume, suppose you want to assign the name resetTrafficVolume to the condition, where inpackets and outpackets each have the value zero. To do so the value definition would be as follows:

```
resetTrafficVolume TrafficVolume ::=
        {
                inpackets 0,
                outpackets 0
        }
```

In the preceding example, resetTrafficVolume represents a value of the type TrafficVolume, in which the variables associated with the type are set to zero. Note that intermediate values are separated from the next by a comma, while the last value in the list simply terminates with its value.

ASN.1 Types

There are four kinds of ASN.1 types, which are summarized in Table 3.1 and will be reviewed in this section. Since only a subset of each type is primarily used in the management framework used to define the rules for describing management information, the description of ASN.1 presented in this chapter will not be focused upon those components of the ASN.1 language used by the Structure of Management Information.

TABLE 3.1 ASN.1 Types

ASN.1 Types	Description
Simple	A set of values without components, such as BOOLEAN and INTEGER.
Structured	A set of values with one or more components, such as SEQUENCE and SEQUENCE OF.
Tagged	An identifier that facilitates the correct interpretation of values associated with other types.
Other	A set of values not included in the above, such as Generalized Time, TCTime, and ObjectDescriptor.

Simple Type

A *simple* type can be considered to represent a set of values without components. That is, a simple type associates only one value at any time even if a list of values is contained in the assignment statement. This concept will become clearer as we examine a few examples of the use of simple types.

Representation The simple ASN.1 types used in the management framework include BIT STRING, INTEGER, NULL, OBJECT IDENTIFIER, and OCTET STRING. Under ASN.1, square brackets ([]) are used to indicate optional terms, braces ({}) are used to group related terms, a bold vertical bar (I) denotes alternatives or a choice within a group while ellipses (. . .) indicate repeated occurrences. In addition, comments are delimited by a pair of hyphens (--) or a pair of hyphens and a line break. Using the previously described meta-structure, let's examine a few examples of specified simple ASN.1 types.

INTEGER Assume you want to associate RingOpenStatus to the integer values 1, 2, and 3 used to denote the conditions Open (1), Closed (2), and LobeFailure (3). To accomplish this using ASN.1, encode the following line:

```
RingStatus ::= INTEGER {Open (1), Closed (2), LobeFailure
(3)}
```

Because of the ability to separate the three components of a type definition from one another by spaces, you could also use the following definition layout:

```
RingStatus ::= INTEGER
    {
        Open (1),
        Closed (2),
        LobeFailure (3)
    }
```

For both of the preceding examples, RingStatus represents an INTEGER whose values 1, 2, and 3 have been named Open, Closed, and LobeFailure, respectively.

OCTET STRING Now suppose you want to assign a MAC address to an OCTET STRING of six octets. To do so you would enter the following:

```
MacAddress ::= OCTET STRING (SIZE(6))
```

BIT STRING The BIT STRING represents a simple type whose values are an ordered sequence of zero or more bits. The value notation for a BIT STRING consists of a binary string surrounded by single quotes and followed by the letter B (for binary) or H (for hexadecimal). Concerning the latter, a hexadecimal representation is valid only when the length of the binary string is a multiple of four. An example of a type definition using BIT STRING is shown below:

```
KeyCode ::= BIT STRING
```

where examples of valid values of BIT STRING could include *10100101*B and *3ABADABA*H.

NULL Perhaps the simplest type of all ASN.1 types is the NULL, which is commonly used as a place holder or when its presence is required to convey a particular meaning. For example,

```
Separator ::= NULL
```

The value notation for the type NULL is also NULL.

OBJECT IDENTIFIER   Although the use of most simple ASN.1 types is relatively straightforward, one—OBJECT IDENTIFIER—deserves special mention.

The OBJECT IDENTIFIER is a simple datatype that provides a mechanism for identifying a node within an inverted tree structure. The OBJECT IDENTIFIER consists of a sequence of non-negative integers, which identifies an object (node) within the inverted tree. That object can represent a registration authority, an algorithm, or another identifier based upon the entries in the naming tree. To illustrate the use of the OBJECT IDENTIFIER requires a tree; thus for illustrative purposes we need one to illustrate the use of this simple type. Fortunately, the *International Organization for Standardization (ISO)* and the *International Telecommunications Union (ITU)*, Telecommunications section (ITU-T) (the latter known until recently as the Consultative Committee for International Telephone and Telegraph (CCITT)) coordinated the development of a global naming tree. This tree, which is partially illustrated in Figure 3.1, provides a mechanism for assigning an identifier to any object which requires naming.

The global naming tree illustrated in Figure 3.1 provides both a labeling mechanism as well as an identifier mechanism, since each object is assigned to a specific node under the root of the tree. Then, describing an OBJECT IDENTIFIER is accomplished by traversing the tree, starting at its root, until the intended object is reached. Several formats can be used to describe an OBJECT IDENTIFIER, with integer values separated by dots most commonly used. That is, to identify the U.S. Department of Defense (dod), its object value in integer notation would become:

```
1.3.6
```

The preceding integer string identifies the object dod located by starting at the root of the tree and first moving to subordinate node 1, followed by moving to the subordinate node 3 under the first subordinate node. Next, moving to the sixth subordinate node under subordinate node 3 results in an integer string that uniquely identifies the U.S. Department of Defense.

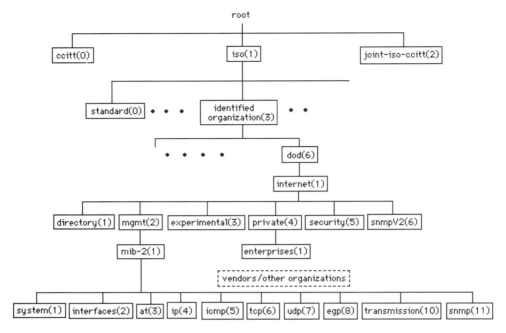

FIGURE 3.1 The ISO/ITU-T (CCITT) global naming tree.

A second method used to identify an object in the global naming tree is accomplished through the use of a text string. This method results in the use of a series of text labels separated from one another by underscores. Thus, dod would be identified by the following text string:

```
iso_identifier-organization_dod
```

The ASN.1 notation for values of the OBJECT IDENTIFIER type is:

```
{[identifier]component₁...componentₙ}
```

where component$_1$ represents an integer or text that corresponds to a node in the global tree path that forms a path to a designated node.

Using ASN.1 notation, you can define a value declaration for the OBJECT IDENTIFIER using the following syntax:

```
object ::= OBJECT IDENTIFIER
```

Thus, you can define the dod subtree as:

```
dod OBJECT IDENTIFIER ::= {1 3 6}
```

Since you can also use textual values or mix integers and textual values, three additional mechanisms for specifying the same object identifier value are:

```
dod OBJECT IDENTIFIER ::= {iso org dod}
dod OBJECT IDENTIFIER ::= {iso org (6)}
dod OBJECT IDENTIFIER ::= {iso 3 6}
```

In examining the global naming tree illustrated in Figure 3.1 you will note that, as you might expect from a structure developed jointly by the ITU-T and ISO, two top-level nodes are administered by each organization as a separate entity, and one node as a jointly administered entity. Under the ISO administered entity, that organization defined the org node as a mechanism to delegate authority to other organizations. One of those organizations just happens to be the U.S. Department of Defense (dod), which funded the development of ARPANet, the predecessor to the Internet. Today the internet subtree under the dod node is controlled by the *Internet Architecture Board* (*IAB*) and administered by the *Internet Assigned Numbers Authority* (*IANA*). As indicated in Figure 3.1, there are six nodes defined under the internet subtree. Of particular interest is the mgmt (management) subtree, since that subtree is the placement area for approved standard network management variables. Note that until a standard network management variable is approved, it is placed under the experimental node. If, after a trial period, it is accepted as a standard, it is then moved to reside under the mgmt node.

Structured Types

A *structured* type under ASN.1 represents a collection of one or more types. Under the management framework, two kinds of structured types are supported—SEQUENCE and SEQUENCE OF.

SEQUENCE The SEQUENCE type denotes an ordered collection or list of one or more elements that represent other ASN.1 types. In ASN.1 notation, a SEQUENCE type has the following format:

```
SEQUENCE   {[identifier₁]Type₁[keyword][{value₁}],
           ...,
           [identifierₙ][Typeₙ][keyword][{valueₙ}]}
```

Here the identifiers are optional and when included function to identify each element. $Type_1 \ldots Type_n$ represent the element type, while $value_1 \ldots value_n$ are optional default values for each element. The keyword can be either OPTIONAL or DEFAULT, or it can be omitted. The use of OPTIONAL indicates that the component's presence is not mandatory. A type can also be followed by the keyword DEFAULT, followed by a value for a component. Although the SEQUENCE type provides a mechanism for denoting an ordered list consisting of different datatypes, it can also be used to present an ordered list of the same datatype.

A common use for the SEQUENCE type is to provide a model of a record structure. For example,

```
PayRecord ::= SEQUENCE
     {
     name      IA5String,
     grade     INTEGER,
     step      INTEGER,
     position  INTEGER{staff (0), manager(1)},
     address   IA5String OPTIONAL
     }
```

An example of a PayRecord value could be:

```
{
name        "Held, Gilbert",
grade       31,
step        14,
position    manager}
```

In the preceding pay record example, note that IA5String references the International Alphabet No. 5 (international ASCII) character string type.

SEQUENCE OF The SEQUENCE OF structured type is similar to the SEQUENCE structured type but is used to model an ordered list of values that belong to a single type. The format of this structured type consists of the keywords SEQUENCE OF followed by a valid type notation, with the value notation consisting of an ordered list of values of the type contained within a pair of braces. For example,

```
DiceRoll ::= SEQUENCE OF INTEGER
```

An example of a DiceRoll value is:

```
{7, 11, 2, 2, 2, 8, 9}
```

A common use of the SEQUENCE OF structured type is to define a table of table entries. Thus, you can view a table under ASN.1 notation as a SEQUENCE OF SEQUENCES, since SEQUENCE simply specifies the list. To illustrate this concept, let me digress and discuss the macro capability of ASN.1 as it relates to the definition of an MIB object.

OBJECT-TYPE Macro Template ASN.1 includes a macro template capability that permits a designer to define a new type notation and an associated new value notation. When applied to SNMP, this capability was used to develop MIB definitions.

The general format of an ASN.1 macro is relatively simple, as indicated below:

```
nameOfValue  MACRO-NAME
    <<definitions>>
::= value
```

When used to develop MIB definitions, the use of a macro template enables a sequence of predefined information to be used to define an MIB object. That information includes:

- The text information used to name an MIB object.
- The datatype the managed object will hold (string, integer, null, etc.).
- Operations allowed (read-create, read-write, read-only, not-accessible).
- A description of the managed object.

To include that information, each MIB-managed object is described using an OBJECT-TYPE macro whose general format is:

```
nameOfValue    OBJECT-TYPE
      SYNTAX
      ACCESS
      STATUS
      DESCRIPTION
      REFERENCE
::= value
```

Returning to the use of SEQUENCE OF, let's cover two topics with one illustration by examining the following OBJECT-TYPE macro template used to describe the IEEE 802.5 statistics table:

```
dot5StatsTable     OBJECT-TYPE
      SYNTAX         SEQUENCE OF Dot5StatsEntry
      ACCESS         Not-accessible
      STATUS         Mandatory
      DESCRIPTION
            A table containing Token-Ring statistics, one
            entry per 802.5 interface.
                All the statistics are defined using the
            syntax Counter as 32-bit wraparound counters.
            Thus, if an interface's hardware maintains these
            statistics in 16-bit counters, then the agent must
            read the hardware's counters frequently enough to
            prevent loss of significance in order to maintain
            32-bit counters in software.
::= {dot5 2}
```

In the preceding macro, the OBJECT IDENTIFIER for dot5-StatsTable is {dot5 2}. From Figure 3.1 the path to the MIB is 1.3.6.1.2. Thus, the OBJECT IDENTIFIER resides at the end of the path specified by 1.3.6.1.2.5.2.

The SYNTAX clause defines the datatype for the object. In the preceding example the SYNTAX for the value dot5StatsTable variable is the SEQUENCE OF Dot5StatsEntry, which means that dot5StatsTable can consist of a table of table entries, the latter defined by Dot5StatsEntry.

The ACCESS clause defines the type of operations that can be performed. In the preceding example, the table ACCESS is not-accessible, which means entries cannot be read or written. This definition is required because the SNMP protocol can retrieve or update only a list of individual variables, while a table represents a logical organization of variables based upon their row and column locations. Including an ACCESS definition of not-accessible means that the table cannot be retrieved in its entirety by transmitting a get command that contains only the OBJECT IDENTIFIER for the table. Instead you can retrieve the entries in the table by transmitting the complete list of OBJECT IDENTIFIERs for the variables in the table, or by walking through the table through the use of a sequence of get-next-request commands.

The STATUS clause tells an implementor whether the definition will soon be made obsolete, is obsolete, is mandatory and must be included in the MIB development, or is optional. In the preceding example, a mandatory STATUS informs an MIB developer that the OBJECT IDENTIFIER must be supported.

The DESCRIPTION clause provides information useful to a developer. Thus, this clause represents a textual description of the managed object.

The REFERENCE clause is optional. This clause is included when one managed object is derived from another, and then identifies the other managed object.

Tagged Types

When a value of an ASN.1 type is transferred, a tag identifying the type is also transferred. That tag is used as a mechanism to permit the receiver to correctly decode the received value. The use of tagging primarily falls into two areas—to distinguish types within an application or to distinguish types within a structured type, such as are obtained through the use of SEQUENCE or SEQUENCE OF.

ASN.1 supports both implicit and explicit tagging. Both methods are based upon the use of universal tags that represent standardized datatypes. Those datatypes were assigned universal tag numbers, with a portion of currently defined ASN.1 universal tags listed in Table 3.2.

Implicit An implicitly tagged type represents a type derived from another type through the modification of an underlying type. To accomplish this, an existing datatype is wrapped within the new datatype through the use of the keyword IMPLICIT.

Under ASN.1 notation the format for implicit tagging is:

```
[[class] number] IMPLICIT Type
```

Class is an optional class name that can be either Universal, Application, or Private. A Universal tag is globally unique and must be defined under ASN.1. An Application class is unique

TABLE 3.2 Examples of ASN.1 Universal Tags

ASN.1 Datatype	Universal Tag (Decimal)	(Hexadecimal)
Boolean	1	01
Integer	2	02
Bit String	3	03
Octet String	4	04
Null	5	05
OBJECT IDENTIFIER	6	06
ObjectDescriptor	7	07
EXTERNAL	8	08
REAL	9	09
ENUMERATED	10	0A
SEQUENCE, SEQUENCE OF	16	10

within an ASN.1 module, while a Private class is unique within a given enterprise. The number represents a tag number within the class, while Type represents a type.

To illustrate the use of implicit tagging, assume you want to define a new datatype named GetRequest-PDU. Further assume you want to use the previously defined SNMP PDU, assigning a tag of zero to the new datatype. To do so, enter the following:

```
GetRequest-PDU ::= [0]IMPLICIT PDU
```

Explicit Through the use of explicit tagging a new type is derived from an existing type by the addition of an outer tag to the underlying type. Similar to implicit tagging, explicit tagging requires the use of a keyword. As you might expect, the keyword for explicit tagging is EXPLICIT.

Under ASN.1 notation the format for an explicit tagged type is:

```
[[class] number]EXPLICIT Type
```

Tagging

One class of tagged types deserves special mention, as it is used to convey a special datatype. That class is the Application class used to transport application-wide datatypes. Application wide datatypes were specially defined for SNMP and are constructed through implicit tagging, as they are derived from simple datatypes. Table 3.3 summarizes the six application wide datatypes defined for SNMP.

To differentiate tags, each 8-bit tag consists of three fields— a class field, format field, and tag number field, as follows:

Class Field	Format Field	Tag Number Field

The Class Field represents the two-high order bits in the 8-bit tag (bits 8 and 7), and their setting denotes the class of the field—universal (00), application-wide (01), context-specific (10), or private (11). Both simple and simply constructed datatypes belong to the Universal class type. Application-wide datatypes belong to the

TABLE 3.3 SNMP Application-Wide Datatypes

Datatype	Description

ipAddress	Represents an IP address defined as four octets:
	
	`IpAddress ::=`
	`  [APPLICATION 0]`
	`    IMPLICIT OCTET STRING (SIZE(4))`

Counter	A non-negative integer that increases to a maximum value of $2^{32}-1$ and then wraps around to 0.
	
	`Counter ::=`
	`  [APPLICATION 1]`
	`    IMPLICIT INTEGER (0..4294967295)`

Gauge	A counting value that can increase or decrease and has a maximum range of 0 to $2^{32}-1$. When it reaches its maximum value a gauge latches and remains there until reset.
	
	`Gauge ::=`
	`  [APPLICATION 2]`
	`    IMPLICIT INTEGER (0..4294967295)`

TimeTicks	A non-negative integer used to record time values in hundredths of a second intervals up to $2^{31}-1$.
	
	`TimeTicks ::=`
	`  [APPLICATION 3]`
	`    IMPLICIT INTEGER (0..4294967295)`

Opaque	A special datatype which enables the exchange of nonstandard information by wrapping it in an OCTET STRING.
	
	`Opaque ::=`
	`  [APPLICATION 4]`
	`    IMPLICIT OCTET STRING`

application-wide class type, while the context-specific class is used to identify a specifically defined constructor type. The fourth class type, private, is used to identify a type defined for a special purpose, such as transporting encrypted data.

The Format field in the tag is represent by bit 6 and identifies the type of tag. When set to 0 it indicates a simple datatype, while when set to a binary 1 it identifies a constructed datatype.

The Tag number field consists of the first 5 low-ordered bits in the tag. Those bits must be used with the 3 high-order bits in the tag to uniquely identify different types of tags. For example, both an integer universal tag and a gauge application-wide class tag have a tag number decimal value of 2. However, an integer is conveyed as a universal class tag and represents a simple datatype. Thus, its 3 high-order bits are 000, and its full tag value is decimal 2. In comparison, a gauge value is conveyed as an application-wide data tag and represents a simple datatype. Thus, its 3 high-order bits are 010, resulting in a tag value of 66 when all 8 bits are considered. Table 3.4 summarizes the bit encoding for the Class, Format, and Tag value fields for the application-wide datatypes and SNMP PDUs used to convey commands.

TABLE 3.4 Application-Wide Datatypes and SNMP PDU Encodings

Datatype/PDU	Class	F	Tag Number	Hex Value
Boolean	000	0	0001	1
Integer	000	0	0010	2
Bit String	000	0	0011	3
Octet String	000	0	0100	4
Null	000	0	0101	5
Object Identifier	000	0	1100	6
Sequence, Sequence Of	001	1	0000	30
IpAddress	010	0	0000	40
Counter	010	0	0001	41
Gauge	010	0	0010	42
TimeTicks	010	0	0011	43
Opaque	010	0	1000	44
Get-Request PDU	101	0	0000	A0
Get-Next-Request PDU	101	0	0001	A1
Get-Response PDU	101	0	0010	A2
Set-Request PDU	101	0	0011	A3
Trap-PDU	101	0	0100	A4

Other Types

The fourth kind of type defined under ASN.1 is the catch all *other*. Examples of *other* types include GeneralizedTime, UTC-Time, and an EXTERNAL type. Since the use of types within the *other* type category are not directly applicable to SNMP, an explanation of their use will not be presented. Thus, let's proceed to the Structure of Management Information prior to probing deeper into the MIB.

STRUCTURE AND IDENTIFICATION OF MANAGEMENT INFORMATION

As noted at the beginning of this chapter, the Structure and Identification of Management Information is the mechanism that defines the rules for describing management information. To accomplish this, RFC 1065 and its successor RFC 1155 (whose titles are similar to the heading of this section) use ASN.1 notation to provide formal descriptions of the defined management structure.

RFC 1065 and its successor RFC 1155 are primarily focused upon two key areas. First, each RFC defines a naming structure for identifying managed objects. Second, each RFC defines a format to define managed objects. Although neither RFC defines objects in the MIB, they both specify the format used by other RFCs to define network management objects. Due to this, those RFCs provide the framework for managing TCP/IP-based internets, commonly referred to as the *Structure of Management Information (SMI)*. This section will first review that portion of the global naming tree applicable to Internet network management, then proceed to the format specified by SMI for defining managed objects, including the syntax specified for defining the abstract data structure corresponding to object types supported by the framework.

Network Management Subtrees

The previous section on ASN.1 briefly reviewed the global naming tree previously illustrated in Figure 3.1. As noted, a sequence of integers that form the path from the root through one or more nodes to an object represents an OBJECT IDENTIFIER. Currently there are six subtrees or nodes defined under the internet node, of which three are most applicable for SNMP network management purposes. Those nodes or subtrees are mgmt, experimental, and private. Each of those nodes or subtrees are identified using the following format:

```
name OBJECT IDENTIFIER ::= {path}
```

Thus, the directory node would be identified as:

```
directory OBJECT IDENTIFIER ::= {1.3.6.1.1.}
```

As an alternative, since the directory node is the first node under the internet node, it can be identified as follows using a combination of text and numeric identifiers:

```
directory OBJECT IDENTIFIER ::= {internet 1}
```

The mgmt Subtree

The mgmt subtree represents the location where objects defined in IAB-approved documents are placed. That is, once an RFC that defines a new version of the Internet-standard MIB is approved, it is assigned an OBJECT IDENTIFIER under the mgmt subtree. Currently only one subtree, mib-2, is defined. That RFC uses the object identifier

```
{mgmt 1}
```

which can also be represented by the path 1.3.6.1.2.1.

The experimental Subtree

The experimental subtree represents the location of objects used in Internet experiments. Newly defined objects are normally placed under the experimental subtree until they successfully pass a trial period during which any necessary revisions are performed. Once this is accomplished the objects are moved under the mgmt subtree.

Objects defined under the experimental subtree have the OBJECT IDENTIFIER prefix

```
experimental OBJECT IDENTIFIER ::= {internet 3}
```

which could also be specified as the path 1.3.6.1.3.

The private Subtree

The private subtree represents a mechanism that enables a standardized expansion of SNMP to accommodate hardware and software developers, universities, and even government entities to define new MIB objects. To accomplish this the subtree enterprises, under the private node, is used by the Assigned Numbers authority for the Internet as a mechanism for registering vendor- or organization-specific MIB objects. To accomplish this the OBJECT IDENTIFIER prefix

```
enterprises OBJECT IDENTIFIER ::= {private 1}
```

which represents the path 1.3.6.1.4.1 in the global naming tree, forms the node under which a vendor or organization's registered MIB objects are placed. To illustrate this concept assume the company Fudrucker manufactures bridges, routers, and gateways. Let's further assume that the Internet Assigned Numbers Authority assigned node 77 to Fudrucker, and the vendor's subtree appears as shown in Figure 3.2. Then, the path to the firm's router MIB would become:

```
1.3.6.1.4.1.77.2
```

Program Utilization Example

Through the use of certain SNMP programs, the structure and use of the global naming tree is facilitated by the generation of a graphic user interface. While such programs hide many of the complexities of SNMP, as we will soon note, knowledge of certain aspects of the tree is required to efficiently operate such programs.

In this section I will illustrate the extraction of information from the private subtree of an RMON probe attached to a dis-

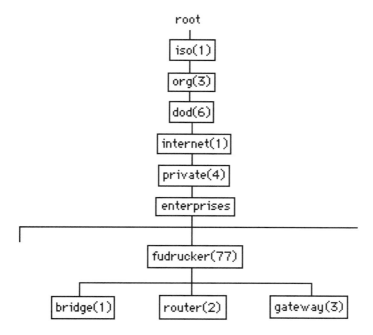

FIGURE 3.2 A hypothetical vendor subtree.

tant network. In doing so I will use SimpleView, a Windows software product from Triticom of Eden Prairie, MN.

Figure 3.3 illustrates the SimpleView screen after an RMON probe at network address 198.78.46.37 was first selected, and the GetNext entry from the Manage menu was next selected. In this example I entered the term *private* as the MIB variable, as I wish to examine the structure and values associated with the private subtree associated with the probe.

Although you can directly enter a subtree name, in the event you forget the name of a subtree or an entry under a subtree, SimpleView contains a powerful MIB walk facility that is initiated either from selecting MIB Browse from the dialog box previously shown in Figure 3.3, or from a View entry from the MIB Database menu. Either action results in the display of a window labeled MIB Walk, which is illustrated in Figure 3.4.

The SimpleView MIB Walk window allows a user to browse through MIB items defined in the MIB database. The program

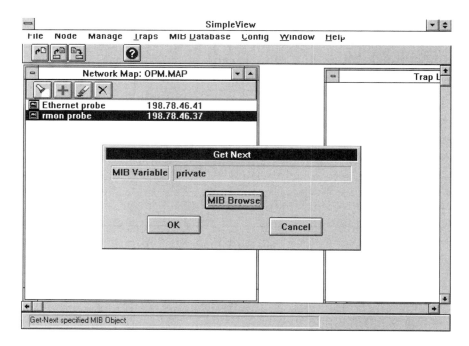

FIGURE 3.3 Using Triticom's SimpleView to display the structure and values of the private subtree of a device on the network.

supports expandable/collapsible trees and leaves that represent MIB objects. Thus, double-clicking on any entry in the window shown in Figure 3.4 would result in an expansion to display level-1 items or objects under the selected subtree. By highlighting an MIB object and clicking on the Select button, the selected object name is copied to the MIB field of GET, GET-NEXT, and SET dialog boxes selected from the Manage menu.

Through the use of a series of GetNext commands, of which the first used the MIB variable private, I was able to walk through the private subtree of the probe whose network address is 198.78.46.37. A portion of this walk through the private subtree is illustrated in Figure 3.5, where the window labeled TrapLog displays the results of a previous sequence of GetNext commands issued through SimpleView. Note that the first two lines in the TrapLog represent the response to the first GetNext command, with the first line of the response listing the address

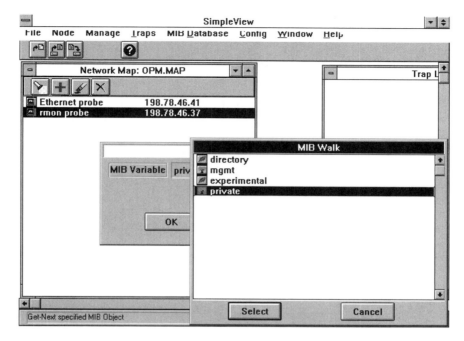

FIGURE 3.4 The SimpleView MIB Walk window enables you to browse through MIB items defined in the MIB, as well as to copy a selected object for use by GET, GET-NEXT, and SET dialog boxes.

that the command was sent to. The second line, which begins "enterprises [209.1.1.01] = cornerstone," tells us that the vendor of the product was registered or assigned node 209 by the Internet Assigned Numbers Authority. Subnode 1.1 under 209 returns the name of the product Cornerstone, while subnode 1.2 under 209 returns the version of the product, which in this example is 1.53. Note that the terminating zero for each displayed response is a mechanism to indicate there is only one value associated with the object, a topic expanded upon later in this section.

Since SimpleView was developed independently of the Cornerstone RMON agent, which is a product of Network General, I had to guess what the values returned from a walk through the private MIB represents—or do the unthinkable and read the RMON agent manual, if one were available, that described its private MIB. Since vendors can essentially do whatever they

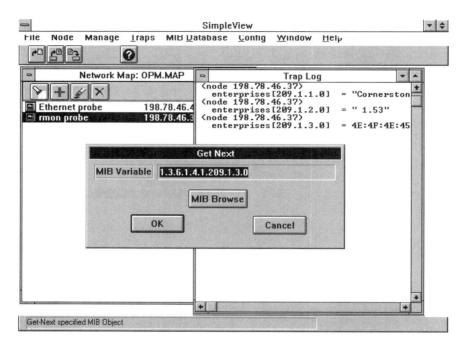

FIGURE 3.5 Walking through the private subtree of an RMON probe.

desire with respect to placing objects in a private MIB, coordination between vendors developing managers and vendors developing agents is best for the MIB-2 portion of the naming tree and can represent the worst aspects of cooperation with respect to the private subtree. This is the price paid for a naming structure that provides a high degree of flexibility, which enables vendors to improve their products beyond standardized functions.

Defining Managed Objects

Under the SMI framework, only a subset of ASN.1 datatypes are supported. For example, only INTEGER, OCTET STRING, OBJECT IDENTIFIER, NULL, and BIT STRING (Version 2) simple types are supported. In addition, several application-wide types are defined. Table 3.3 previously summarized the application-wide datatypes defined by the SMI.

Defining MIB Objects

Earlier, this chapter examined the use of an OBJECT-TYPE macro to define an MIB managed object. That example noted that each definition commences with a name and ends with the assignment of an OBJECT IDENTIFIER. Now we'll proceed further to examine how tables are defined and manipulated as well as how singular entities representing a one-of-a-kind object that is not part of a table are defined and manipulated.

Under the SMI framework, SEQUENCE and SEQUENCE OF constructed types are supported. A row consisting of one or more types can be defined as follows:

```
<row> ::=
     SEQUENCE {<type₁>,...<typeₙ>}
```

Here each type is simple or application-wide, and the defined sequence forms a row in a table. Then, a table takes the following form:

```
<table> ::=
     SEQUENCE OF <row>
```

Under the SMI framework each row has an identical number of objects, with one or more objects defined as an index for accessing an entry in the table.

To differentiate an object that is not part of a table, the naming convention specifies that a dot zero (.0) is appended to the object path. Thus, an object path which includes the suffix .0 indicates only one instance or value is associated with the object. Another method by which you can note the presence and location of a one-of-a-kind object is via viewing exploded subtrees of the global naming tree. Since a one-of-a-kind object cannot have subnodes, it must reside at an endpoint or leaf of the tree. Thus, another term used to indicate a one-of-a-kind object is a *leaf*.

For readers familiar with the manipulation of array elements via a programming language, the manipulation of SNMP table elements is much more restrictive. Under the SMI framework, only instances of columnar objects that form the cells of a table can be manipulated. Thus, a set of clauses was developed that define the method by which columnar objects are retrieved. The key clause is INDEX, which is used to define the instance of tabular objects. To accomplish this the INDEX value for a particular table is located by referring to the table's ENTRY definition, which always follows each table definition in a MIB. Here the ENTRY definition defines a row in a table by listing its columns. Then, the INDEX clause of the ENTRY definition functions as the key for manipulating the rows in the table. To illustrate an example of the preceding, let's examine the buffer Control Table that represents a SEQUENCE OF entries. The MIB table definition from RFC 1757 covering the Remote Network Monitoring MIB is as follows:

```
bufferControlTable  OBJECT-TYPE
    SYNTAX      SEQUENCE OF BufferControlEntry
    ACCESS      not-accessible
    STATUS      mandatory
    DESCRIPTION
        "A list of buffers control entries."
    ::= {capture 1}
```

The bufferControlTable, like all SNMP tables, is a SEQUENCE OF entries. The definition of an entry in that table follows:

```
bufferControlEntry  OBJECT-TYPE
    SYNTAX      BufferControlEntry
    ACCESS      not-accessible
    STATUS      mandatory
    DESCRIPTION
        "A set of parameters...."
    INDEX       { bufferControlIndex }
    ::= { bufferControlTable 1 }
```

From the preceding the bufferControlEntry definition points to the BufferControlEntry definition (note the capital B) to locate the list of variables in the row (column elements). A portion of those variables are defined as follows:

```
BufferControlEntry ::= SEQUENCE {
   bufferControlIndex        INTEGER (1...65535),
   bufferControlChannelIndex     INTEGER (1...65535),
   bufferControlFullStatus INTEGER,
   .    .                    .
   .    .                    .
   }
```

Once the variables are defined the datatype for each variable is listed. For example:

```
bufferControlIndex      OBJECT-TYPE
SYNTAX     INTEGER (1..65535)
ACCESS     read-only
STATUS     mandatory
DESCRIPTION
    "An index that..."
    ::= {bufferControlEntry 1}
```

By pointing to the bufferControlIndex and issuing a series of GET-NEXT commands, you obtain the ability to walk through the table, retrieving the instances of each object.

MIB

In concluding this chapter I will present a summary of the objects located in the current standard MIB, mib-2, whose location in the global naming tree is 1.3.6.1.2.1. As illustrated in Figure 3.1, located under that node are ten MIB groups. After briefly reviewing the objects in the first few MIB groups to include a few examples showing the retrieval of object instances from some groups, I will essentially provide a general overview of the remaining groups and focus upon the SNMP group. Although certain MIB groups are essentially skipped over while other groups are limited to a general explanation of their objects, a complete reference to MIB groups can be found in Appendix B. In addition, in succeeding chapters readers will find information concerning the use of different MIB groups as I focus upon managing different LAN protocols, equipment, and transmission facilities used to interconnect networks. Those chapters covering different MIB groups commence with Chapter 6, since Chapter 4 provides characteristics of Ethernet and Token-Ring networks, while Chapter 5 is focused upon the management of those networks with RMON probes.

System Group

The *system group* contains seven objects used to describe configuration information about the managed device. The OBJECT IDENTIFIER for the system group is {mib-2 1}. The individual objects within the system group have an OBJECT IDENTIFIER of {system *n*}, with *n* having a value of 1 to 7. A brief description of the instance of each object is contained in Table 3.5, while Appendix B includes the formal definition of objects in the system group.

From Figure 3.1 you will note that the system subtree is located at 1.3.6.1.2.1.1. Thus, I can illustrate the object iden-

TABLE 3.5 System Group

Object Identifier	Access	Description
sysDescr (1.3.6.1.2.1.1.1)	r	Description of the device
sysObjectID (1.3.6.1.2.1.1.2)	r	Identification of an agent's hardware, software, and/or resources
sysUpTime (1.3.6.1.2.1.1.3)	r	Length of the time since the agent was started or restarted
sysContact (1.3.6.1.2.1.1.4)	r-w	Name of the contact person responsible for the node
sysName (1.3.6.1.2.1.1.5)	r-w	Device name
sysLocation (1.3.6.1.2.1.1.6)	r-w	Physical location of the device
sysServices (1.3.6.1.2.1.1.7)	r	Coded number that identifies the set of services provided by the device

tifiers under that subtree in a tree diagram, as illustrated in Figure 3.6.

Through the use of SimpleView or a similar SNMP management program, the global naming tree can, to a large degree, become hidden through the use of a program's graphic user interface. An example of this is shown in Figure 3.7, in which the SimpleView View option from the program's MIB Database menu was selected to obtain a view of the entries within the system group. As indicated earlier in this chapter, after selecting a desired object from the SimpleView MIB Walk window, you could use the GET, GET-NEXT, or SET entries from the program's Manage menu to perform a desired operation on a selected MIB object. By selecting the system group entry and issuing a series of GET-NEXT commands, you can walk through the system group of the selected device. The result of this operation, which in effect results in a dump of the object instances of the system group for the selected device at address 198.78.46.37, is shown in Figure 3.8. In this example the selected object at address 198.78.46.37 is a Network General RMON probe, more formally referred to as a Cornerstone Agent, which is its system name.

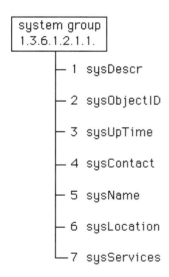

FIGURE 3.6 The system group MIB objects.

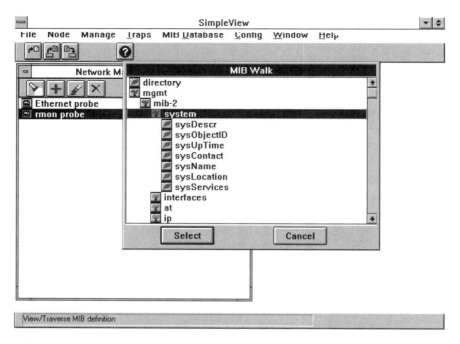

FIGURE 3.7   Using SimpleView to select an object in the system group.

Interfaces Group

The *interface* group consists of 23 object identifiers that provide generic performance, configuration, and status information for any type of interface. Although this generic information can provide insight into the activity at an interface, by its nature generic information is not specific enough for many management applications. For example, although a count of inbound and outbound octets is relevant to both Ethernet and Token-Ring networks, you could not have a generic collision count, as it would not be applicable to Token-Ring networks. Recognizing this, the SNMP developers used the transmission subgroup as a location to define a set of interface-specific MIB groups.

Since a managed device can have more than one interface, a mechanism was required to identify the interface attachment to a device. Thus, the interfaces subtree is structured so that the first identifier (ifNumber) serves as a pointer to the interface. Informa-

```
(node 198.78.46.37)
  sysDescr[0] = "RMON CA Win Version 2.5c"
(node 198.78.46.37)
  sysObjectID[0] = enterprises[209.1.1.0] =  1.3.6.1.4.1.209.1.1.0
(node 198.78.46.37)
  sysUpTime[0] = 169830286 (19 days, 15:45:02)
(node 198.78.46.37)
  sysContact[0] = "Network Administrator"
(node 198.78.46.37)
  sysName[0] = "Cornerstone Agent"
(node 198.78.46.37)
  sysLocation[0] = "Network Services Dept"
(node 198.78.46.37)
  sysServices[0] = 72
```

FIGURE 3.8 The results obtained from using SimpleView to walk through the system group of a selected device.

tion about a specific interface is included in a table consisting of 22 entries. Table 3.6 lists the object identifiers that provide information concerning the state of an interface, as well as a brief description of each identifier. Note that the ifType object identifier is used to indicate the specific type of interface. Currently over 50 types of network interfaces are defined, ranging from a version of X.25 (interface type 4) to ATM Adaption Layer 5 (interface type 49).

To illustrate the retrieval of instances from the Interface group I will again turn to the use of SimpleView. Figure 3.9 illustrates the result obtained from *exploding* the interfaces entry in the program's MIB Walk window. By selecting the interfaces entry and using a series of GET-NEXT requests, I was able to walk through the interfaces group of the remote RMON probe. The results of this operation are shown in Figure 3.10.

An examination of the instances of many of the object identifiers of the interfaces group can provide you with information that can be a valuable assistant in determining the health of a network component. From the results of the MIB Walk shown in Figure 3.10, note that the probe is operational (ifOperStatus=1) and no errors (ifInErrors=0 and ifOutErrors=0) were detected. Thus, a quick glance at a few of the instances of objects in the interface group tells us that the RMON probe is operational and no input or output errors were encountered.

TABLE 3.6 Interface Group

Object Identifier	Access	Description
ifIndex (1.3.6.1.2.1.2.2.1)	r	Interface number
ifDeser (1.3.6.1.2.1.2.2.2)	r	Text describing the interface
ifType (1.3.6.1.2.1.2.2.3)	r	Numeric identifier that defines the type of interface
ifMtu (1.3.6.1.2.1.2.2.4)	r	Largest PDU in octets that can be sent or received
ifSpeed (1.3.6.1.2.1.2.2.5)	r	Transmission rate in bps
ifPhysAddress (1.3.6.1.2.1.2.2.6)	r	Media-specific address
ifAdminStatus (1.3.6.1.2.1.2.2.7)	r	Desired interface state
ifOperStatus (1.3.6.1.2.1.2.2.8)	r	Current interface state
ifLastChange (1.3.6.1.2.1.2.2.9)	r	Time when the interface state changed last
ifInOctets (1.3.6.1.2.1.2.2.10)	r	Total octets received, including framing
ifInUcastPkts (1.3.6.1.2.1.2.2.11)	r	Number of unicast packets delivered
ifInNUcastPkts (1.3.6.1.2.1.2.2.12)	r	Number of nonunicast packets delivered
ifInDiscards (1.3.6.1.2.1.2.2.13)	r	Number of inbound packets discarded due to resource limitations
ifInErrors (1.3.6.1.2.1.2.2.14)	r	Number of inbound packets discarded due to being in error
ifInUnknownProtos (1.3.6.1.2.1.2.2.15)	r	Number of inbound packets discarded because they were directed to an unknown protocol
ifOutOctets (1.3.6.1.2.1.2.2.16)	r	Total number of transmitted octets, including framing
ifOutUcastPkts (1.3.6.1.2.1.2.2.17)	r	Total number of unicast packets transmitted

TABLE 3.6   Interface Group (*cont.*)

Object Identifier	Access	Description
ifOutNUcastPkts (1.3.6.1.2.1.2.2.18)	r	Total broadcast or multicast packets transmitted
ifOutDiscards (1.3.6.1.2.1.2.2.19)	r	Total number of outbound packets discarded due to resource limitations
ifOutErrors (1.3.6.1.2.1.2.2.20)	r	Number of outbound packets discarded due to error
ifOutQLen (1.3.6.1.2.1.2.2.21)	r	Number of packets in the output queue
ifSpecific (1.3.6.1.2.1.2.2.22)	r	Identifier for an MIB that contains additional information related to the interface type

One of the more interesting aspects of the Interfaces table is its last OBJECT IDENTIFIER, ifSpecific. If additional variables for the interface exist, ifSpecific will function as a pointer to an MIB subtree where additional variables can be read. For example, if the ifType is Token-Ring, the value of ifSpecific could be set to identify the MIB subtree, defining objects specific to Token-Ring. If there is no additional information for ifSpecific to point to, its value would be set to zero. Since the RMON probe just queried is attached to an Ethernet LAN, as you might expect, its ifSpecific value is zero. Readers are referred to Appendix B for detailed information concerning the OBJECT IDENTIFIERs for the interfaces group.

Address Translation Group

The *address translation* group provides a mapping of the internetwork layer address (for example, its IP address) of a device to its physical or interface layer address. This group uses a single table for mapping, with each row containing three columns. Those columns contain instances for atIfIndex (the interface number), atPhysAddress (the media address), and atNetAddress (the IP address). Readers are referred to Appendix B for detailed information concerning this MIB group.

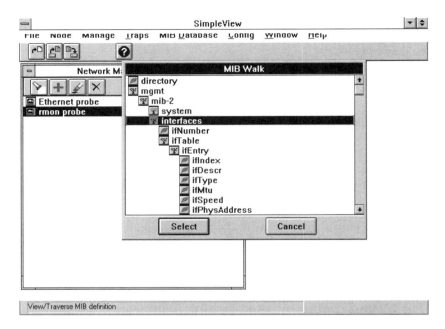

FIGURE 3.9 Using SimpleView to examine the object entries within the interfaces group.

Internet Protocol Group

The *Internet Protocol* (*IP*) group contains the managed objects that provide information about the IP subsystem of a managed node. Included in this group are 19 scalars and four tables whose instances provide such IP information as the state of routing tables and address conversion tables. The IP group OBJECT IDENTIFIER is {mib 4}, which results in a full naming tree address of 1.3.6.1.2.4. Table 3.7 lists the 19 scalar objects defined within the IP group to include a short description of their use.

The tables in the IP group include address, route, and address translation. The IP address table is used to keep track of addresses associated with the managed node, while the address translation table tracks the mapping between IP and the physical address of the managed node. The routing table tracks IP routes associated with the managed node. Table 3.8 lists the OBJECT IDENTIFIERs for the IP group address and address translation tables. Readers are referred to Appendix B

```
(node 198.78.46.37)
  ifIndex[1] = 1
(node 198.78.46.37)
  ifDescr[1] = "ProTools, Inc. Cornerstone Agent Serial No.
NONE Ver. 1.53"
(node 198.78.46.37)
  ifType[1] = 9
(node 198.78.46.37)
  ifMtu[1] = 1500
(node 198.78.46.37)
  ifSpeed[1] = 4194304
(node 198.78.46.37)
  ifPhysAddress[1] = 00:00:F6:2B:5D:B7
(node 198.78.46.37)
  ifAdminStatus[1] = 1
(node 198.78.46.37)
  ifOperStatus[1]
(node 198.78.46.37)
  ifLastChange[1] = 1428 (00:00:14)
(node 198.78.46.37)
  ifInOctets[1] = 1186429611
(node 198.78.46.37)
  ifInUcastPkts[1] = 141222
(node 198.78.46.37)
  ifInNucastPkts[1] = 141216
(node 198.78.46.37)
  ifInDiscards[1] = 0
(node 198.78.46.37)
  ifInErrors[1] = 0
(node 198.78.46.37)
  ifInUnknownProtos[1] = 2270730
(node 198.78.46.37)
  ifOutOctets[1] = 350199
(node 198.78.46.37)
  ifOutNUcastPkts[1] = 1266
(node 198.78.46.37)
  ifOutDiscards[1] = 0
(node 198.78.46.37)
  ifOutErrors[1] = 0
(node 198.78.46.37)
  ifOutQLen[1] = 1
(node 198.78.46.37)
  if Specific[1] = 0.0
```

FIGURE 3.10 The results obtained from a walk through the interfaces group of an RMON probe.

TABLE 3.7 Internet Protocol Group Scalar Objects

Object Identifier	Access	Description
ipForwarding (1.3.6.1.2.1.4.1)	r-w	Whether the entry is acting as a gateway with respect to forwarding packets
ipDefaultTTL (1.3.6.1.2.1.4.2)	r-w	Default Time-To-Live value of the IP header
ipInReceives (1.3.6.1.2.1.4.3)	r	Number of input datagrams received, including those in error
ipInHdrErrors (1.3.6.1.2.1.4.4)	r	Number of input datagrams discarded due to errors in their IP headers
ipInAddrErrors (1.3.6.1.2.1.4.5)	r	Number of input datagrams discarded due to IP address not valid
ipForwDatagrams (1.3.6.1.2.1.4.6)	r	Number of forwarded datagram
ipInUnknownProtos (1.3.6.1.2.1.4.7)	r	Number of datagrams discarded because of an unknown or unsupported protocol
ipInDiscards (1.3.6.1.2.1.4.8)	r	Number of datagrams discarded due to device resource imitations; that is, buffer space
ipInDelivers (1.3.6.1.2.1.4.9)	r	Number of datagrams successfully delivered
ipOutRequests (1.3.6.1.2.1.4.10)	r	Number of IP datagrams that local IP user protocols supplied to IP in request for transmission
ipOutDiscards (1.3.6.1.2.1.4.11)	r	Number of datagrams discarded due to lack of resources
ipOutNoRoutes (1.3.6.1.2.1.4.12)	r	Number of datagrams discarded due to no route
ipReasmTimeout (1.3.6.1.2.1.4.13)	r	Maximum number of seconds that received fragments held while awaiting reassembly
ipReasmReqds (1.3.6.1.2.1.4.14)	r	Number of IP fragments received requiring reassembly
ipReasmOKs (1.3.6.1.2.1.4.15)	r	Number of IP datagrams successfully reassembled
ipReasmFails (1.3.6.1.2.1.4.16)	r	Number of failures detected by the IP reassembly algorithm
ipFragOKs (1.3.6.1.2.1.4.17)	r	Number of IP datagrams successfully fragmented
ipFragFails (1.3.6.1.2.1.4.18)	r	Number of IP datagrams needing fragmentation but could not be fragmented
ipFragCreates (1.3.6.1.2.1.4.19)	r	Number of IP fragments generated

TABLE 3.8 Internet Protocol Address and Address Translation Table Object Identifiers

Address Table	Access	Object Identifier Description
ipAdEntAddr (1.3.6.1.2.1.4.20.1.1)	r	IP address
ipAdEntIfIndex (1.3.6.1.2.1.4.20.1.2)	r	Interface number
ipAdEntNetMask (1.3.6.1.2.1.4.20.1.3)	r	Subnet-mask for the IP address
ipAdEntBeastAddr (1.3.6.1.2.1.4.20.1.4)	r	Least significant bit of the IP broadcast address
ipAdEntReasmMaxSize (1.3.6.1.2.1.4.20.1.5)	r	Largest IP datagram that can be reassembled
Address Translation Table		
ipNetToMediaIfIndex (1.3.6.1.2.1.4.22.1.1)	r-w	Interface number
ipNetToMediaPhysAddress (1.3.6.1.2.1.4.22.1.2)	r-w	Media address of mapping
ipNetToMediaNetAddress (1.3.6.1.2.1.4.22.1.3)	r-w	IP address of mapping
ipNetToMediaType (1.3.6.1.2.1.4.22.1.4)	r-w	Method by which mapping occurred

for detailed information concerning the OBJECT IDENTIFIERs for the Internet Protocol group.

Internet Control Message Protocol Group

The *Internet Control Message Protocol* group is responsible for handling error and control messages normally generated by gateways and hosts to report problems to the originators of datagrams. The Internet Control Message Protocol Group provides statistics and error counts for the ICMP protocol. This group has the OBJECT IDENTIFIER {mib 5}, while its numeric global naming tree address is 1.3.6.1.2.5. Readers are referred to Appendix B for information concerning the OBJECT IDENTIFIERs for the Internet Control Message Protocol Group.

Transmission Group

The *transmission* group is one of the more interesting MIB groups because it is not actually a group. Instead, it represents a node in the global naming tree, under which media-specific transmission groups are located.

The OBJECT IDENTIFIER for the Transmission Group is {mib 10}, while its position in the global naming tree is 1.3.6. 1.2.1.10. Directly under the Transmission Group node are 12 currently defined MIB groups. Figure 3.11 illustrates the relationship of the currently defined MIB groups under the transmission group node to that node. Later in this book I will examine several

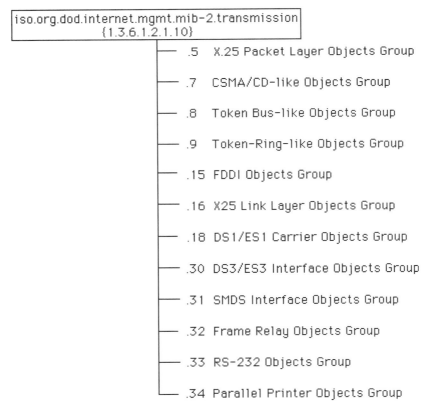

iso.org.dod.internet.mgmt.mib-2.transmission
{1.3.6.1.2.1.10}

- .5 X.25 Packet Layer Objects Group
- .7 CSMA/CD-like Objects Group
- .8 Token Bus-like Objects Group
- .9 Token-Ring-like Objects Group
- .15 FDDI Objects Group
- .16 X25 Link Layer Objects Group
- .18 DS1/ES1 Carrier Objects Group
- .30 DS3/ES3 Interface Objects Group
- .31 SMDS Interface Objects Group
- .32 Frame Relay Objects Group
- .33 RS-232 Objects Group
- .34 Parallel Printer Objects Group

FIGURE 3.11 Currently defined MIB transmission groups.

of the MIB transmission groups illustrated in Figure 3.11 in detail, including noting the information retrievable and what different OBJECT IDENTIFIER instances might suggest concerning the operation of a device or transmission facility. Readers are referred to Appendix A for a list of RFCs associated with each of the currently defined transmission groups.

Transmission Control Protocol Group

The *Transmission Control Protocol (TCP)* group provides statistics about the TCP connection that represents the operation of the layer-4 protocol. The TCP group has the OBJECT IDENTIFIER {mib 6}, while its numeric global naming tree identifier is 1.3.6.1.2.6. Readers are referred to Appendix B for information concerning the OBJECT IDENTIFIERs associated with the TCP Group.

User Datagram Protocol Group

Statistics and information about the TCP/IP layer-4 protocol, known as the *User Datagram Protocol*, are maintained in the object identifiers associated with this group, which is a subtree under the MIB and has an OBJECT IDENTIFIER of {mib 7}, while its global naming tree numeric address is 1.3.6.2.1.7. Readers are referred to Appendix B for a complete description of the OBJECT IDENTIFIERs associated with this group.

Exterior Gateway Protocol Group

The *Exterior Gateway Protocol (EGP)* represents a communications protocol that permits neighboring routers in different domains to exchange routing information. The protocol is defined in RFC 904, and the Exterior Gateway Protocol group's OBJECT IDENTIFIERs provide statistical information about the EGP as well as a table of neighbor information.

The Exterior Gateway Protocol group has the OBJECT IDENTIFIER {mib 8}, while its global naming tree numeric address is 1.3.6.2.1.8. Readers are referred to Appendix B for a complete description of object identifiers associated with this group.

SNMP Group

In concluding this section I will examine the SNMP MIB group whose OBJECT IDENTIFIER is {mib 11}, while its global naming tree address is 1.3.6.1.2.11. Although the SNMP group is similar to other MIB groups covered in this chapter with respect to their OBJECT IDENTIFIERs (as fully described in Appendix B), due to the importance of those identifiers in examining the effectiveness of SNMP operations, as well as the effect of SNMP on a LAN's nonmanagement data flow, I will examine the use of the group's identifiers in some detail in this section.

If you examine the group's MIB definitions listed in Appendix B you will note that this group has 28 identifiers, with identifiers ranging from 1 to 30, as 7 and 23 are currently not used. Identifiers 1 and 3 through 19 perform traffic counts for incoming SNMP messages, while identifiers 2 and 20 through 29 provide traffic counts for outgoing SNMP messages. While all of the preceding identifiers are limited to read-only access, identifier 30, which has read-write access, governs the enabling or disabling of authentication traps.

Authentication Traps

When a station is properly configured, the enabling of the OBJECT IDENTIFIER snmpEnableAuthenTraps will result in the transmission of a trap whenever an improperly authenticated message is received by the station. Although you will normally want to enable this identifier, upon occasion it can result in the generation of a large amount of repetitive traffic that can interfere with network operations.

To illustrate the preceding, consider the community naming process. For a manager to be able to correctly interoperate with each agent, the community names, in the form of strings configured for each managed device, must exactly match the configured string of the manager, since the community name functions as a password. Figure 3.12 illustrates the community dialog box for the SimpleView manager. In this example, the SNMP GET, SET, and TRAP communities are each set to PUBLIC; which for many internal networks connected to public facilities can represent a poor choice, since PUBLIC is a commonly used default set-

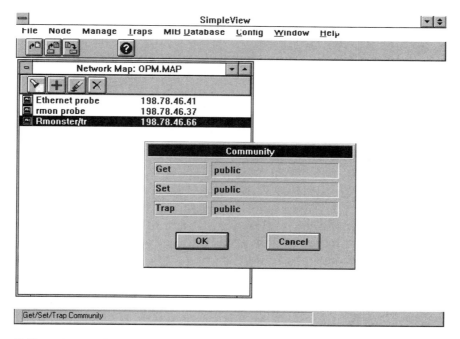

FIGURE 3.12 The community names assigned to the management platform must match agent community names for the manager and agent to interoperate with each other.

ting. Although you may not care who retrieves information from your agents, it is doubtful if you want any person with a bit of SNMP knowledge to be able to modify an agent via the use of the SET command. Thus, at the very least, you should consider modifying the manager and each agent's SET community name to an alphanumeric string that would be difficult to guess.

Returning to our traffic generation problem, consider a management station inadvertently configured with one or more community names that do not match agent names. If the management station is configured to poll agents on a predefined basis, enabling snmpEnableAuthenTraps will result in the generation of a large number of authentication-failure traffic, which becomes more of a nuisance than being of assistance—especially if you have to manually reset each trap received by a management station. Another trap-associated problem can occur if you use two or more management platforms and segmented your network with respect to the control of agents by each management platform. If you leave the string for the TRAP community name blank, many management platforms will display every trap received in their trap log, which may not be your intention. Now that I have covered the only SNMP OBJECT IDENTIFIER that has read-write access capability, let's focus upon incoming and outgoing SNMP traffic counts.

Incoming Traffic Counts

Table 3.9 lists 16 SNMP object identifiers as well as a brief description of those identifiers used to provide incoming traffic counts for a managed object. In examining the entries in Table 3.9, note that the first identifier indicates the total number of SNMP messages delivered to the managed agent, while the second through tenth identifiers listed in the table represent error conditions. The eleventh through fifteenth identifiers provide a summary of commands accepted and processed by the managed agent, while the 16th identifier indicates the number of traps accepted and processed. By examining the count of error condition identifiers, and comparing that count to the number of SNMP messages tracked by snmpInPkts, you can obtain an appreciation of the performance of your network management platform, your communications infrastructure, and the operation of your managed agent.

Since SNMP is transported by UDP, you can reasonably expect the snmpInGenErrs count to reflect the error rate on your communications infrastructure, which should be relatively low. Thus, a comparison of the values for the identifiers snmpInPkts and snmpInGenErrs permits you to determine if the error rate for other than defined SNMP errors is within an acceptable range. Concerning the defined SNMP errors listed in Table 3.9, by examining the count of different identifiers you can determine if the manager and agent are configured correctly, if a manager is performing correctly, and if the agent and manager provide support for the same version of SNMP. For example, a count for snmpInBadVersions indicates incompatibility between SNMP manager and agent support levels, while a count for snmpInBad-CommunityNames indicates a configuration problem between the manager and agent.

TABLE 3.9 Incoming SNMP Traffic Counts

Object Identifier	Access	Description
snmpInPkts (1.3.6.1.2.1.11.1)	r	Number of SNMP messages delivered by the transport service
snmpInBadVersions (1.3.6.1.2.1.11.3)	r	Number of SNMP messages delivered for an unsupported SNMP version
snmpInBadCommunityNames (1.3.6.1.2.1.11.4)	r	Number of SNMP messages that used an unknown community name
snmpInBadCommunityUses (1.3.6.1.2.1.11.5)	r	Number of SNMP messages requesting an unsupported operation by the community name
snmpInASNParseErrs (1.3.6.1.2.1.11.6)	r	Number of ASN.1 or BER errors encountered when decoding a message
snmpInTooBigs (1.3.6.1.2.1.11.8)	r	Number of SNMP message responses that could not fit in the largest message size supported by the manager and agent
snmpInNoSuchNames (1.3.6.1.2.1.11.9)	r	Number of messages that indicate a requested object is not supported by the agent
snmpInBadValues (1.3.6.1.2.1.11.10)	r	Number of SET-REQUEST commands that had an improper value
snmpInReadOnlys (1.3.6.1.2.1.11.11)	r	Number of messages indicating a local implementation error resulting from an incorrect SET-REQUEST command
snmpInGenErrs (1.3.6.1.2.1.11.12)	r	Number of messages with errors different from those listed previously
snmpInTotalReqVars (1.3.6.1.2.1.11.13)	r	Number of MIB objects successfully retrieved in response to GET-REQUEST and GET-NEXT-REQUEST commands
snmpInTotalSetVars (1.3.6.1.2.1.11.14)	r	Number of MIB objects successfully updated as a result of SET-REQUESTs
snmpInGetRequests (1.3.6.1.2.1.11.15)	r	Number of GET commands accepted and processed
snmpInGetNexts (1.3.6.1.2.1.11.16)	r	Number of GET-NEXT commands accepted and processed
snmpInSetRequests (1.3.6.1.2.1.11.17)	r	Number of SET-REQUEST commands accepted and processed
snmpInGetResponses (1.3.6.1.2.1.11.18)	r	Number of GET-RESPONSE commands accepted and processed
snmpInTraps (1.3.6.1.2.1.11.19)	r	Number of traps accepted and processed

Outgoing Traffic Counts

Similar to the incoming SNMP traffic counts, the SNMP group has a number of identifiers used to track outgoing traffic. Table 3.10 lists the nine identifiers used to track outgoing SNMP traffic, including a brief description of each identifier.

In examining the entries in Table 3.10 note that they are also subdivided into error counts and traffic counts. The first identifier listed in Table 3.10 provides a count of outbound messages from the agent, while the second through fifth identifiers listed in the table provide a traffic count for different types of error conditions. The last four identifiers listed in Table 3.10 provide a distribution of outgoing SNMP traffic counts based upon the type of outgoing message. Thus, an examination of the traffic counts listed in Table 3.9 provides you with the ability to analyze communications between a manager and agent, while an analysis of the traffic count identifiers listed in Table 3.10 provides a mechanism for analyzing communications between the managed agent and the manager.

To illustrate the use of SNMP identifiers, I used SimpleView to walk through the SNMP group for an agent. The result of my MIB walk through the agent at address 198.78.46.37 is illustrated in Figure 3.13, which represents the listing of Simple-View's trap log after my MIB walk.

In examining the entries in Figure 3.13, note that the value of snmpInPkts was 1279, while the value of snmpOutPkts was 1272 when I started my walk through the SNMP group. Although you would expect the two to equate to one another, note that the value of snmpInBadCommunityNames was 7. Thus, out of the 1279 received packets only 1272 were valid and received responses. Another set of values in Figure 3.13 that may appear questionable and deserves a degree of explanation are the values for snmpInGetRequests and snmpInGetNexts, which are shown as 40 and 1246, respectively. The total for those two identifiers is 1286; however, note that 14 operations were required between retrieving the value for snmpInPkts to retrieving the value of snmpInGetNexts during the walk through the SNMP group. Since seven of the 1279 input packets were bad, the 1279+14−7 equals 40+1246, which explains how the total for snmpInGetRequests and snmpInGetNexts became 1286.

Although it's important to understand why the values

TABLE 3.10 Outgoing SNMP Traffic Counts

Oject Identifier	Access	Description
snmpOutPkts (1.3.6.1.2.1.11.2)	r	Number of messages passed to the transport service
snmpOutTooBigs (1.3.6.1.2.1.11.20)	r	Number of messages sent with the error status field set to *tooBig*, indicating the message could not fit in the largest message size supported by the manager and agent
snmpOutNoSuchNames (1.3.6.1.2.1.11.21)	r	Number of messages sent with the error status field set to *noSuchName*, which indicates a requested object is not supported by the agent
snmpOutBad (1.3.6.1.2.1.11.22)	r	Number of messages sent with the error status field set to *badValue*, which indicates number of SET REQUEST commands sent with an improper value
snmpOutGenErrs (1.3.6.1.2.1.11.24)	r	Number of messages sent with the error status field set to *genErr*, indicating errors different from those previously listed Number of outgoing GET REQUEST
snmpOutGetRequests (1.3.6.1.2.1.11.25)	r	commands transmitted
snmpOutGetNexts (1.3.6.1.2.1.11.26)	r	Number of outgoing GET-NEXT-REQUEST commands transmitted
snmpOutSetRequests (1.3.6.1.2.1.11.27)	r	Number of SET-REQUEST commands transmitted
snmpOutGetResponses (1.3.6.1.2.1.11.28	r	Number of GET-RESPONSE commands transmitted
snmpOutTraps (1.3.6.1.2.1.11.29)	r	Number of traps transmitted

retrieved from an SNMP group during an MIB walk may appear awkward when compared to other identifier values, the real value obtained from retrieving information about this group's values is in verifying configuration settings and focusing upon correcting errors. Thus, retrieving SNMP identifier values can provide information necessary to identify SNMP problems, as well as provide an indication of the type of problem, which can be valuable when attempting to correct.

```
(node 198.78.46.37)
  snmpInPkts[0] = 1279
(node 198.78.46.37)
  snmpOutPkts[0] = 1272
(node 198.78.46.37)
  snmpInnBadVersions[0] = 0
(node 198.78.46.37)
  snmpInBadCommunityNames[0] = 7
(node 198.78.46.37)
  snmpInBadCommunityUses[0] = 0
(node 198.78.46.37)
  snmpInASNParseErrs[0] = 0
(node 198.78.46.37)
  snmpInTooBigs[0] = 0
(node 198.78.46.37)
  snmpInNoSuchNames[0] = 0
(node 198.78.46.37)
  snmpInBadValues[0] = 0
(node 198.78.46.37)
  snmpInReadOnlys[0] = 0
(node 198.78.46.37)
  snmpInGenErrs[0] = 0
(node 198.78.46.37)
  snmpInTotalReqVars[0] = 0
(node 198.78.46.37)
  snmpInTotalSetVars[0] = 0
(node 198.78.46.37)
  snmpInGetRequests[0] = 40
(node 198.78.46.37)
  snmpInGetNexts[0] = 1246
(node 198.78.46.37)
  snmpInSetRequests[0] = 0
(node 198.78.46.37)
  snmpInGetResponses[0] = 0
(node 198.78.46.37)
  snmpInTraps[0] = 0
(node 198.78.46.37)
  snmpOutTooBigs[0] = 0
(node 198.78.46.37)
  snmpOutNoSuchNames[0] = 283
```

FIGURE 3.13 The SimpleView trap log obtained from a walk through an agent's SNMP group.

```
(node 198.78.46.37)
  snmpOutBadValues[0] = 0
(node 198.78.46.37)
  snmpOutGenErrs[0] = 0
(node 198.78.46.37)
  snmpOutGetRequests[0] = 0
(node 198.78.46.37)
  snmpOutGetNexts[0] = 0
(node 198.78.46.37)
  snmpOutSetRequests[0] = 0
(node 198.78.46.37)
  snmpOutGetResponses[0] = 1265
(node 198.78.46.37)
  snmpOutTraps[0] = 0
(node 198.78.46.37)
  snmpEnableAuthenTraps[0] = 1
```

FIGURE 3.13   (*continued*)

SNMP MESSAGE FORMAT

In concluding this chapter I will attempt to put several loose ends together by focusing upon the SNMP message format. In doing so my goal is to provide a general indication of how commands and responses are transported between a manager and agent, and how traps are conveyed from an agent to manager. Once again, readers are reminded that the purpose of this book is to understand the operation of SNMP, not to be a developer's guide. Thus, the concluding information will provide a good indication of the method by which SNMP commands, responses, and traps are conveyed, without requiring many of the intricate details necessary to program a manager or agent.

Figure 3.14 illustrates the general format of an SNMP message. An SNMP message value consists of three subfields. The first indicates the version of SNMP and provides a mechanism to determine compatibility between an agent and manager. Unlike other protocols, SNMP does not support negotiation, and the receipt of an incorrect version results in the message being discarded.

The Community Name field is an octet string that functions as a password for authentication of access to an agent. If a received community name does not match an agent's community name, the message will be discarded. The third subfield of the SNMP message value field is the PDU field. As indicated in Figure 3.14, that field consists of three subfields—a PDU tag, PDU length, and a PDU field value. The last subfield, PDU Field Value, consists of four subfields if it is a nontrap PDU, or six subfields if it represents a trap PDU. Since nontrap PDUs significantly differ from trap PDUs, let me focus attention on each separately.

Nontrap PDUs

The RequestID field provides a mechanism to number or identify requests sent from a manager to an agent. This enables the manager to match a subsequently received GetResponse PDU from an agent to a Get, Get Next, or Set command. The Error Status field is limited to use by an agent transmitting a GetResponse PDU, and indicates the status of a previously received command. Thus, this field is set to a value of zero in a Get, Get Next, or Set command. Table 3.11 summarizes the values supported by the Error Status field.

The Error Index field is similar to the Error Status field in that it is used only by an agent in a GetResponse PDU. Thus, this field is also set to a value of zero in a Get, Get Next, or Set command.

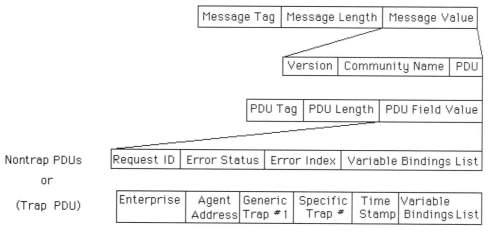

FIGURE 3.14 The SNMP message format.

TABLE 3.11 Error Status Field Values

Field Value	Status Name
0	noError
1	tooBig
2	noSuchName
3	badValue
4	readOnly
5	genError

When responding to a Get, Get Next, or Set command that caused an error, an agent places a value in the Error Index field, which functions as a pointer to a variable in the Variable Bindings List that caused the error condition. Figure 3.15 illustrates the subfields included in the Variable Bindings List field.

The Variable Bindings List represents the instances of the managed objects that are operated on by the message's command, and the Error Index pointer provides the location of the variable in the list that caused an error condition, enabling the manager to obtain additional information concerning the cause of the error.

Trap PDU

The Trap PDU illustrated in the lower portion of Figure 3.14 has a PDU field consisting of six subfields. The Enterprise field contains the OBJECT IDENTIFIER for the network device that

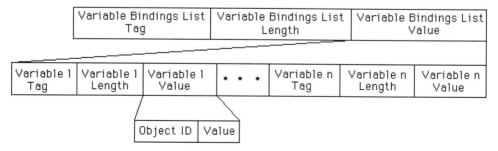

FIGURE 3.15 Variable Bindings List field format.

TABLE 3.12 Generic Traps

Trap	Identifier
coldStart	1
warmStart	2
linkDown	3
linkUp	4
authenticationFailure	5
egpNeighborLoss	6
enterpriseSpecific	7

generated the trap, permitting the management station to identify the trap source. The actual value of this field is obtained from the sysObjectID in the System Group for the device generating the trap. The second field, Agent Address, represents the agent's IP address and further identifies the trap originator to the manager. The third subfield, Generic Trap Number, contains an integer value that represents one of the seven generic traps defined in RFC 1157. Table 3.12 summarizes the seven generic traps and their integer values.

If a value of 7 is included in the Generic Trap field, this indicates that the Specific Trap field contains an enterprise-specific trap. The value in the Specific Trap field then represents a value defined for a specific enterprise. Thus, a management platform constructed independently of an agent may not be able to recognize a specific trap number.

The Time Stamp field indicates the time the trap was generated, and provides a manager with the ability to store and retrieve traps based upon type and time of occurrence when appropriately programmed. The last field, Variable Bindings List, has the same format as that used for nonTrap PDUs, and was previously illustrated in Figure 3.15.

Ethernet and Token-Ring Operations

The ability to effectively manage local area networks using SNMP requires knowledge concerning how LANs operate, including their access methods, cabling infrastructure, and the composition of frames used to transport information. In writing this book, space constraints, as well as the availability of my previously published books covering Ethernet and Token-Ring networks, precluded a full review of Ethernet and Token-Ring LAN characteristics. Instead, I primarily concentrated on providing a review of the composition of Ethernet and Token-Ring frame operations. I felt this would be more appropriate, as a majority of network related problems can be detected by either observing the flow of frames or the display of network management information which relates to various frame fields. Thus, readers requiring detailed information covering Ethernet and Token-Ring access protocols and their cabling infrastructure are referred to my previously published books, *Ethernet Networks 2ED* and *Token-Ring Networks*, both published by John Wiley & Sons.

This chapter will first focus upon the composition of different types of Ethernet frames. In reality, there is only one Ethernet frame, while the CSMA/CD frame format standardized by the IEEE is technically referred to as an 802.3 frame. As noted later in this chapter, the physical 802.3 frame can have several logical formats. For consistency and ease of reference, I will refer to Carrier Sense Multiple Access/Collision Detection (CSMA/CD) operations collectively as Ethernet and, when appropriate, indicate differences between Ethernet and the IEEE 802.3 Ethernet-based CSMA/CD standards. After describing the general composition of Ethernet and IEEE 802.3 frames, I will examine the function of the fields within each frame, as well as the manner by which the placement of frames on the media is controlled—a process known as *media access control*. This will be followed by a similar examination oriented toward the Token-Ring frame format and the function of each frame field within a Token-Ring frame. In doing so, I will cover the three types of Token-Ring frames defined by the IEEE 802.5 standard. I will then turn in Chapter 5 to the operation and utilization of Ethernet and Token-Ring RMON probes, including a detailed examination of the use of identifiers tracked by each type of probe.

ETHERNET FRAME COMPOSITION

Figure 4.1 illustrates the general frame composition of Ethernet and IEEE 802.3 frames. Note that they differ slightly. An Ethernet frame contains an 8-byte preamble, while the IEEE 802.3 frame contains a 7-byte preamble followed by a 1-byte start of frame delimiter field. A second difference between the composition of Ethernet and IEEE 802.3 frames concerns the 2-byte Ethernet type field. That field is used by Ethernet to specify the protocol carried in the frame, enabling several protocols to be carried independently of one another. Under the IEEE 802.3 frame format, the type field was replaced by a 2-byte length field that specifies the number of bytes that follow that field as data. In addition, to enable different types of protocols to be carried in a frame and correctly identified, the 802.3 frame format subdivides the data field into subfields. Those subfields include a *Destination Service Access Point* (*DSAP*), *Source Service Access Point* (*SSAP*), and *Control field* which prefixes a reduced data field. The use of those fields defines a *Logical Link Control* (*LLC*) layer residing within an 802.3 frame, which will be discussed later in this chapter along with some common framing variations.

Ethernet

Preamble	Destination Address	Source Address	Type	Data	Frame Check Sequence
8 bytes	6 bytes	6 bytes	2 bytes	46-1500 bytes	4 bytes

IEEE 802.3

Preamble	Start of Frame Delimiter	Destination Address	Source Address	Length	Data	Frame Check Sequence
7 bytes	1 byte	2/6 bytes	2/6 bytes	2 bytes	46-1500 bytes	4 bytes

FIGURE 4.1 Ethernet and IEEE 802.4 frame formats.

The differences between Ethernet and IEEE 802.3 frames, while minor, make the two incompatible with one another. This means that your network must contain all Ethernet-compatible network interface cards (NICs), all IEEE 802.3-compatible NICs, or adapter cards that can examine the frame and automatically determine its type, a process described later in this chapter. Fortunately, the fact that the IEEE 802.3 frame format represents a standard means that most vendors now market 802.3-compliant hardware and software. Although a few vendors continue to manufacture Ethernet or dual functioning Ethernet/IEEE 802.3 hardware, such products are primarily used to provide organizations with the ability to expand previously developed networks without requiring the wholesale replacement of NICs. Although the IEEE 802.3 standard has essentially replaced Ethernet, because of their similarities and the fact that 802.3 was based upon Ethernet we will consider both to be Ethernet.

Now that we have an overview of the structure of Ethernet and 802.3 frames, let's probe deeper and examine the composition of each frame field. We will take advantage of the similarity between Ethernet and IEEE 802.3 frames to examine the fields of each frame on a composite basis, noting the differences between the two when appropriate.

Preamble Field

The *preamble* field consists of 8 (Ethernet) or 7 (IEEE 802.3) bytes of alternating 1 and 0 bits. The Ethernet chip set contained on the network interface adapter places the preamble and following start-of-frame delimiter on the front of each frame transmitted on the network.

The purpose of the preamble field is to announce the frame and to enable all receivers on the network to synchronize themselves to the incoming frame. In addition, this field by itself (under Ethernet) or in conjunction with the start-of-frame delimiter field (under the IEEE 802.3 standard) ensures there is a minimum spacing period of 9.6 ms between frames for error detection and recovery operations.

Start-of-Frame Delimiter Field

The *start-of-frame delimiter* field is applicable only to the IEEE 802.3 standard, and can be viewed as a continuation of the preamble. In fact, the composition of this field continues in the same manner as the format of the preamble, with alternating 1 and 0 bits used for the first six bit positions of this 1-byte field. The last two bit positions of this field are 11—this breaks the synchronization pattern and alerts the receiver that frame data follows.

Both the preamble field and the start-of-frame delimiter field are removed by the Ethernet chip set or controller when it places a received frame in its buffer. Similarly, when a controller transmits a frame, it prefixes the frame with those two fields (if it is transmitting an IEEE 802.3 frame) or a preamble field (if it is transmitting a true Ethernet frame).

Destination Address Field

The *destination address* field identifies the recipient of the frame. Although this may appear to be a simple field, in reality its length can vary between IEEE 802.3 and Ethernet frames. In addition, each field can consist of two or more subfields, whose settings govern such network operations as the type of addressing used on the LAN, and whether the frame is addressed to a specific station or more than one station. To obtain an appreciation for the use of this field, let's examine how this field is used under the IEEE 802.3 standard as one of the two field formats applicable to Ethernet.

Figure 4.2 illustrates the composition of the source and destination address fields. As indicated, the 2-byte source and destination address fields are applicable only to IEEE 802.3 networks, while the 6-byte source and destination address fields are applicable to both Ethernet and IEEE 802.3 networks. A user can select either a 2- or 6-byte destination address field; however, with IEEE 802.3 equipment, all stations on the LAN must use the same addressing structure. Today, almost all 802.3 networks use 6-byte addressing, since the inclusion of a 2-byte

A. 2-byte field (IEEE 802.3)

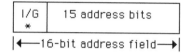

B. 6-byte field (Ethernet and IEEE 802.3)

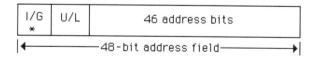

I/G bit subfield   '0' = Individual address   '1' = Group address
U/L bit subfield   '0' = Universally administrated addressing
                   '1' = Locally administrated addressing

* Set to '0' in source address field

FIGURE 4.2   Source and destination address field formats.

field option was designed primarily to accommodate early LANs that use 16-bit address fields.

I/G Subfield

The 1-bit I/G subfield is set to a 0 to indicate that the frame is destined to an individual station, or 1 to indicate that the frame is addressed to more than one station—a group address. One special example of a group address is the assignment of all 1s to the address field. Hex FF-FF-FF-FF-FF-FF is recognized as a broadcast address, and each station on the network will receive and accept frames with that destination address.

When a destination address specifies a single station, the address is referred to as a unicast address. A group address that defines multiple stations is known as a *multicast address*, while a group address that specifies all stations on the network is, as previously mentioned, referred to as a *broadcast address*.

U/L Subfield

The U/L subfield is applicable only to the 6-byte destination address field. The setting of this field's bit position indicates whether the destination address is an address that was assigned by the IEEE (universally administered) or assigned by the organization via software (locally administered).

Universal versus Locally Administered Addressing

Each Ethernet Network Interface Card (NIC) contains a unique address burned into its read-only memory (ROM) at the time of manufacture. To ensure this universally administered address is not duplicated, the IEEE assigns blocks of addresses to each manufacturer. These addresses normally include a 3-byte prefix that identifies the manufacturer and is assigned by the IEEE, and a 3-byte suffix that is assigned by the adapter manufacturer to its NIC. For example, the prefix hex 02-60-8C identifies an NIC manufactured by 3Com.

Table 4.1 lists the 3-byte identifiers associated with ten manufacturers of Ethernet network interface cards. Through the use of a table of 3-byte identifiers and associated manufacturer names, diagnostic hardware or software can be programmed to read the source and destination address fields within frames, and identify the manufacturer of the originating and destination adapter cards.

Although the use of universally administered addressing eliminates the potential for duplicate network addresses, it does not provide the flexibility obtainable from locally administered addressing. For example, under locally administered addressing, you can configure mainframe software to work with a predefined group of addresses via a gateway PC. Then, as you add new stations to your LAN, you simply use your installation program to assign a locally administered address to the NIC, instead of using its universally administered address. As long as your mainframe computer has a pool of locally administered addresses that includes your recent assignment, you do not have to modify your mainframe communications software configuration. Since the modification of mainframe communications software typically requires recompiling and reloading, the attached network must become inoperative for a short period of time. Because a large mainframe may service hundreds to thousands of users, such changes are normally performed late in the evening or on a weekend. Thus, the changes required for locally administered addressing are more responsive to users than those required for universally administered addressing.

TABLE 4.1 Representative Ethernet Manufacturer IDs

Manufacturer	3-Byte Identifiers
3COM	02-60-8C
Cabletron	00-00-1D
Excelan	08-00-14
NEC	00-00-4C
NeXT	00-00-0F
Novell	00-00-1B
Synoptics (Bay Networks)	00-00-81
Western Digital	00-00-C0
Xerox	00-00-AA
Xircom	00-80-C7

Source Address Field

The *source address field* identifies the station that transmitted the frame. Like the destination address field, the source address can be either 2 or 6 bytes in length.

The 2-byte source address is supported only under the IEEE 802.3 standard and requires the use of a 2-byte destination address; all stations on the network must use 2-byte addressing fields. The 6-byte source address field is supported by both Ethernet and the IEEE 802.3 standard. When a 6-byte address is used, the first 3 bytes represent the address assigned by the IEEE to the manufacturer for incorporation into each NIC's ROM. The vendor then normally assigns the last 3 bytes for each of its NICs.

Type Field

The 2-byte *type field* is applicable only to the Ethernet frame. This field identifies the higher-level protocol contained in the data field. Thus, this field tells the receiving device how to interpret the data field.

Under Ethernet, multiple protocols can exist on the LAN at the same time. Xerox served as the custodian of Ethernet address ranges licensed to NIC manufacturers and defined the protocols supported by the assignment of type field values. Table 4.2 lists five common Ethernet Type field identifiers, including their hex values. Note that the value of the type field always exceeds decimal 1500 (hex 05-DC) and provides a mechanism for a receiving station to determine the type of frame on

TABLE 4.2 Ethernet Type Field Identifiers

Protocol Specified	*Hex Value*
Address Resolution Protocol (ARP)	08-06
AppleTalk	80-9B
AppleTalk ARM	80-F3
Netware IPX/SPX	81-37

the network, since a length field (described in the following) cannot exceed decimal 1500. Under the IEEE 802.3 standard, the type field was replaced by a length field, which precludes compatibility between pure Ethernet and 802.3 frames.

Length Field

The 2-byte *length field*, applicable to the IEEE 802.3 standard, defines the number of bytes contained in the data field. Under both Ethernet and IEEE 802.3 standards, the minimum size frame must be 64 bytes in length from preamble through FCS fields. This minimum size frame ensures that there is sufficient transmission time to enable Ethernet NICs to detect collisions accurately, based on the maximum Ethernet cable length specified for a network and the time required for a frame to propagate the length of the cable. Based on the minimum frame length of 64 bytes and the possibility of using 2-byte addressing fields, each data field must be a minimum of 46 bytes in length.

Because the data field cannot exceed 1500 bytes, the length field's maximum value cannot exceed 1500 decimal. Concerning its minimum value, when the data field contains less than 46 bytes, the data field is padded to reach 46 bytes in length. However, the length field does not include padding and reflects the actual number of characters in the data field.

Data Field

As previously discussed, the *data field* must be a minimum of 46 bytes in length to ensure that the frame is at least 64 bytes in length. This means that the transmission of 1 byte of information must be carried within a 46-byte data field; if the information to be placed in the field is less than 46 bytes, the remainder of the field must be padded. Although some publications subdivide the data field to include a PAD subfield, the latter actually represents optional fill characters that are added to the information in the data field to ensure a length of 46 bytes. The maximum length of the data field is 1500 bytes.

Frame Check Sequence Field

The *frame check sequence field*, applicable to both Ethernet and the IEEE 802.3 standard, provides a mechanism for error detection. Each chip set transmitter computes a *cyclic redundancy check (CRC)* that covers both address fields, the type/length field, and the data field. The transmitter then places the computed CRC in the 4-byte FCS field.

The CRC treats the previously mentioned fields as one, long binary number. The n bits to be covered by the CRC are considered to represent the coefficients of a polynomial $M(X)$ of degree $n-1$. Here, the first bit in the destination address field corresponds to the X^{n-1} term, while the last bit in the data field corresponds to the X^0 term. Next, $M(X)$ is multiplied by X^{32}, and the result of that multiplication process is divided by the following polynomial:

$$G(X)=X^{32}+X^{26}+X^{23}+X^{22}+X^{16}+X^{12}+X^{11}+X^{10}+X^8+X^7+X^5+X^4+X^2+X+1$$

Note that the term X^n represents the setting of a bit to a 1 in position n. Thus, part of the generating polynomial $X^5+X^4+X^2+X^1$ represents the binary value 11011.

This division produces a quotient and remainder. The quotient is discarded, and the remainder becomes the CRC value placed in the 4-byte FCS field. This 32-bit CRC reduces the probability of an undetected error to 1 bit in every 4.3 billion, or approximately 1 bit in 2^{32-1} bits.

Once a frame reaches its destination, the chip set's receiver uses the same polynomial to perform the same operation upon the received data. If the CRC computed by the receiver matches the CRC in the FCS field, the frame is accepted. Otherwise, the receiver discards the received frame, as it is considered to have one or more bits in error. The receiver will also consider a received frame to be invalid and discard it under two additional conditions. Those conditions occur when the frame does not contain an integral number of bytes, or when the length of the data field does not match the value contained in the length field. The latter condition obviously is applicable only to the 802.3 standard, since an Ethernet frame uses a type field instead of a length field.

ETHERNET MEDIA ACCESS CONTROL

Under the IEEE 802 series of standards, the data link layer of the OSI Reference Model was subdivided into two sublayers— logical link control (LLC) and medium access control (MAC). The frame formats previously examined represent the manner in which LLC information is transported. Directly under the LLC sublayer is the MAC sublayer.

Functions

The MAC sublayer, which is the focus of this section, is responsible for checking the channel and transmitting data if the channel is idle, checking for the occurrence of a collision and taking a series of predefined steps if a collision is detected. Thus, this layer provides the required logic to control the network.

Figure 4.3 illustrates the relationship between the physical and LLC layers with respect to the MAC layer. The MAC layer is an interface between user data and the physical placement and retrieval of data on the network. To better understand the functions performed by the MAC layer, let us examine the four major functions performed by that layer—transmitting data operations, transmitting medium access management, receiving data operations, and receiving medium access management. Each of those four functions can be viewed as a functional area, since a group of activities is associated with each area.

Table 4.3 lists the four MAC functional areas and the activities associated with each area. Although the transmission and reception of data operations activities are self-explanatory, the transmission and reception of media access management require some elaboration. Therefore, let's focus on the activities associated with each of those functional areas.

Transmit Media Access Management

CSMA/CD can be described as a *listen-before-acting* access method. Thus, the first function associated with transmit media access management is to find out whether any data is already being transmitted on the network and, if so, to defer transmis-

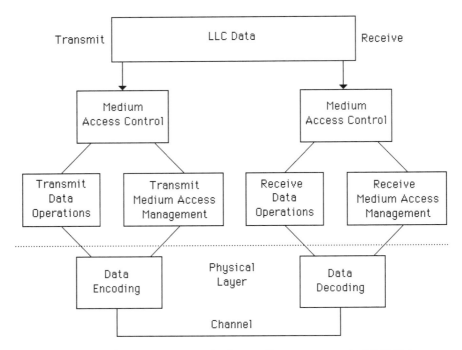

FIGURE 4.3 Medium access control. The medium access control (MAC) layer can be considered an interface between user data and the physical placement and retrieval of data on the network.

sion. During the listening process, each station attempts to sense the carrier signal of another station, hence the prefix *carrier sense (CS)* for this access method. Although broadband networks use RF modems that generate a carrier signal, a baseband network has no carrier signal in the conventional sense of a carrier as a periodic waveform altered to convey information. Thus, you may question how the MAC sublayer on a baseband network can sense a carrier signal if there is no carrier. The answer lies in the use of a digital signaling method known as *Manchester encoding*, by which a station can monitor to note whether another station is transmitting.

To understand the Manchester encoding signaling method used by baseband Ethernet LANs, let us first review the method of digital signaling used by computers and terminal devices. In that signaling method, a positive voltage is used to represent a

TABLE 4.3 MAC Functional Areas

Transmit Data Operations	• Accept data from the LLC sublayer and construct a frame by appending preamble and start-of-frame delimiter; insert destination and source address, length count; if frame is less than 64 bytes, insert sufficient PAD characters in the data field. • Calculate the CRC and place in the FCS field.
Transmit Media Access Management	• Defer transmission if the medium is busy. • Delay transmission for a specified interframe gap period. • Present a serial bit stream to the physical layer for transmission. • Halt transmission when a collision is detected. • Transmit a jam signal to ensure that news of a collision propagates throughout the network. • Reschedule retransmissions after a collision until successful, or a specified retry limit is reached.
Receive Data Operations	• Discard all frames not addressed to the receiving station. • Recognize all broadcast frames and frames specifically addressed to station. • Perform a CRC check. • Remove preamble, start-of-frame delimiter, destination and source addresses, length count, FCS; if necessary, remove PAD fill characters. • Pass data to LLC sublayer.
Receive Media Access Management	• Receive a serial bit stream from the physical layer. • Verify byte boundary and length of frame. • Discard frames not an even 8 bits in length or less than the minimum frame length.

binary 1, while the absence of voltage (0 volts) is used to represent a binary 0. If two successive 1 bits occur, two successive bit positions then have a similar positive voltage level or a similar zero voltage level. Since the signal goes from 0 to some positive voltage and does not return to 0 between successive binary 1s, it is referred to as a *unipolar nonreturn to zero signal (NRZ)*. This signaling technique is illustrated at the top of Figure 4.4.

Although unipolar nonreturn to zero signaling is easy to

implement, its use for transmission has several disadvantages. One of the major disadvantages associated with this signaling method involves determining where one bit ends and another begins. Overcoming this problem requires synchronization between a transmitter and receiver by the use of *clocking circuitry*, which can be relatively expensive.

To overcome the need for clocking, baseband LANs use Manchester or Differential Manchester encoding. In Manchester encoding, a timing transition always occurs in the middle of each bit, while an equal amount of positive and negative voltage is used to represent each bit. This coding technique provides a good timing signal for clock recovery from received data due to its timing transitions. In addition, since the Manchester code always maintains an equal amount of positive and negative voltage, it prevents direct current (DC) voltage buildup, enabling repeaters to be spaced farther apart from one another.

Unipolar Nonreturn to Zero

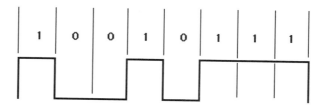

Manchester Coding

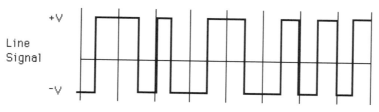

FIGURE 4.4 Unipolar nonreturn to zero signaling and Manchester coding. In Manchester coding, a timing transition occurs in the middle of each bit, and the line code maintains an equal amount of positive and negative voltage.

The lower portion of Figure 4.4 illustrates an example of Manchester coding. Note that a low-to-high voltage transition represents a binary 1, while a high-to-low voltage transition represents a binary 0. Although NRZI encoding is used on broadband networks, the actual data is modulated after it is encoded. Thus, the presence or absence of a carrier is directly indicated by the presence or absence of a carrier signal on a broadband network.

Collision Detection

As previously discussed, under Manchester coding a binary 1 is represented by a high-to-low transition, while a binary 0 is represented by a low-to-high voltage transition. Thus, an examination of the voltage on the medium of a baseband network enables a station to determine whether a carrier signal is present.

If a carrier signal is found, the station with data to transmit will continue to monitor the channel. When the current transmission ends, the station will then transmit its data while checking the channel for collisions. Since Ethernet and IEEE 802.3 Manchester encoded signals have a 1-volt average DC voltage level, a collision results in an average DC level of 2 volts. Thus, a transceiver or network interface card can detect collisions by monitoring the voltage level of the Manchester line signal.

Jam Pattern

If a collision is detected during transmission, the transmitting station will cease transmission of data and initiate transmission of a jam pattern. The jam pattern consists of 32 to 48 bits. These bits can have any value other than the CRC value that corresponds to the partial frame transmitted before the jam. The transmission of the jam pattern ensures that the collision lasts long enough to be detected by all stations on the network.

Wait Time

Once a collision is detected, the transmitting station waits a random number of slot times before attempting to retransmit. Here the term *slot* represents 512 bits on a 10-Mbps network, or a minimum frame length of 64 bytes. The actual number of slot times the station waits is selected by a randomization process, formerly known as a *truncated binary exponential backoff*. Under this randomization process, a random integer r defines the number of slot times the station waits before listening to determine whether the channel is clear. If it is, the station begins to retransmit the frame while listening for another collision.

If the station transmits the complete frame successfully and has additional data to transmit, it will again listen to the channel as it prepares another frame for transmission. If a collision occurs on a retransmission attempt, a slightly different procedure is followed. After a jam signal is transmitted, the station simply doubles the previously generated random number and then waits the prescribed number of slot intervals prior to attempting a retransmission. Up to 16 retransmission attempts can occur before the station aborts the transmission and declares the occurrence of a multiple collision error condition.

Figure 4.5 illustrates the collision detection process by which a station can determine that a frame was not successfully transmitted. At time t_0 both stations A and B are listening and fail to detect the occurrence of a collision, and at time t_1 station A commences the transmission of a frame. As station A's frame begins to propagate down the bus in both directions, station B begins the transmission of a frame, since at time t_2 it appears to station B that there is no activity on the network.

Shortly after time t_2 the frames transmitted by stations A and B collide, resulting in a doubling of the Manchester encoded signal level for a very short period of time. This doubling of the Manchester encoded signal's voltage level is detected by station B at time t_3, since station B is closer to the collision than station A. Station B then generates a jam pattern that is detected by station A.

ETHERNET LOGICAL LINK CONTROL

The logical link control (LLC) sublayer was defined under the IEEE 802.2 standard to make the method of link control independent of a specific access method. Thus, the 802.2 method of

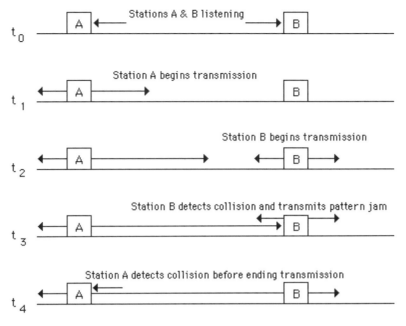

FIGURE 4.5 Collision detection.

link control spans Ethernet (IEEE 802.3), Token Bus (IEEE 802.4), and Token-Ring (IEEE 802.5) local area networks. Functions performed by the LLC include generating and interpreting commands to control the flow of data, including recovery operations for when a transmission error is detected.

Link control information is carried within the data field of an IEEE 802.3 frame as an LLC Protocol Data Unit. Figure 4.6 illustrates the relationship between the IEEE 802.3 frame and the LLC Protocol Data Unit.

LLC Protocol Data Unit

Service Access Points (SAPs) function much like a mailbox. Since the LLC layer is bounded below the MAC sublayer and bounded above by the network layer, SAPs provide a mechanism for exchanging information between the LLC layer and the MAC and network layers. For example, from the network layer

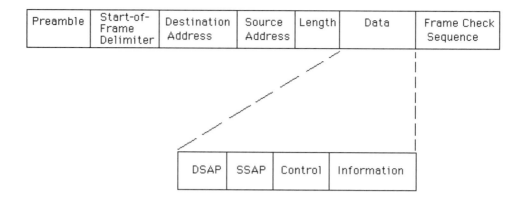

Legend:
    DSAP Destination Service Access Point
    SSAP Source Service Access Point

FIGURE 4.6 Formation of LLC protocol data unit. Control information is carried within a MAC frame.

perspective, a SAP represents the place to leave messages about the services requested by an application.

The *Destination Services Access Point* (*DSAP*) is 1 byte in length, and is used to specify the receiving network layer process, which is an IEEE term to denote the destination upper-layer protocol. The *Source Service Access Point* (*SSAP*) is also 1 byte in length. The SSAP specifies the sending network layer process that is in effect the source upper-layer protocol. Both DSAP and SSAP addresses are assigned by the IEEE and are always the same since destination and source protocols must always be the same. For example, hex address FF represents a DSAP broadcast address.

The control field provides information that can indicate the type of service and protocol format. For example, if the frame is transporting NetWare data, the control field will contain the hex value 03, which indicates that the frame uses the unnumbered format for connectionless services. Prior to discussing the types and classes of service defined by the 802.2 standard, let us examine two additional IEEE 802.3 logical frame formats.

Ethernet_SNAP Frame

The *Ethernet_SNAP* (*Subnetwork Access Protocol*) frame provides a mechanism for obtaining a type field identifier associated with a pure Ethernet frame in an IEEE 802.3 frame. To accomplish this, the data field is subdivided similarly to the previously illustrated LLC protocol data unit shown in Figure 4.6; however, two additional subfields are added after the control field. Those fields are an organization code of 3 bytes and an Ethernet type field of 2 bytes. Figure 4.7 illustrates the format of an Ethernet_SNAP frame.

A value of hex AA is placed in the DSAP and SSAP fields to indicate that the frame is an Ethernet_SNAP frame. The control field functions similarly to the previously described LLC protocol data unit, indicating the type and class of service, where hex 03 would indicate a connectionless service unnumbered format.

The organization code field references the assigner of the value in the following Ethernet type field. For most situations, a hex value of 00-00-00 is used to indicate that the Ethernet type field value was assigned by Xerox. When the organization code is hex 00-00-00, the Ethernet type field will contain one of the entries previously listed in Table 4.2.

NetWare Ethernet_802.3 Frame

One additional logical variation of the IEEE 802.3 frame format that warrants an elaboration is known as the *NetWare Ether-*

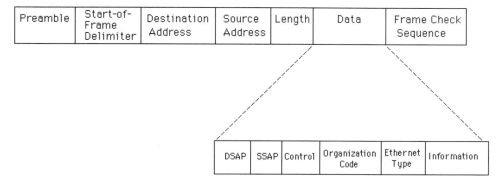

FIGURE 4.7   Ethernet_SNAP frame format.

net_802.3 frame. Instead of using the IEEE 802.2 subfields to form an LLC protocol data unit, Novell places the IPX header immediately after the length field, reducing the maximum data field length by 30 bytes. The NetWare Ethernet_802.3 frame can be used only to transport NetWare IPX traffic, and represents a common level of frustration when an administrator attempts to use this frame format to transport a different protocol.

Receiver Frame Determination

A receiving station can distinguish between different types of Ethernet frames and correctly interpret data transported in those frames. To do so, it must examine the value of the field following the source address field, which is either a type or length field. If the field value exceeds 1500 decimals, the field must be a type subfield. Thus, the frame is a *raw* Ethernet frame. If the value is less than 1500, the field is a length field and the 2 bytes following that field, which represent the first 2 bytes of an IEEE 802.3 frame's data field, must be examined. If those 2 bytes have the value hex FF-FF, the frame is a NetWare Ethernet_802.3 frame used to transport IPX. If the value of the 2 bytes is hex AA-AA, the frame is an Ethernet_SNAP frame. Any other value in those bytes means the frame is an IEEE_802.3 frame.

It is important during the LAN installation process to bind the appropriate protocol to the frame type capable of transporting the protocol. Table 4.4 lists several examples of protocols that can be bonded to different types of Ethernet frames.

TABLE 4.4 Protocols versus Frame Type

Frame Type	Protocols That Can Be Bound
Ethernet	NetWare, AppleTalk, Phase I, TCP/IP
IEEE 802.3	NetWare, FTAM
NetWare Ethernet_802.3	NetWare only
Ethernet-SNAP	NetWare, AppleTalk, Phase II, TCP/IP

Type 1 Unacknowledged connectionless service

Type 2 Connection-oriented service

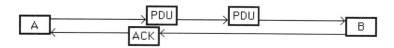

Type 3 Acknowledged connectionless source

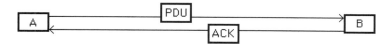

Legend:
PDU = Protocol data unit
ACK = Acknowledgement
A,B = Stations on the network

FIGURE 4.8 Local link control service types.

Types And Classes of Service

Under the 802.2 standard, there are three types of services available for sending and receiving LLC data. These types are discussed in the next three sections. Figure 4.8 provides a visual summary of the operation of each LLC service type.

Type 1

Type 1 is an *unacknowledged connectionless service*. The term *connectionless* refers to the fact that transmission does not occur between two devices as if a logical connection were established.

Instead, transmission flows on the channel to all stations; however, only the destination address acts upon the data. As the name of this service implies, there are no provisions for the acknowledgment of frames or for flow control or error recovery. Therefore, this is an unreliable service.

Despite those shortcomings, Type 1 is the most commonly used service, since most protocol suites use a reliable transport mechanism at the transport layer, thus eliminating the need for reliability at the link layer. In addition, by eliminating the time needed to establish a virtual link and the overhead of acknowledgments, a Type 1 service can provide a greater throughput than other LLC types of services.

Type 2

The Type 2 *connection-oriented* service requires that a logical link be established between the sender and the receiver prior to information transfer. Once the logical connection is established, data will flow between the sender and receiver until either party terminates the connection. During data transfer, a Type 2 LLC service provides all of the functions lacking in a Type 1 service, using a sliding window for flow control.

Type 3

The Type 3 *acknowledged connectionless* service contains provision for the setup and disconnection of transmission; it acknowledges individual frames using the *stop-and-wait* flow control method. Type 3 service is primarily used in an automated factory process-control environment, where one central computer communicates with many remote devices that typically have a limited storage capacity.

Classes of Service

All logical link control stations support Type 1 operations. This level of support is known as *Class I* service. The classes of service supported by LLC indicate the combinations of the three LLC service types supported by a station. Class I supports Type 1 service, *Class II* supports both Type 1 and Type 2, *Class III* supports Type 1 and Type 3 service, while *Class IV* supports all three service types. Since service Type 1 is supported by all classes, it can be considered a least common denominator, enabling all stations to communicate using a common form of service.

TOKEN-RING FRAME OPERATIONS

This section will examine Token-Ring frame operations, enabling us to understand the manner in which different frame fields are used for such functions as access control, error checking, routing of data between interconnected networks, and other Token-Ring network functions. In addition, by obtaining an understanding of the composition of Token-Ring frames, we will obtain the ability to better understand the meaning associated with values obtained from the retrieval of Ethernet and Token-Ring MIB identifiers.

A *Token-Ring network* consists of ring stations representing devices that attach to a ring and an attaching medium. Concerning the latter, the attaching medium can be *shielded, twisted-pair*, or *fiber optic* cable, each having constraints concerning transmission distance and number of stations allowed on the network.

A *ring station*, also referred to as a *station* or *workstation*, transfers data to the ring in a transmission unit referred to as a *frame*. Frames are transmitted sequentially from one station to another physically active station in a clockwise direction. The next active station is referred to as the *downstream neighbor*, which regenerates the frame as well as performs MAC address checking and other functions. In performing a Media Access Control (MAC) address check, the station compares its address to the destination address contained in the frame. If the two match or if the station has a functional address that matches the frame destination's address, the station copies the data contained in the frame. While performing the previously described operations, the station performs a number of error checks based upon the composition of data in the frame, and reports errors via the generation of different types of error reporting frames. Thus, it is important to understand the composition of the fields within the Token-Ring frames, as they govern the operation of a Token-Ring network.

Transmission Formats

Three types of transmission formats are supported on a Token-Ring network—*token*, *abort*, and *frame*. The token format, as illustrated in the top of Figure 4.9, is the mechanism by which access to the ring is passed from one computer attached to the network to another device connected to the network. Here the token format consists of 3 bytes, of which the starting and ending delimiters are used to indicate the beginning and end of a token frame. The middle byte of a token frame is an access control byte; 3 bits are used as a priority indicator, 3 bits are used as a reservation indicator, while 1 bit is used for the token bit, and another bit position functions as the monitor bit.

When the token bit is set to a binary 0, it indicates that the transmission is a token. When it is set to a binary 1, it indicates that data in the form of a frame is being transmitted.

The second Token-Ring frame format signifies an abort token. In actuality there is no token, since this format is indicated by a starting delimiter followed by an ending delimiter. The transmission of an abort token is used to abort a previous transmission. The format of an abort token is illustrated in Figure 4.9.

The third type of Token-Ring frame format occurs when a station seizes a free token. At that time the token format is converted into a frame that includes the addition of frame control, addressing data, an error detection field, and a frame status field. The format of a Token-Ring frame is illustrated in Figure 4.9C. At any given point in time, only one token can reside on a ring, represented either as a token format, abort token format, or frame. By examining each of the fields in the frame we will also examine the token and token abort frames due to the commonality of fields between each frame.

Starting/Ending Delimiters

The starting and ending delimiters mark the beginning and ending of a token or frame. Each delimiter consists of a unique code pattern that identifies it to the network. To understand the composition of the starting and ending delimiter fields requires us to review the method by which data is represented on a Token-Ring network using Differential Manchester encoding.

A. Token Format

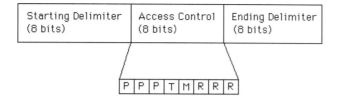

B. Abort Token Format

Starting Delimiter	Ending Delimiter

C. Frame Format

Starting Delimiter (8 bits)	Access Control (8 bits)	Frame Control (8 bits)	Destination Address (48 bits)	Source Address (48 bits)	Routing Information (optional)

Information Variable	Frame Check Sequence (32 bits)	Ending Delimiter (8 bits)	Frame Status (8 bits)

FIGURE 4.9 Token, abort, and frame formats (P: priority bits, T: token bit, M: monitor bit, R: reservation bits).

Differential Manchester Encoding Figure 4.10 illustrates the use of Differential Manchester encoding, comparing its operation to non-return to zero (NRZ) and conventional Manchester encoding.

At the top of Figure 4.10, NRZ coding illustrates the representation of data by holding a voltage low (–V) to represent a binary 0, and high (+V) to represent a binary 1. This method of signaling is called *nonreturn to zero*, since there is no return to a 0 V position after each data bit is coded.

To avoid the necessity of building clocking circuitry into devices, a mechanism is required for encoded data to carry clocking information. One method by which encoded data carries clocking information is obtained from the use of Manchester encoding, which is illustrated in Figure 4.10 and which represents the signaling method used by Ethernet. In Manchester encoding, each data bit consists of a half-bit time signal at a low voltage (–V), and another half-bit time signal at the opposite positive voltage (+V). Every binary 0 is represented by a half-bit time at a low voltage, and the remaining bit time at a high voltage. Every binary 1 is represented by a half-bit time at a high voltage, followed by a half-bit time at a low voltage. By changing the voltage for every binary digit, Manchester encoding ensures that the signal carries self-clocking information.

In Figure 4.10C, Differential Manchester encoding is illustrated. The difference between Manchester encoding and Differential Manchester encoding occurs in the method by which binary 1s are encoded. In Differential Manchester encoding, the direction of the signal's voltage transition changes whenever a binary 1 is transmitted, but remains the same for a binary 0. The IEEE 802.5 standard specifies the use of Differential Manchester encoding, and this encoding technique is used on Token-Ring networks at the physical layer to transmit and detect four distinct symbols—a binary 0, a binary 1, and two nondata symbols.

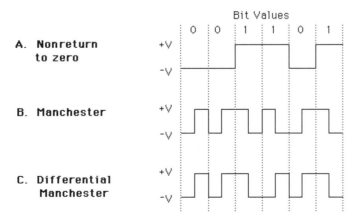

FIGURE 4.10 Differential Manchester encoding. In differential Manchester encoding, the direction of the signal's voltage transition changes whenever a binary 1 is transmitted, but remains the same for a binary 0.

Nondata Symbols

Under Manchester and Differential Manchester encoding there are two possible code violations that can occur. Each code violation produces what is known as a *nondata symbol*, and is used in the Token-Ring frame to denote starting and ending delimiters similar to the use of the flag in an HDLC frame. However, unlike the flag, whose bit composition 01111110 is uniquely maintained by inserting a 0 bit after every sequence of five set bits and removing a 0 following every sequence of five set bits, Differential Manchester encoding maintains the uniqueness of frames by the use of nondata J and nondata K symbols. This eliminates the bit-stuffing operations required by HDLC.

The two nondata symbols each consists of two half-bit times without a voltage change. The J symbol occurs when the voltage is the same as that of the last signal, while the K symbol occurs when the voltage becomes opposite of that of the last signal. Figure 4.11 illustrates the occurrence of the J and K nondata symbols based upon different last bit voltages. Readers will note in comparing Figure 4.11 to Figure 4.10(C) that the J and K nondata symbols are distinct code violations that cannot be mistaken for either a binary 0 or a binary 1.

Now that we have an understanding of the operation of Differential Manchester encoding and the composition of the J and

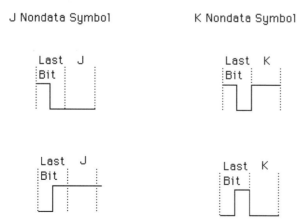

FIGURE 4.11   J and K nondata symbol composition. J and K nondata symbols are distinct code violations that cannot be mistaken for data.

K nondata symbols, we can focus upon the actual format of each frame delimiter.

The start delimiter field marks the beginning of a frame. The composition of this field is the bits and nondata symbols JK0JK000. The end delimiter field marks the end of a frame as well as denotes whether the frame is the last frame of a multiple frame sequence using a single token, or if there are additional frames following this frame.

The format of the end delimiter field is JK1JK1IE, where I is the intermediate frame bit. If I is set to 0, this indicates it is the last frame transmitted by a station. If I is set to 1, this indicates that additional frames follow this frame.

E is an error-detected bit. The E bit is initially set to 0 by the station transmitting a frame, token, or abort sequence. As the frame circulates the ring, each station checks the transmission for errors. Upon detection of a Frame Check Sequence (FCS) error, inappropriate nondata symbol, illegal framing, or another type of error, the first station detecting the error will set the E bit to a value of 1. Since stations keep track of the number of times they set the E bit to a value of 1, it becomes possible to use this information as a guide to locating possible cable errors. For example, if one workstation accounted for a very large percentage of E bit settings in a network, there is a high degree of probability that there is a problem with the lobe cable to that workstation. The problem could be a crimped cable or a loose connector and represents a logical place to commence an investigation in an attempt to reduce E bit errors.

Access Control Field

The second field in both token and frame formats is the access control byte. As illustrated at the top of Figure 4.9, this byte consists of four subfields and serves as the controlling mechanism for gaining access to the network. When a free token circulates the network, the access control field represents one-third of the length of the frame, since it is prefixed by the start delimiter and suffixed by the end delimiter.

The lowest priority that can be specified by the priority bits in the access control byte is 0 (000), while the highest is 7 (111), providing eight levels of priority. Table 4.5 lists the normal use of the priority bits in the access control field. Workstations have a default priority of 3, while bridges have a default priority of 4.

To reserve a token, a workstation will attempt to insert its priority level in the priority reservation subfield. Unless another station with a higher priority bumps the requesting station, the reservation will be honored and the requesting station will obtain the token. If the token bit is set to 1, this serves as an indication that a frame follows instead of the ending delimiter.

A station that needs to transmit a frame at a given priority can use any available token that has a priority level equal to or less than the priority level of the frame to be transmitted. When a token of equal or lower priority is not available, the ring station can reserve a token of the required priority through the use of the reservation bits. In doing so the station must follow two rules. First, if a passing token has a higher priority reservation than the reservation level desired by the workstation, the station will not alter the reservation field contents. Second, if the reservation bits have not been set or indicate a lower priority than that desired by the station, the station can now set the reservation bits to the required priority level.

Once a frame is removed by its originating station, the reservation bits in the header will be checked. If those bits have a nonzero value, the station must release a nonzero priority token, with the actual priority assigned based upon the priority

TABLE 4.5 Priority Bit Settings

Priority Bits	Priority
000	Normal user priority, MAC frames that do not require a token and response type MAC frames
001	Normal user priority
010	Normal user priority
011	Normal user priority and MAC frames that require tokens
100	Bridge
101	Reserved
110	Reserved
111	Specialized Station Management

used by the station for the recently transmitted frame, the reservation bit settings received upon the return of the frame, and any stored priority.

On occasion, the Token-Ring protocol will result in the transmission of a new token by a station prior to that station having the ability to verify the settings of the access control field in a returned frame. When this situation arises, the token will

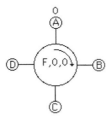

A. Station A generates a frame using a nonpriority token P,R=0,0.

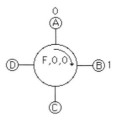

B. Station B reserves a priority 1 in the reservation bits in the frame P,R=0,1: Station A enters a priority–hold state.

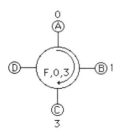

C. Station C reserves a priority of 3, overriding B's reservation of 1: P,R=0,3.

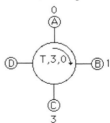

D. Station A removes its frame and generates a token at reserved priority level 3: P,R=3,0.

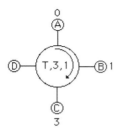

E. Station B repeats priority token and makes a new reservation of priority level 1: P,R=3,1.

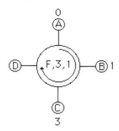

F. Station C grabs token and transmits a frame with a priority of 3: P,R=3,1.

FIGURE 4.12 Priority and reservation field utilization.

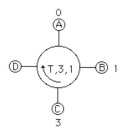

G. Upon return of frame to Station C
it's removed. Station C generates a
token at the priority just used: P,R=3,1.

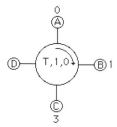

H. Station A in a priority-hold state
grabs token and changes its
priority to 1: P,R=1,0. Station A
stays in priority-hold state until
priority reduced to 0.

Legend:

Ⓐ, Ⓑ, Ⓒ, Ⓓ = Stations

Numeric outside station identifier
indicates priority level.

FIGURE 4.12   (*continued*)

be issued according to the priority and reservation bit settings
in the access control field of the transmitted frame.

Figure 4.12 illustrates the operation of the priority (P) and
reservation (R) bit fields in the access control field. In this example, the prevention of a high-priority station from monopolizing
the network is illustrated by station A entering a priority-hold
state. This occurs when a station originates a token at a higher
priority than the last token it generated. Once in a priority-hold
state, the station will issue tokens that will bring the priority
level eventually down to zero as a mechanism to prevent a high-
priority station from monopolizing the network.

Monitor Bit   The *monitor bit* is used to prevent a token with a
priority exceeding zero or a frame from continuously circulating
on the Token-Ring. This bit is transmitted as a 0 in all tokens
and frames, except for a device on the network that functions as
an active monitor and thus obtains the capability to inspect and
modify that bit.

When a token or frame is examined by the active monitor, it will set the monitor bit to a 1 if it was previously found to be set to 0. If a token or frame is found to have the monitor bit already set to 1, this indicates that the token or frame has already made at least one revolution around the ring and an error condition has occurred, usually caused by the failure of a station to remove its transmission from the ring or the failure of a high-priority station to seize a token. When the active monitor finds a monitor bit set to 1, it assumes an error condition has occurred. The active monitor then purges the token or frame and releases a new token onto the ring. Now that we have an understanding of the role of the monitor bit in the access control field, and the operation of the active monitor on that bit, let's focus upon the active monitor.

Active Monitor The *active monitor* is the device that has the highest address on the network. All other stations on the network are considered standby monitors that watch the active monitor.

As previously explained, the function of the active monitor is to determine if a token or frame is continuously circulating the ring in error. To accomplish this the active monitor sets the monitor count bit as a token or frame goes by. If a destination workstation fails or has its power turned off, the frame will circulate back to the active monitor, where it is then removed from the network. In the event the active monitor should fail or be turned off, the standby monitors watch the active monitor by looking for an active monitor frame. If one does not appear within seven seconds, the standby monitor that has the highest network address then takes over as the active monitor.

In addition to detecting and removing frames that might otherwise continue to circulate the ring, the active monitor performs several other ring management functions. Those functions include the detection and recovery of multiple tokens and the loss of a token or frame on the ring, as well as initiation of a token when a ring is started. The loss of a token or frame is detected by the expiration of a timer whose time-out value exceeds the time required for the longest possible frame to circulate the ring. The active monitor restarts this time and each time it transmits a starting delimiter that precedes every frame and token. Thus, if the timer expires without the appearance of a frame or token, the active monitor will assume the frame or token was lost and initiate a purge operation, which is described later in this section.

Frame Control Field

The frame control field informs a receiving device on the network of the type of frame that was transmitted and how it should be interpreted. Frames can be either logical link control (LLC) or reference physical link functions, according to the IEEE 802.5 media access control (MAC) standard. A media access control frame carries network control information and responses, while a logical link control frame carries data.

The 8-bit frame control field has the format FFZZZZZZ, where FF are frame definition bits. The top of Table 4.6 indicates the possible settings of the frame bits and the assignment of those settings. The ZZZZZZ bits convey media access control (MAC) buffering information when the FF bits are set to 00.

TABLE 4.6 Frame Control Field Subfields

Frame Type Field	
F Bit Settings	Assignment
00	MAC frame
01	LLC frame
10	Undefined (reserved for future use)
11	Undefined (reserved for future use)
Z Bit Settings	Assignment*
000	Normal buffering
001	Remove ring station
010	Beacon
011	Claim token
100	Ring purge
101	Active monitor present
110	Standby monitor present

*When F bits are set to 00, Z bits are used to notify an adapter that the frame is to be expressed buffered.

When the FF bits are set to 01 to indicate an LLC frame, the ZZZZZZ bits are split into two fields, designated rrrYYY. Currently, the rrr bits are reserved for future use and are set to 000. The YYY bits indicate the priority of the logical link control (LLC) data. The lower portion of Table 4.6 indicates the value of the Z bits when used in MAC frames to notify a Token-Ring adapter that the frame is to be expressed buffered.

Destination Address Field

Although the IEEE 802.5 standard supports both 16-bit and 48-bit address fields, IBM's implementation requires the use of 48-bit address fields. IBM's destination address field is made up of five subfields, as illustrated in Figure 4.13. The first bit in the destination address identifies the destination as an individual station (bit set to 0) or as a group (bit set to 1) of one or more stations. The latter provides the capability for a message to be broadcast to a group of stations.

Universally Administered Address Similar to an Ethernet universally administered address, a Token-Ring universally administered address is a unique address permanently encoded into an adapter's ROM. Because it is placed into ROM, it is also known as a *burned-in address*. The IEEE assigns blocks of addresses to each vendor manufacturing Token-Ring equipment, which ensures that Token-Ring adapter cards manufactured by different vendors are uniquely defined. Token-Ring adapter manufacturers are assigned universal addresses that contain an organizationally unique identifier. This identifier consists of the first six hex digits of the adapter card address, and is also referred to as the *manufacturer identification*. For example, cards

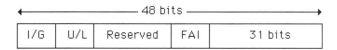

FIGURE 4.13 Destination address subfields (I/G: individual or group bit address identifiers; U/L: universally or locally administered bit identifier; FAI: functional address indicator). The reserved field contains the manufacturer's identification in 22 bits represented by 6 hex digits.

manufactured by IBM will begin with the hex address 08-00-5A or 10-00-5A, whereas adapter cards manufactured by Texas Instruments will begin with the address 40-00-14.

Locally Administered Address A key problem with the use of universally administered addresses is the requirement to change software coding in a mainframe computer whenever a workstation connected to the mainframe via a gateway is added or removed from the network. To avoid constant software changes, locally administered addressing can be used. This type of addressing functions similarly to its operation on an Ethernet LAN, temporarily overriding universally administered addressing; however, the user is now responsible for ensuring the uniqueness of each address. To accomplish locally administered addressing, a statement is inserted into a configuration file that sets the adapter's address at adapter-open time, normally when a station is powered on or a system reset operation is performed.

Functional Address Indicator The *functional address indicator* subfield in the destination address identifies the function associated with the destination address, such as a bridge, active monitor, or configuration report server.

The functional address indicator indicates a functional address when set to 0 and the I/G bit position is set to a 1—the latter indicating a group address. This condition can occur only when the U/L bit position is also set to a 1 and results in the ability to generate locally administered group addresses that are called *functional addresses*. Table 4.7 lists the functional addresses defined by the IEEE. Currently, 21 functional addresses have been defined out of a total of 31 that are available for use, with the remaining addresses available for user definitions or reserved for future use.

Address Values The range of addresses that can be used on a Token-Ring primarily depends upon the settings of the I/G, U/L, and FAI bit positions. When the I/G and U/L bit positions are set to 00 the manufacturer's universal address is used. When the I/G and U/L bits are set to 01, individual locally administered addresses are used in the defined range listed in Table 4.7.

TABLE 4.7 IEEE Functional Addresses

Active Monitor	C0-00-00-00-00-01
Ring Parameter Server	C0-00-00-00-00-02
Network Server Heartbeat	C0-00-00-00-00-04
Ring Error Monitor	C0-00-00-00-00-08
Configuration Report Server	C0-00-00-00-00-10
Synchronous Bandwidth Manager	C0-00-00-00-00-20
Locate—Directory Server	C0-00-00-00-00-40
NETBIOS	C0-00-00-00-00-80
Bridge	C0-00-00-00-01-00
IMPL Server	C0-00-00-00-02-00
Ring Authorization Server	C0-00-00-00-04-00
LAN Gateway	C0-00-00-00-08-00
Ring Wiring Concentrator	C0-00-00-00-10-00
LAN Manager	C0-00-00-00-20-00
User-defined	C0-00-00-00-80-00
through	
	C0-00-40-00-00-00
ISO OSI ALL ES	C0-00-00-00-40-00
ISO OSI ALL IS	C0-00-00-00-80-00
IBM discovery nonserver	C0-00-00-01-00-00
IBM resource manager	C0-00-00-02-00-00
TCP/IP	C0-00-00-04-00-00
6611-DECnet	C0-00-20-00-00-00
LAN Network Manager	C0-00-40-00-00-00

When all three bit positions are set, this situation indicates a group address within the range contained in Table 4.8. If the I/G and U/L bits are set to 11 but the FAI bit is set to 0, this indicates that the address is a functional address. In this situation the range of addresses is bit-sensitive, permitting only those functional addresses previously listed in Table 4.7.

A number of destination ring stations can be identified through the use of a group address. Table 4.9 lists a few of the standard group addresses that have been defined when the I/G, U/L, and FAI bits are set to one.

In addition to the previously mentioned addresses, there are two special destination address values that are defined. An address of all 1s (FF-FF-FF-FF-FF-FF) identifies all stations as destination stations. If a null address is used in which all bits are set to 0 (00-00-00-00-00), the frame is not addressed to any workstation. In this situation it can be transmitted but not received, enabling you to test the ability of the active monitor to purge this type of frame from the network.

Source Address Field

The *source address field* always represents an individual address that specifies the adapter card responsible for the transmission. The source address field consists of three major subfields, as illustrated in Figure 4.14. When locally administered addressing occurs, only 24 bits in the address field are used, since the 22 manufacturer identification bit positions are not used.

The routing information bit identifier identifies the fact that routing information is contained in an optional routing information field. This bit is set when a frame is routed across a bridge using IBM's source routing technique.

TABLE 4.8   Token-Ring Addresses

	Bit Settings			
	I/G	U/L	FAI	Address/Address Range
Individual, universally administered	0	0	0/1	Manufacturer's serial no.
Individual, locally administered	0	1	0	40-00-00-00-00-00 - 40-00-7F-FF-FF-FF
Group address	1	1	1	40-00-80-00-00-00 - 40-00-FF-FF-FF-FF
Functional address	1	1	0	C0-00-00-00-00-01 - C0-00-FF-FF-FF-FF (bit-sensitive)
All stations broadcast	1	1	1	FF-FF-FF-FF-FF-FF
Null address	0	0	0	00-00-00-00-00-00

TABLE 4.9 Representative Standardized Group Addresses

Bridge	80-02-43-00-00-00
Bridge Management	80-01-43-00-00-08
Novell IPX	90-00-72-00-00-40
Hewlett Packard probe	90-00-90-00-00-80
Vitalink gateway	90-00-3C-A0-00-80
Customer use	D5-00-20-00-XX-XX
DECnet phase IV station addresses	55-00-20-00-XX-XX

Routing Information Field

The *routing information field* is optional and is included in a frame when the RI bit of the source address field is set. Figure 4.15 illustrates the format of the optional routing information field. If this field is omitted, the frame cannot leave the ring it was originated on under IBM's source routing bridging method. Under transparent bridging, the frame can be transmitted onto another ring. The routing information field is of variable length and contains a control subfield and one or more 2-byte route designator fields when included in a frame, as the latter are required to control the flow of frames across one or more bridges.

The maximum length of the routing information field (RIF) is 18 bytes. Since each RIF field must contain a 2-byte routing control field, this leaves a maximum of 16 bytes available for use by up to eight route designators. As illustrated in Figure 4.15, each 2-byte route designator consists of a 12-bit ring number and a 4-bit bridge number. Thus, a maximum total of 16 bridges can be used to join any two rings in an Enterprise Token-Ring network.

FIGURE 4.14 Source address field (RI: routing information bit identifier; U/L: universally.or locally administered bit identifier). The 46 address bits consist of 22 manufacturer identification bits and 24 universally administered bits when the U/L bit is set to 0. If set to 1, a 31-bit locally administered address is used with the manufacturer's identification bit set to 0.

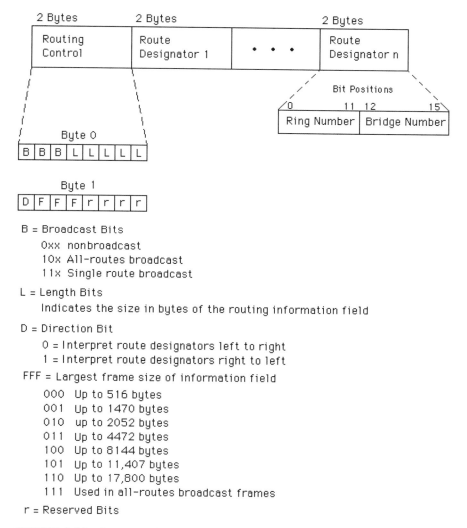

FIGURE 4.15 Routing information field.

Information Field

The *information field* is used to contain Token-Ring commands and responses, as well as carry user data. The type of data carried by the information field depends upon the F bit settings in the frame type field. If the F bits are set to 00, the information field carries media access control (MAC) commands and responses that are used for network management operations. If the F bits are set to 01, the information field carries logical link control (LLC) or user data. Such data can be in the form of portions of a file being transferred on the network, or an electronic mail message being routed to another workstation on the network. The information field is of variable length and can be considered to represent the higher level protocol enveloped in a Token-Ring frame.

In the IBM implementation of the IEEE 802.5 Token-Ring standard, the maximum length of the information field depends upon the Token-Ring adapter used and the operating rate of the network. Token-Ring adapters with 64 Kbytes of memory can handle up to 4.5 Kbytes on a 4 Mbps network, and up to 18 Kbytes on a 16 Mbps network.

Frame Check Sequence Field

The *frame check sequence field* contains 4 bytes that provide the mechanism for checking the accuracy of frames flowing on the network. The cyclic redundancy check data included in the frame check sequence field covers the frame control, destination address, source address, routing information, and information fields. If an adapter computes a cyclic redundancy check that does not match the data contained in the frame check sequence field of a frame, the destination adapter discards the frame information and sets an error bit (E bit) indicator. This error bit indicator, as previously discussed, actually represents a ninth bit position of the ending delimiter, and serves to inform the transmitting station that the data was received in error.

Frame Status Field

The *frame status field* serves as a mechanism to indicate the results of a frame's circulation around a ring to the station that initiated the frame. Figure 4.16 indicates the format of the frame status field. The frame status field contains three subfields that are duplicated for accuracy purposes since they reside outside of CRC checking. One field (A) is used to denote whether an address was recognized, while a second field (C) indicates whether the frame was copied at its destination. Each of these fields is 1 bit in length. The third field, which is two bit positions in length (rr), is currently reserved for future use.

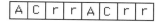

A = Address-Recognized Bits
B = Frame-Copied Bits
r = Reserved Bits

FIGURE 4.16 Frame status field. The frame status field denotes whether the destination address was recognized and whether the frame was copied. Since this field is outside the CRC checking, its subfields are duplicated for accuracy.

TOKEN-RING MEDIUM ACCESS CONTROL

As previously discussed, a MAC frame is used to transport network commands and responses. As such, the MAC layer controls the routing of information between the LLC and the physical network. Examples of MAC protocol functions include the recognition of adapter addresses, physical medium access management, and message verification and status generation. A MAC frame is indicated by the setting of the first 2 bits in the frame control field to 00. When this situation occurs, the contents of the information field that carries MAC data is known as a *vector*.

Vectors and Subvectors

Only one vector is permitted per MAC frame. That vector consists of a major vector length (VL), a major vector identifier (VI), and zero or more subvectors.

As indicated in Figure 4.17, there can be multiple subvectors within a vector. The vector length (VL) is a 16-bit number that gives the length of the vector, including the VL subfield in bytes. VL can vary between decimal 4 and 65 535 in value. The minimum value that can be assigned to VL results from the fact that the smallest information field must contain both VL and VI subfields. Since each subfield is two bytes in length, the minimum value of VL is 4.

When one or more subvectors are contained in a MAC information field, each subvector contains three fields. The subvector length (SVL) is an 8-bit number that indicates the length of the subvector. Since an 8-bit number has a maximum value of 255

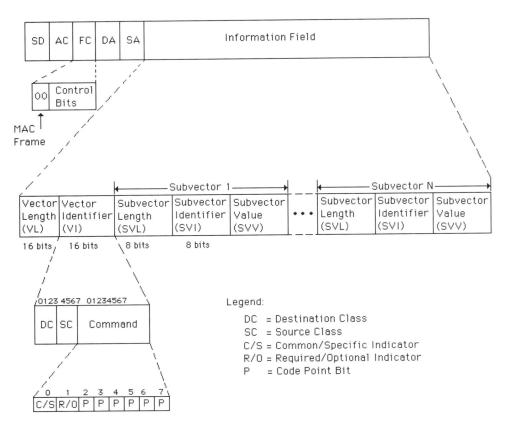

FIGURE 4.17 MAC frame information field format.

and cannot indicate a length exceeding 256 bytes (0-255), a method was required to accommodate subvector values (SVV) longer than 254 bytes. The method used is the placement of hex FF in the SVL field to indicate that SVV exceeds 254 bytes. Then, the actual length is placed in the first 2 bytes following SVL. Finally, each SVV contains the data to be transmitted. The command field within the major vector identifier contains bit values referred to as *code points* that uniquely identify the type of MAC frame. Figure 4.17 illustrates the format of the MAC frame information field, while Table 4.10 lists currently defined vector identifier codes for six MAC control frames defined under the IEEE 802.5 standard.

MAC Control

As previously discussed, each ring has a station known as the active monitor that is responsible for monitoring tokens and taking action to prevent the endless circulation of a token on a ring. Other stations function as standby monitors, and one such station will assume the functions of the active monitor if that device should fail or be removed from the ring. For the standby monitor with the highest network address to take over the functions of the active monitor, the standby monitor needs to know there is a problem with the active monitor. If no frames are circulating on the ring but the active monitor is operating, the standby monitor might falsely presume the active monitor has failed. Thus, the active monitor will periodically issue an active monitor present (AMP) MAC frame. This frame must be issued every seven seconds to inform the standby monitors that the active monitor is operational. Similarly, standby monitors periodically issue a standby monitor present (SMP) MAC frame to denote they are operational.

If an active monitor fails to send an AMP frame within the required time interval, the standby monitor with the highest network address will continuously transmit claim token (CL_TK) MAC frames in an attempt to become the active monitor. The standby monitor will continue to transmit CL_TK MAC frames until one of three conditions occurs:

TABLE 4.10 Vector Identifier Codes

Code Value	MAC Frame Meaning
010	Beacon (BCN)
011	Claim token (CL_TK)
100	Purge MAC frame (PRG)
101	Active monitor present (AMP)
110	Standby monitor present (SMP)
111	Duplicate address test (DAT)

- A MAC CL_TK frame is received and the sender's address exceeds the standby monitor's station address.
- A MAC beacon (BCN) frame is received.
- A MAC purge (PRG) frame is received.

If one of the preceding conditions occurs, the standby monitor will cease its transmission of CL_TK frames and resume its standby function.

Purge Frame

If a CL_TK frame issued by a standby monitor is received back without modification and neither a beacon nor purge frame is received in response to the CL_TK frame, the standby monitor becomes the active monitor and transmits a purge MAC frame. The purge frame is also transmitted by the active monitor each time a ring is initialized or if a token is lost. Once a purge frame is transmitted, the transmitting device will place a token back on the ring.

Beacon Frame

In the event of a major ring failure, such as a cable break or the continuous transmission by one station (known as *jabbering*), a beacon frame will be transmitted. The transmission of BCN frames can be used to isolate ring faults. For an example of the use of a beacon frame, consider Figure 4.18 in which a cable fault results in a ring break. When a station detects a serious problem with the ring, such as the failure to receive a frame or token, it transmits a *beacon frame*. That frame defines a *failure domain* that consists of the station reporting the failure via the transmission of a beacon and its *nearest active upstream neighbor (NAUN)*, as well as everything between the two.

If a beacon frame makes its way back to the issuing station, that station will remove itself from the ring and perform a series of diagnostic tests to determine if it should attempt to reinsert itself into the ring. This procedure ensures that a ring error caused by a beaconing station can be compensated for by having that station remove itself from the ring. Since beacon frames indicate a general area where a failure occurred, they also initi-

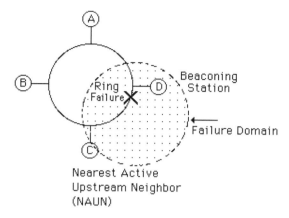

FIGURE 4.18 Beaconing. A beaconing frame indicates a failure occurring between the beaconing station and its nearest active upstream neighbor—an area referred to as a failure domain.

ate a process known as *autoreconfiguration*. The first step in the autoreconfiguration process is the diagnostic testing of the beaconing station's adapter. Other steps in the autoreconfiguration process include diagnostic tests performed by other nodes located in the failure domain in an attempt to reconfigure a ring around a failed area.

Duplicate Address Test Frame

The last type of MAC command frame is the *duplicate address test* (*DAT*) frame. This frame is transmitted during a station initialization process when a station joins a ring. The station joining the ring transmits a MAC DAT frame with its own address in the frame's destination address field. If the frame returns to the originating station with its address-recognized (A) bit in the frame control field set to 1, this means that another station on the ring is assigned that address. The station attempting to join the ring will send a message to the ring network manager concerning this situation and will not join the network.

Station Insertion

Depending upon the type of LAN adapter installed in your workstation, you may observe a series of messages at the format *Phase X,* followed by the message *Completed* or *Passed* when you power on your computer. Those messages reference a five-phase ring insertion process, during which your workstation's Token-Ring adapter attempts to become a participant on the ring. Table 4.11 lists the steps in the ring insertion process.

During the lobe testing phase, the adapter transmits a series of Lobe Media Test MAC frames to the *multistation access unit (MAU)*. Those frames should be wrapped at the MAU, resulting in their return to the adapter. Assuming the returned frames are received correctly, the adapter sends a five-volt DC current, which opens a relay at the MAU port and results in an attachment to the ring.

After the station attaches to the ring, it sets a value in a timer, known as the *Insert-timer*, and watches for an AMP, SMP, or Purge MAC frame prior to the timer expiring. If the timer expires, a token-claiming process is initiated. If the station is the first station on the ring, it then becomes the active monitor.

Once the Monitor Check Phase is completed, the station transmits a Duplicate Address Test frame, during which the destination and source address fields are set to the station's universal address. If a duplicate address is found when the A bit is set to 1, the station cannot become a participant on the ring and detaches itself from the ring.

Assuming the station has a unique address, it next begins the neighbor notification process. During this ring insertion phase, the station learns the address of its nearest active upstream neighbor (NAUN) and reports its address to its nearest active downstream neighbor.

TABLE 4.11 Ring Station Insertion Process

Phase 0:	Lobe testing
Phase 1:	Monitor check
Phase 2:	Duplicate address check
Phase 3:	Participation in neighbor notification
Phase 4:	Request initialization

The address learning process begins when the active monitor transmits an AMP frame. The first station that receives the frame and is able to copy it sets the address-recognized (A) and frame-copied (C) bits to 1. The station then saves the source - address from the copied frame as the NAUN address, and initiates a Notification-Response timer. As the frame circulates the ring, other active stations only repeat it as its A and C bits were set.

When the Notification-Response timer of the first station downstream from the active monitor expires, it broadcasts an SMP frame. The next station downstream copies its NAUN address from the source address field of the SMP frame, and sets the A and C bits in the frame to 1. Then, it starts its own Notification-Response time that, upon expiration, results in that station transmitting its SMP frame. As the SMP frames originate from different stations, the notification process proceeds around the ring until the active monitor copies its NAUN address from an SMP frame. At this point, the active monitor sets its Neighbor-Notification Complete flag to 1, which indicates that the neighbor notification process was successfully completed.

The final phase in the ring insertion process occurs after the neighbor notification process is completed. During this phase, the station's adapter transmits a Request Initialization frame to the ring parameter server. The server responds with an Initialize-Ring-Station frame that contains values that enable all stations on the ring to use the same ring number and soft error report time value, thereby completing the insertion process.

TOKEN-RING LOGICAL LINK CONTROL

In concluding this chapter, I will examine the flow of information within a Token-Ring network at the logical link control (LLC) sublayer. Similar to Ethernet, the Token-Ring LLC sublayer is responsible for performing routing, error control, and flow control. In addition, this sublayer is responsible for providing a consistent view of a LAN to upper OSI layers, regardless of the type of media and protocols used on the network.

Figure 4.19 illustrates the format of an LLC frame that is carried within the information field of the Token-Ring frame. As previously discussed in this chapter, the setting of the first two bits in the frame control field of a Token-Ring frame to 01 indicates that the information field should be interpreted as an LLC frame. The portion of the Token-Ring frame which carries LLC information is known as a protocol data unit and consists of either three or four fields, depending upon the inclusion or omission of an optional information field. The control field is similar

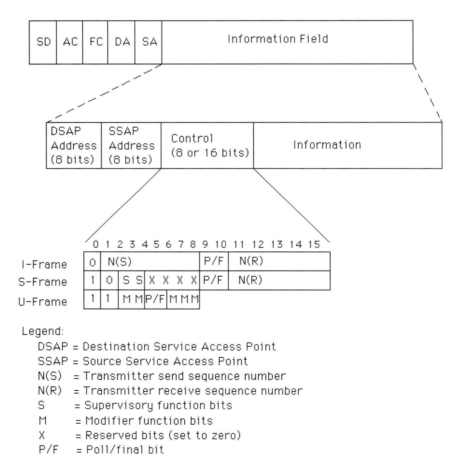

FIGURE 4.19 Logical link control frame format.

to the control field used in the HDLC protocol and defines three types of frames—information (I-frames) are used for sequenced messages, supervisory (S-frames) are used for status and flow control, while unnumbered (U-frames) are used for unsequenced, unacknowledged messages.

Service Access Points

Service access points (SAPs) can be considered interfaces to the upper layers of the OSI Reference Model, such as the network layer protocols. A station can have one or more SAPs associated with it for a specific layer, and can have one or more active sessions initiated through a single SAP. Thus, we can consider a SAP to function similarly in scope to a mailbox, containing an address that enables many types of mailings to reach the box. However, instead of mail, SAP addresses identify different network layer processes or protocols and function as locations where messages can be left concerning desired network services.

DSAP

The first field in the LLC protocol data unit is the destination services access point (DSAP). The DSAP address field identifies one or more service access points for which information is to be delivered.

SSAP

The second field in the LLC protocol data unit is the source services access point (SSAP). The SSAP address field identifies the service access point that transmitted the frame. Both DSAP and SSAP addresses are assigned to vendors by the IEEE to ensure that each is unique.

Both DSAPs and SSAPs are 8-bit fields; however, only 7 bits are used for addressing, which results in a maximum of 128 distinct addresses available for each service access point. The eighth DSAP bit indicates whether the destination is an individual or a group address, while the eighth SSAP bit indicates whether the PDU contains a request or a response.

The control field contains information that defines how the LLC frame will be handled. U-frames are used for what is known as connectionless service, in which frames are not acknowledged, while I-frames are used for connection-oriented services, in which frames are acknowledged.

Types and Classes of Service

The types and classes of service supported by Token-Ring are the same as those supported by Ethernet, which was described in the earlier section on Ethernet logical link control. Thus, readers are referred to that section for information concerning the types and classes of service supported by a Token-Ring LAN.

5

Managing Ethernet and Token-Ring LANs

Chapter 4 examined the operations of Ethernet and Token-Ring LANs with respect to the flow of frames on each type of network. That chapter noted a variety of error conditions resulting from the flow of frames on each type of network. Using that information as a base, we will now focus upon the use of SNMP and RMON to manage Ethernet and Token-Ring LANs. In doing so, I will use Triticom's SimpleView and ProTool's Foundation Manager with Triticom's RMONster and ProTool's Cornerstone RMON probes. This will provide a visual insight concerning the operation of managers and agents, as well as the interoperability of different network management products.

Although the title of this chapter indicates the management of Ethernet and Token-Ring LANs will be examined, note that my coverage is not intended to be all inclusive. Primary focus in this chapter is upon the flow of frames on both networks, and excludes the management of certain devices that can be connected to either type of LAN, such as bridges, hubs, Uninterruptible Power Supply (UPS), and other devices that are covered in later chapters.

SNMP MANAGEMENT

Although the agent and manager are important components of SNMP, it is the MIB that governs your ability to obtain an insight into LAN operations. Thus, this section will discuss and describe two common LAN MIBs. First, the Ethernet MIB, including statistics computed and optional chip set statistics. This will be followed by an examination of the Token-Ring MIB. However, prior to doing so let me answer a question that may be in the mind of many readers—How do I actually perform SNMP management?

Performing SNMP Management

As discussed previously the three key SNMP components are a manager, agent, and MIB. Figure 5.1 illustrates this relationship for an Ethernet bus-structured network. Although many network and network-related devices, such as bridges, routers, DSUs/CSUs, and UPS systems, may contain both an agent and built-in MIB, the majority of workstations on networks do not include either. Thus, the counting of frame flow information is normally accomplished by a separate device that includes both an agent and MIB. That device is normally referred to as a *probe*.

RMON probes can be connected to a local LAN and will provide the ability to capture the full set of statistical information

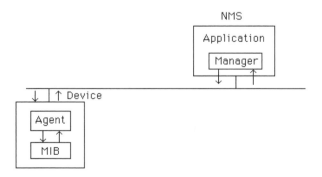

Legend: MIB —Management Information Base
NMS —Network Management System

FIGURE 5.1 SNMP component relationship.

concerning the flow of frames on the LAN. Thus, you may consider using an RMON probe on both your local LAN and remote LANs to obtain an insight concerning the operation of both types of networks. Concerning such probes, you can acquire them as a software product that operates on a PC or as a bundled hardware-software solution. Concerning the latter, although the bundles solution may be more expensive, some products provide the capability to monitor multiple LANs, which may reduce the cost per monitored interface below that of competitive products.

Ethernet MIB

RFC 1650, dated August 1994, resulted in the definition of managed objects for Ethernet-like interfaces using SNMPv2. The MIB defined in the referenced RFC updates RFC 1398, as well as respecifies the RFC 1398 MIB so that it is compliant with SNMPv2 and SNMPv1. The actual title of RFC 1650 is *Definitions of Managed Objects of the Ethernet-like Interface Types using SMIv1*. The term *Ethernet-like* in the title acknowledges the fact that there are several variations to the original technology defined by Xerox, Digital Computer, and Intel during the 1970s, and standardized by the IEEE 802 committee. RFC 1650 supports the original Ethernet frame format as well as IEEE frame formats described in Chapter 4.

Statistics

Under RFC 1650, 12 32-bit counters are used to record statistics for a particular interface, while five optional statistics for an Ethernet chip set are defined. Table 5.1 lists the object identifiers for the Ethernet MIB statistics table, as well as provides a brief description of each statistics counter. Table 5.2 provides similar information for the optional Ethernet Collision Statistics Group.

The MIB defined by RFC 1650 is located under the transmission subtree of the mib-2 node, in the group labeled *dot3*, which has the address 1.3.6.1.2.1.10.7. The mandatory Ethernet statistics table summarized in Table 5.1 has the address {dot3 2}, which equates to the global naming tree address 1.3.6.1.2.1.10.7.2. In examining the global naming tree addresses listed in Table 5.1, note that entries 12, 14, and 15 are unassigned, which explains their absence from the referenced table.

The identifiers listed in Table 5.1 can be used individually or in conjunction with other identifiers to provide an insight to the operational status of an Ethernet LAN. For example, adding the count for dot3StatsExcessiveCollisions and dot3StatsInternalMacTransmitErrors would result in a count of frames for which transmission on a particular interface failed due to either excessive collisions or an internal MAC sublayer transmit error.

The optional Ethernet Collision Statistics Group summarized in Table 5.2 has the address {dot3 5}. This group, when implemented, provides information that can be used by a management station to construct a collision histogram chart. This is accomplished by an entry in the table counting the number of frames for which there were x collisions prior to the frame being transmitted or the transmission attempt being abandoned. By plotting the number of frames that had a collision (frequency) by the number of collisions reported (count), a two-dimensional collision histogram can be generated.

Tests

Although it is important to examine statistics, by themselves they may not provide a complete story concerning the operational status of a complex network. Recognizing this fact, RFC 1650 includes a *Time-Domain Reflectometry (TDR)* test as well as a *loopback* test. Those tests are defined in the dot3Tests group located under the sixth node in the dot3 group {dot3 6}. The TDR test whose identifier is {dot3 Tests 1} is applicable to only coaxial cable Ethernet, and returns a time interval measured in 100 nsec units between the start of a TDR test and the subsequent detection of a collision or deassertion of a carrier signal. The loopback test whose identifier is {dot3 Tests 2} results in an internal loopback test of memory, data paths, and MAC chip logic; however, it can be performed only if the interface is offline. If an error occurs during a loopback test, the object ifTestResult defined in RFC 1573 will be set to failed (7). You can obtain additional information by retrieving values for the variable ifExtnsTestCode from the OBJECT IDENTIFIERs {dot3 Errors 1} and {dot3 Errors 2}, where the dot3Errors group entries are located under the seventh node in the dot3 group {dot3 7}. The first identifier, whose full address is 1.3.6.1.2.1.10.7.7.1, indicates

TABLE 5.1 Ethernet MIB Statistics

Object Identifier	Access	Description
dot3StatsIndex (1.3.6.1.2.1.10.7.2.1.1)	r	Index for the interface
dot3StatsAlignmentErrors (1.3.6.1.2.1.10.7.2.1.2)	r	Frames that are not an even number of octets in length and do not pass the FCS check
dot3StatsFCSErrors (1.3.6.1.2.1.10.7.2.1.3)	r	Count of frames that are an integral number of octets in length but do not pass the FCS check
dot3StatsSingleCollisionFrames (1.3.6.1.2.1.10.7.2.1.4)	r	Count of successfully transmitted frames for which transmission was inhibited by exactly one collision
dot3StatsMultipleCollisionFrames (1.3.6.1.2.1.10.7.2.1.5)	r	Count of successfully transmitted frames for which transmission was blocked by more than one collision
dot3StatsSQETestErrors (1.3.6.1.2.1.10.7.2.1.6)	r	Count of the number of times an SQE test error message is generated
dot3StatsDeferredTransmissions (1.3.6.1.2.1.10.7.2.1.7)	r	Count of frames for which the first transmission attempt is delayed because the medium is busy
dot3StatsLateCollisions (1.3.6.1.2.1.10.7.2.1.8)		Count of the number of times a collision is detected later than 512 bit-times into the transmission of a frame
dot3StatsExcessiveCollisions (1.3.6.1.2.1.10.7.2.1.9)	r	Count of the number of frames for which transmission fails due to excessive collisions
dot3StatsInternalMacTransmitErrors (1.3.6.1.2.1.10.7.2.1.10)	r	Count of frames for which transmission fails due to an internal MAC sublayer transmit error
dot3StatsCarrierSenseErrors (1.3.6.1.2.1.10.7.2.1.11)	r	Count of the number of times the carrier sense condition was lost or never asserted when attempting to transmit a frame
dot3StatsFrameTooLong (1.3.6.1.2.1.10.7.2.1.13)	r	Count of frames received whose length exceed the maximum permitted frame size
dot3StatsInternalMacReceiveErrors (1.3.6.1.2.1.10.7.2.1.14)	r	Count of frames for which reception fails due to an internal MAC sublayer receive error

Legend: r read-only

that the error results from an inability to initialize a MAC chip for test; while the second identifier, whose address is 1.3.6.1.2.1.10.7.7.2, indicates that the error results from either the expected data not received or not received correctly.

By examining the types of Ethernet statistics counted by SNMP you can appreciate the ability of this network management tool to provide assistance with respect to isolating and resolving network problems. Although most of the entries in Tables 5.1 and 5.2 are appropriately described, the late collisions counter deserves a degree of elaboration. At a 10-Mbps operating rate, 512 bit-times corresponds to 51.2 microseconds, which results in the detection of a collision beyond 64 octets into the transmission. When this situation occurs the late collision is also counted as a generic collision and is then included in other appropriate collision-related statistics, such as excessive collisions.

Token-Ring MIB

Similar to Ethernet, SNMP defines a MIB for a Token-Ring interface. This MIB was originally defined in RFC 1231, which

TABLE 5.2 Ethernet Collision Statistics Group

Object Identifier	Access	Description
dot3CollTable (1.3.6.1.2.1.10.7.5)	n/a	Collection of collision histograms for a particular set of interfaces
dot3CollEntry per-(1.3.6.1.2.1.10.7.5.1)	r	Cell in the histogram of frame collisions for a particular interface
dot3CollCount (1.3.6.1.2.1.10.7.5.2)	r	Number of per-frame media collisions for which a particular collision histogram cell represents the frequency on a particular interface
dot3CollFrequencies (1.3.6.1.2.1.10.7.5.3)	r	Count of individual MAC frames for which transmission occurs after the frame experienced exactly the number of collisions in the associated collision count object

Legend: n/a not accessible
      r read-only

TABLE 5.3 Token-Ring Interface Table

Object Identifier	Access	Description
dot5IfIndex (1.3.6.1.2.1.10.9.1.1.1)	r	Identifies the 802.5 interface for which the entry contains management information.
dot5Commands (1.3.6.1.2.1.10.9.1.1.2)	r-w	Used to set the state of the station.
dot5RingStatus (1.3.6.1.2.1.10.9.1.1.3)	r	Current interface status that can be used to diagnose problems after a station is added to a ring.
dot5RingState (1.3.6.1.2.1.10.9.1.1.4)	r	Current interface state with respect to a station entering or leaving the ring
dot5RingOpenStatus (1.3.6.1.2.1.10.9.1.1.5)	r	Indicates the success or reason for failure of the station's most recent attempt to enter the ring
dot5RingSpeed (1.3.6.1.2.1.10.9.1.1.6)	r-w	Operating rate of the ring
dot5UpStream (1.3.6.1.2.1.10.9.1.1.7)	r	MAC address of the upstream neighbor station in the ring
dot5ActiveMonParticipate (1.3.6.1.2.1.10.9.1.1.8)	r-w	Returns information concerning whether the interface will participate in the active monitor selection process.
dot5Functional (1.3.6.1.2.1.10.9.1.1.9)	r-w	Controls the bit mask of all Token-Ring addresses for which the interface accepts frames.

Legend: r read-only
r-w read-write

was made obsolete by RFC 1743 and includes several mandatory tables and an optional table. Mandatory tables include Token-Ring configuration parameters and a table of statistics and error counters. The option table consists of timer values that govern network management on the ring-by-ring stations.

Mandatory Information

Table 5.3 provides an overview of the contents of the Token-Ring interface table. This table stores configuration and status information applicable to a Token-Ring interface, including the sta-

TABLE 5.4 Token-Ring MIB Status and Parameters Values

Object Type/Values	Description
Commands:	
1 (no-op)	No effect upon station
2 (open)	Station goes into open state and joins ring
3 (reset)	Station goes into a reset state
4 (close)	Station is removed from ring
Ring Status:	
0	No problems detected
32	Ring Recovery
64	Single Station
256	Remove Received
512	Reserved
1024	AutoRemoval Error
2048	Lobe Wire Fault
4096	Transmit Beacon
8192	Soft Error
16384	Hard Error
32768	Signal Loss
131072	No status; open not completed
Ring State:	
1	Opened
2	Closed
3	Opening
4	Closing
5	Open Failure
6	Ring Failure
Ring Open Status:	
1	No open attempt
2	Bad Parameter
3	Lobe Failed
4	Signal Loss
5	Insertion Time-out
6	Ring Failed
7	Beaconing
8	Duplicate MAC
9	Request Failed
10	Remove Received
11	Open

TABLE 5.4 (*continued*)

Object Type/Values	Description
Ring Speed:	
1	Unknown
2	1 Mbps
3	4 Mbps
4	16 Mbps
Active Monitor Participate:	
1	True
2	False

tus of the ring, its operating speed, whether the interface is joining or leaving the ring, as well as other information concerning what is occurring at the interface. The Token-Ring MIB is built into essentially some Token-Ring adapter cards, resulting in the ability to retrieve information from such devices as servers, PCs, routers, bridges, and even such products as a 3174 communications controller when such devices include a manageable Token-Ring adapter and are participants on a Token-Ring network. The Token-Ring interface table summarized in Table 5.3 is located in the dot5 group under the transmission subtree, resulting in its address becoming 1.3.6.1.2.1.10.9.1.1 in the global naming tree. The index is at entry 1, with succeeding OBJECT IDENTIFIERs listed in Table 5.3 having entries through 9. Thus, the global naming tree address of the OBJECT IDENTIFIER for dot5Functional becomes 1.3.6.1.2.1.10.9.1.1.9.

Table 5.4 lists the values associated with the identifiers listed in Table 5.3, as well as provides a brief description of the event associated with each identifier value. The Commands object type is composed of integer values that reference the particular command included in parentheses in Table 5.4. Access to the Command object is read-write, which enables a management station to control the state of a station.

The Ring Status object type is restricted to read-only access, as this object defines the current interface status. By examining this object a management station can determine a specific type of error. The Ring State object is also restricted to read-only access. This object type provides state information about opening (joining the ring) and closing (leaving the ring).

The Ring Open Status object type is also restricted to read-only access, providing information that indicates whether the last attempt to enter a ring was successful; and if not, why not. The Ring Speed object indicates the operating rate of the ring and has read-write access. This permits a management station to reset the speed if a station uses an adapter that was improperly configured.

I did not list in Table 5.4 the UpStream and Functional identifiers described in Table 5.3, as those object types, while included in the interface table, represent single table entries. The Up-Stream identifier is the MAC address of the upstream neighbor, while the Functional object type is a bit mask for a MAC address and is used to identify all functional addresses for the interface.

Statistics Table The Token-Ring statistics table provides a comprehensive count of error conditions that can be extremely useful in determining the cause of current problems or possible evolving problems. Table 5.5 lists the Token-Ring statistics table counters, as well as provides a brief description of the object tracked by the counter.

The Token-Ring statistics table summarized in Table 5.5 has its index located at 1.3.6.1.2.1.10.9.2.1.1 in the global naming tree, with the counters listed in Table 5.5 varying from entry 2 for line errors through 19 for frequency errors. As indicated in Table 5.5, each OBJECT IDENTIFIER counter is limited to read-only access.

In examining the entries in Table 5.5 it is important to review the contents of the Token-Ring frame's Ending Delimiter (ED) field whose contents govern several error conditions, such as Line Errors, AC Errors, and Frame Copied Errors. Thus, you may wish to consider reviewing the Token-Ring frame operation information presented in Chapter 4 to obtain an appreciation for the previously mentioned error conditions.

Optional Timer Table The implementation of the Token-Ring Timer table is optional and when included provides access to the values of many timers measured in units of 100-microsecond intervals. The timers are uniquely applicable to Token-Ring operations and are an option to the Token-Ring MIB. Table 5.6 lists the Token-Ring Timer table entries, as well as provides a brief description of each timer. Since the Token-Ring Timer table was designed to track the value of different timers required for Token-Ring operations, as you might expect, access to each object is restricted to read-only. The index to the Token-Ring Timer Table is located at 1.3.6.1.2.1.10.9.5.1 in the global naming tree, while the entries in Table 5.6 are located at 2 through 11 with respect to the index location.

The retrieval of identifier instances from both the Ethernet and Token-Ring MIBs would be accomplished in a manner similar to the retrieval of other instances previously illustrated in this book. That is, you would use the GET or GET-NEXT command and specify the IP address of the managed device and the global naming tree identifier of the MIB entry you wish to retrieve from the device. Since several examples of the retrieval of MIB entries were previously illustrated in this book I will focus the hands-on illustrations in this chapter on the coverage of RMON, which is presented in the next section. Doing so will illustrate how you can use an RMON probe to obtain information about both local and remotely located networks.

RMON

Although SNMP can provide significant information about network attached devices, to do so it must poll public and private MIBs. While this action may not require a relatively large portion of bandwidth when occurring on a single LAN or LANs connected by local bridges, as soon as a network expands to encompass geographically separated networks connected by a WAN, polling can represent a significant bandwidth problem. Recognizing this problem, RMON was developed as a mechanism to support proactive monitoring of LAN traffic.

RMON was developed by the *Internet Engineering Task Force (IETF)* and became a standard in 1992 as RFC number 1271 for Ethernet, and then later defined RFC number 1513 for Token-Ring. The most recent update to RMON at the time this

TABLE 5.5 Token-Ring MIB Statistics Table

Object Identifier	Access	Description
dot5StatsIfIndex (1.3.6.1.2.1.10.9.2.1.1)	r	Index for the interface.
dot5StatsLineErrors (1.3.6.1.2.1.10.9.2.1.2)	r	Counter incremented if there is a nondata bit (J or K symbol) between starting and ending delimiters of token or frame, or an FCS error in the frame.
dot5StatsBurstErrors (1.3.6.1.2.1.10.9.2.1.3)	r	Counter incremented when a station detects the absence of transitions for five half-bit timers.
dot5StatsACErrors (1.3.6.1.2.1.10.9.2.1.4)	r	Counter incremented when a station receives an Active Monitor Present (AMP) or Standby Monitor Present (SMP) frame in which A and C bits equal 0, and then receives another SMP frame with A and C bits equal to 0 without first receiving an AMP frame.
dot5StatsAbortTransErrors (1.3.6.1.2.1.10.9.2.1.5)	r	Counter incremented when a station transmits an abort delimiter while transmitting.
dot5StatsInternalErrors (1.3.6.1.2.1.10.9.2.1.6)	r	Counter incremented when a station recognizes an internal error.
dot5StatsLostFrameErrors (1.3.6.1.2.1.10.9.2.1.7)	r	Counter incremented when a station is transmitting and its Return-to-Report (TRR) timer expires.
dot5StatsReceiveCongestions (1.3.6.1.2.1.10.9.2.1.8)	r	Counter incremented when a station recognizes a frame addressed to it but has no available buffer space, indicating the station is congested.
dot5StatsFrameCopiedErrors (1.3.6.1.2.1.10.9.2.1.9)	r	Counter incremented when a station recognizes a frame addressed to its address and detects the A bits set to 1, indicating a possible line hit or duplicate address.
dot5StatsTokenErrors (1.3.6.1.2.1.10.9.2.1.10)	r	Counter incremented when a station acting as an active monitor recognizes an error condition that requires the transmission of a token.
dot5StatsSoftErrors (1.3.6.1.2.1.10.9.2.1.11)	r	Counter incremented when a Soft Error (recoverable by the MAC layer protocols) occurs.

TABLE 5.5 (*continued*)

Object Identifier	Access	Description
dot5StatsHardErrors (1.3.6.1.2.1.10.9.2.1.12)	r	Counter incremented when an immediately recoverable fatal error occurs. The Counter notes number of times the interface is either transmitting or receiving beacon MAC frames.
dot5StatsSignalLoss (1.3.6.1.2.1.10.9.2.1.13)	r	Counter incremented when the loss of signal condition is detected.
dot5StatsTransmitBeacons (1.3.6.1.2.1.10.9.2.1.14)	r	Counter incremented when a beacon frame transmitted.
dot5StatsRecoverys (1.3.6.1.2.1.10.9.2.1.15)	r	Counter incremented when a Claim Token MAC frame transmitted or received after a Ring Purge MAC frame received. This counter indicates the number of times the ring was purged and recovered back to a normal operating state.
dot5StatsLobeWires (1.3.6.1.2.1.10.9.2.1.16)	r	Counter increments when an open or short circuit in the lobe data path is detected.
dot5StatsRemoves (1.3.6.1.2.1.10.9.2.1.17)	r	Counter incremented when a Remove Ring Station MAC frame request is received, resulting in a close state condition.
dot5StatsSingles (1.3.6.1.2.1.10.9.2.1.18)	r	Counter incremented when the interface senses it is the only station on the ring.
dot5StatsFrequencyErrors (1.3.6.1.2.1.10.9.2.1.19)	r	Counter incremented when the interface detects that the frequency of the incoming signal differs from the expected frequency by more than the IEEE 802.5 standard.

Legend: r read-only

book was written was RFC 1757, issued in February 1995, which obsoleted RFC number 1271. Under RFCs 1271 and 1513, RMON includes an *Alarm Group* that enables thresholds to be set for critical network parameters. Then, when those thresholds are reached an alert will be automatically transmitted to the network management station.

The actual RMON MIB is located under subtree 16 of the mib-2 tree, resulting in the path to this MIB becoming 1.3.6.1. 2.1.16. As I examine the use of management stations to retrieve

RMON information and discuss the use of different RMON groups, I will also denote the location in the global naming tree of different RMON groups and, for certain key groups, the OBJECT IDENTIFIER and global naming tree address of entries in the group.

TABLE 5.6 The Optional Token-Ring Timer Table

Object Identifier	Access	Description
dot5TimerIpIndex (1.3.6.1.2.1.10.9.5.1.1)	r	Index for the interface
dot5TimerReturnRepeat (1.3.6.1.2.1.10.9.5.1.2)	r	Time-out value used to ensure the interface returns to its repeat state
dot5TimerHolding (1.3.6.1.2.1.10.9.5.1.3)	r	Maximum period of time a station is permitted to transmit frames after capturing a token
dot5TimerQueue (1.3.6.1.2.1.10.9.5.1.4)	r	Time-out value for queuing a Standby Monitor Present message for transmission after receiving an Active Monitor Present or Standby Monitor Present frame
dot5TimerValidTransmit (1.3.6.1.2.1.10.9.5.1.5)	r	Time-out value used by the active monitor to detect the absence of valid ttransmissions
dot5TimerNoToken (1.3.6.1.2.1.10.9.5.1.6)	r	Time-out value used to detect a lost token
dot5TimerActiveMon (1.3.6.1.2.1.10.9.5.1.7)	r	Time-out value used by the Active Monitor to generate Active Monitor Present frames
dot5TimerStandbyMon (1.3.6.1.2.1.10.9.5.1.8)	r	Time-out value used by the standby monitors to ensure there is an active monitor on the ring
dot5TimerErrorReport (1.3.6.1.2.1.10.9.5.1.9)	r	Time-out value that defines how often a station sends a Report Error frame to report the values in its error counters
dot5TimerBeaconTransmit (1.3.6.1.2.1.10.9.5.1.10)	r	Time-out value that defines how long a station continues beaconing prior to entering the bypass state
dot5TimerBeaconReceive (1.3.6.1.2.1.10.9.5.1.11)	r	Time-out value that determines how long a station will receive beacon frames from its downstream neighbor prior to entering the bypass state

Legend: r read-only

An RMON agent can be either hardware or software based, operating on a computer connected to a LAN segment, a self-contained probe, or built into another LAN device, such as a router. In addition to an Alarm Group, RMON provides a standard set of MIBs that provide valuable network statistical information.

Through RMON you obtain a common platform from which you can monitor equipment from different vendors at the data link and physical layer. Hardware- and software-based RMON probes monitor all data packets transmitted and received, maintaining a historical record of events that can be used for fault diagnosis, performance tuning, and even network planning.

RMON Groups

There are nine RMON groups considered to be generally common to both Ethernet and Token-Ring networks, while a tenth group is applicable only to the latter network. Table 5.7 lists the ten RMON groups and includes a brief description or overview of the function of each group. While most of the MIB group objects in the first nine groups are applicable for the management of any type of network, some objects in different groups are applicable only to a particular type of LAN. For example, the Traffic Matrix Group provides statistics based upon pairs of nodes at the MAC layer, resulting in a count of packets and errors received and transmitted. Thus, the Traffic Matrix Group is very similar for both Ethernet and Token-Ring. In comparison, the Statistics Group varies considerably between Ethernet and Token-Ring RMON MIB groups due to the key differences between the operation of each type of LAN, which results in different access methods requiring different methods of tracking.

In examining the groups listed in Table 5.7, I will defer a discussion of specific statistics maintained by Token-Ring RMON probes until later in this section. Doing so will facilitate a review of the use of Ethernet RMON probes prior to covering the use of Token-Ring probes.

The Ethernet RMON MIB is located at node 16 under the mib-2 node, resulting in its global naming tree position becoming 1.3.6.1.2.1.16. The nine groups within the Ethernet RMON MIB are located at subnodes 1 through 9 and correspond to the first nine entries in Table 5.7.

TABLE 5.7 Ethernet and Token-Ring RMON MIB Groups

Common Groups	Description
Statistics	Collects cumulative traffic and error statistics for the segment.
History	Collects and provides general traffic statistics based on user-defined sampling interval.
Alarm	Permits users to define thresholds and sampling intervals to generate alarms on any segment monitored by RMON agent.
Host Table	Collects traffic statistics for each network node (device) in the table format.
Host Top N	Extends the host table by providing sorted host statistics based upon user-defined data selected, duration, and number of devices (N).
Matrix	Collects amount of traffic and number of errors occurring between pairs of nodes at the MAC layer using a traffic matrix.
Filters	Permits capturing of packets that match a predefined criteria.
Packet Capture	Captures all packets or those meeting filtering criteria. Packets can be requested by the NMS and subsequently decoded.
Event	Creates entries in a log using packet matches and alarms. SNMP traps can be defined for any event for transmission to the NMS.
Ring Station Statistics	Applicable only to Token-Ring LANs; captures ring station control, status information, order of stations on monitored rings, configuration, and source routing data.

The Token-Ring RMON MIB is specified in the form of extensions to the original RMON MIB developed for Ethernet. The extension is located at node 10 under the mib-2 node, resulting in its global naming tree position becoming 1.3.6.1.2.1.10. This extension defines several groups that are unique to Token-Ring operations, such as Statistics, History, Ring Station, Token-Ring Ring Station Station Order, and Token-Ring Source Routing. In examining the groups listed in Table 5.7, I will first focus upon Ethernet, examining its Statistics Group in detail while providing an overview of the other groups. Then I will focus upon Token-Ring, examining its Statistics group in detail while providing an overview of the other groups contained in the RMON MIB extension.

Ethernet

This section will examine the Ethernet RMON Statistics Group in detail, as well as present an overview of other groups in the RMON MIB. Doing so will illustrate the use of Ethernet probes via the use of two management station products.

Statistics Group Table 5.8 provides a summary of the identifiers contained in the Ethernet *Statistics Group* in the RMON MIB. In examining the entries contained in Table 5.8, note that the identifiers in the group provide counts of data traffic, specific types of packets, different error conditions, and the distribution of packet counts. Although I used the term *frame* in Chapter 4 to indicate formatted units of data transported at the data link layer, SNMP standards documents use the term *packets* to reference frames. Thus, I decided to be consistent with my inconsistency by using the term *packet* in SNMP descriptions and references to table entries even though I correctly described the formatted data units as frames in Chapter 4. Since layer 3 information is normally referred to as packets, I hesitate to denote frames and packets as synonyms. Instead think of them as being used in a similar context to describe monitored data at the data link layer.

To illustrate the retrieval and display of portions of the Ethernet RMON Statistics Group, I will use the Foundation Manager management platform developed by ProTools, Inc., a wholly owned subsidiary of Network General Corporation. Later in this chapter, I will use the Triticom SimpleView network manager to illustrate how to query selected portions of a probe's RMON MIB.

Figure 5.2 illustrates the operation of Foundation Manager in its Remote Ethernet Monitoring mode after a remote probe's address was configured into the program, and the device was selected from the program's station selection dialog box. In Fig-

TABLE 5.8 Ethernet Statistics Group

Object Identifier	Access	Description
etherStatsIndex (1.3.6.1.2.1.16.1.1.1.1)	r	Identifier of the entry
etherStatsDataSource (1.3.6.1.2.1.16.1.1.1.2)	r-w	Source of the data (interface) the entry is configured to analyze
etherStatsDropEvents (1.3.6.1.2.1.16.1.1.1.3)	r	Number of times packets dropped due to lack of resources
etherStatsOctets (1.3.6.1.2.1.16.1.1.1.4)	r	Total number of octets of data received to include bad packets
etherStatsPkts (1.3.6.1.2.1.16.1.1.1.5)	r	Total number of packets received, including those in error
etherStatsBroadcastPkts (1.3.6.1.2.1.16.1.1.1.6)	r	Total number of good packets received directed to a broadcast address
etherStatsMulticastPkts (1.3.6.1.2.1.16.1.1.1.7)	r	Total number of good packets received directed to a multicast address
etherStatsCRCAlignErrors (1.3.6.1.2.1.16.1.1.1.8)	r	Total number of packets received with a length between 64 and 1518 octets that had a bad CRC or were not an integral number of octets in length
etherStatsUndersizePkts (1.3.6.1.2.1.16.1.1.1.9)	r	Total number of otherwise well-formed packets that were less than 64 octets long
etherStatsOversizePkts (1.3.6.1.2.1.16.1.1.1.10)	r	Total number of otherwise well-formed packets that were longer than 1518 octets
etherStatsFragments (1.3.6.1.2.1.16.1.1.1.11)	r	Total number of packets received that were not an integral number of octets in length, or were less than 64 octets in length
etherStatsJabbers (1.3.6.1.2.1.16.1.1.1.12)	r	Total number of packets longer than 1518 octets and were not an integral number of octets or had a bad FCS
etherStatsCollisions (1.3.6.1.2.1.16.1.1.1.13)	r	Best estimate of the total number of collisions on this segment
etherStatsPkts64Octets (1.3.6.1.2.1.16.1.1.1.14)	r	Total number of packets received, including those in error that were 64 octets in length
etherStatsPkts65to127Octets (1.3.6.1.2.1.16.1.1.1.15)	r	Total number of packets received, including those in error that were 65 to 127 octets in length

TABLE 5.8 (*continued*)

Object Identifier	Access	Description
etherStatsPkts128to255Octets r (1.3.6.1.2.1.16.1.1.1.16)		Total number of packets received, including those in error that were 128 to 255 octets in length
etherStatsPkts256to511Octets (1.3.6.1.2.1.16.1.1.1.17)	r	Total number of packets received, including those in error that were 256 to 511 octets in length
etherStatsPkts512to1023Octets (1.3.6.1.2.1.16.1.1.1.18)	r	Total number of packets received, including those in error that were 512 to 1023 octets in length
etherStatsPkts1024to1518Octets (1.3.6.1.2.1.16.1.1.1.19)	r	Total number of packets received, including those in error that were 1024 to 1518 octets in length
etherStatsOwner (1.3.6.1.2.1.16.1.1.1.20)	r-w	Entity that configured the entity as is, using the resources assigned to it
etherStatsStatus (1.3.6.1.2.1.16.1.1.1.21)	r-w	Status of this etherStats entry

ure 5.2, note the two series of bar charts that run horizontally across the screen. The display of each bar chart sequence resulted from clicking on two icons in the program's solution bar that contains the second row of icons at the top of the screen. Clicking on the solution set icon labeled Net, which is to the right of the stop sign icon, results in the display of a bar chart indicating the current remote segment usage, plus a breakdown of the different types of errors that might appear on the segment. If you compare the labels of the bar chart to the entries in Table 5.8, you will note that the Foundation Manager program divides the value of etherStatsOctets by the number of elapsed seconds to generate the Ether Bytes/sec display, divides the value of ether-StatsPkts by the number of elapsed seconds to generate the Ethernet Frames/sec display and so on. Also note that Foundation Manager uses *bytes* and *frames* instead of *octets* and *packets*.

The lower window containing a horizontal series of bar charts resulted from clicking on the icon labeled Size in the program's solution set. Once again, a comparison of the entries in Table 5.8 to the labels on the series of bar charts in the lower window in Figure 5.2 illustrates the manner by which the Pro-Tool's Foundation Manager uses the Ethernet Statistics Group in its program displays.

Through the use of the two statistics charts shown in Figure 5.2 you can obtain a quick visual indication of the health of the segment being monitored as well as an indication of the type of traffic being transported. Concerning the latter, since interactive traffic is primarily transported by relatively short frames while file transfers are transported by relatively long frames, the distribution of the frame sizes provides an indication of the type of traffic transported on the remote segment.

To obtain another view of the Statistics Group, I used Foundation Manager's Remote QuickStats solution set. Figure 5.3 illustrates the initial retrieval effort of Foundation Manager in gathering statistics from the Ethernet probe. In examining Fig-

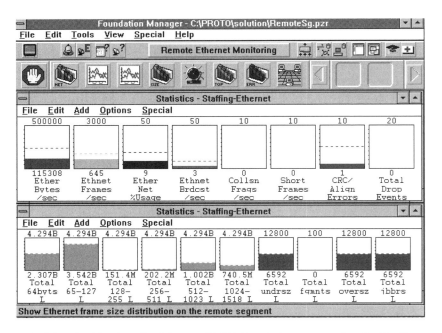

FIGURE 5.2 Viewing the Ethernet RMON Statistics group using ProTool's Foundation Manager program.

ure 5.3, note the icon labeled Working displayed in the frame size distribution window, as the program was in the process of retrieving the required information when the screen was displayed. In Figure 5.4 the Remote QuickStats Statistics screen was expanded to its full size after the program initially displayed frame distribution data elements from the probe. In examining Figures 5.3 and 5.4, note that statistical dial panes or gauges are used to display four statistics that are updated every five seconds, while the percentage of network usage and broadcast frames are plotted over time in the form of a trend graph at the bottom of the display. Thus, this program provides several methods by which to view information from the Statistics Group.

History Group   The *History Group* provides historical views of the statistics collected by the Statistics group. To do so, the History group collects statistics based upon default or user-defined sampling intervals and bucket counters.

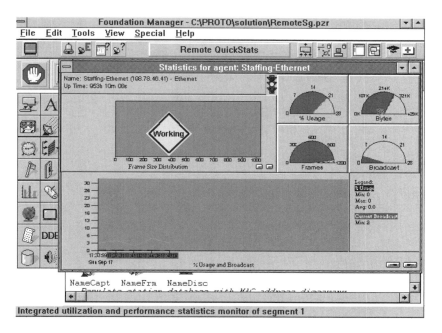

FIGURE 5.3 Initiating a ProTool's Foundation Manager Remote QuickStats display.

The RMON MIB has two defaults for trend analysis. The first provides 50 buckets or samples of 30-second sampling intervals over a period of 25 minutes. The second supports 50 buckets of 30-minute sampling intervals over a period of 25 hours. You can modify either default or add additional intervals to meet your specific requirement for historical analysis, varying the sample interval from one second to one hour.

Host Table Group The *Host Table Group* maintains a series of traffic statistics in table form, including cumulative errors that represent a combination of all statistics error conditions. A host timetable maintains the relative order by which each host was discovered by the agent. This feature assists in providing the management station with newly discovered addresses it is not yet aware of, reducing unnecessary SNMP polling traffic on the network.

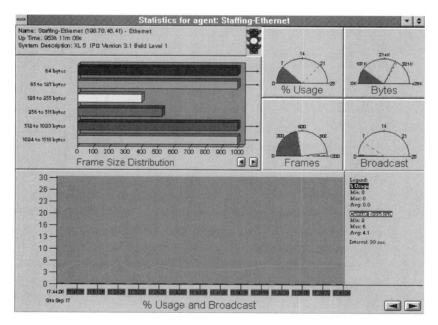

FIGURE 5.4 An exploded view of ProTool's Foundation Manager's QuickStats display.

Host Top N Group This group extends the Host Table Group by providing sorted host statistics for N statistics. You can define data to be sorted and the duration of the study through the use of the network management station.

Host Top N counters maintain the statistics you select for study, while non-selected statistics over the same interval will not be available for later study. The actual number of studies you can invoke is limited by the resources of the RMON agent. The effect of the RMON agent maintaining the Host Top N counters is similar to the effect of the History and Host Table groups, reducing SNMP traffic as well as the processing load on the management station. Examples of the use of the Top N Hosts group would be retrieving the five nodes with the highest number of errors transmitted during the past eight hours, or the ten nodes that transmitted or received the most traffic in octets during the past hour.

Traffic Matrix Group The *Traffic Matrix Group* is used to store the amount of traffic and number of errors between pairs of nodes, with each node pair consisting of one source and one destination address. For each address pair, the RMON MIB maintains counters for the number of packets, number of octets, and error packets occurring between the node pair. Data generated by retrieving Traffic Matrix Group information can be extremely useful in attempting to determine if one or a few workstations are responsible for a majority of network traffic, if errors are primarily attributable to a specific workstation, and similar information that can significantly assist network managers and administrators in testing, troubleshooting, and performance-tuning operations.

Alarms Group Through the use of the *Alarms Group* you can set thresholds that when reached generate an alarm. Both rising and falling thresholds can be set using either the absolute value of a statistic or its delta value. Here the latter can be used to provide notification of a rapid change in a monitored value, which could indicate a potential problem is about to occur. Since alarms are proactively generated without SNMP polling, once again SNMP traffic is reduced.

Events Group The *Events Group* provides a mechanism to specify the number of events that can be stored in a probe and periodically transmitted to the network management station. Here the term *event* represents the occurrence of a trap condition. RF 1157 specifies seven SNMP traps: link up, link down, warm start, cold start, authentication failure, Exterior Gateway Protocol (EGP) neighbor loss, and enterprise-specific. Three additional traps—rising threshold, falling threshold, and packet match—are specified in the RMON MIB, resulting in up to ten distinct traps for which the Events group can provide a notification of occurrence.

When a trap occurs the Events group time-stamps each event and adds a description of the event written by the manufacturer of the probe. This information is stored in a circular log in the probe, which can result in events becoming lost by overwriting unless they are periodically uploaded to the management station.

Filters Group Through the use of the *Filters Group* you can define packets to be captured. RMON supports the use of AND and NOT operations, and allows multiple filters to be combined through the use of the OR operator. By the use of one or more filters, you can capture packets that meet a predefined address criteria, error condition, or another criteria that can assist your analysis of activity on a distant LAN segment.

Packet Capture Group Through the *Packet Capture Group* you obtain the ability to create one or more capture buffers, as well as control recording of information into those buffers.

The actual placement of packets into a capture buffer is controlled by filters created through the use of the Filters Group. When a packet matches a filter, it can be used to initiate a trigger to perform a trace, resulting in trace data filling a designated buffer. In comparison, the Packet Capture Group lets you assign matched filtered objects to one or more capture buffers, and control whether trace buffers will wrap back to the beginning (circular buffer) and overwrite previously captured packets or stop when the buffer is full.

Using a Management Platform   Although knowledge of global naming tree identifiers can be helpful, especially when you're developing a program, many programs hide the naming tree and identifiers from view. For example, consider Figure 5.5, which illustrates the display of ProTool's Foundation Manager's Map display. This display, which appears as a matrix indicating the flow of packets from source to destination MAC address, was obtained by clicking on the mesh-structed icon containing three small computers. Although the window is labeled Map, followed by the name of the probe being queried, the map is actually a matrix that will display the latest 20 conversation pairs on the network. The information displayed is obtained from the Ethernet Matrix Group. Similarly, clicking on the alarm icon in the program's solution bar results in a window labeled Alarm being displayed. This window is shown in the upper left portion of Figure 5.6.

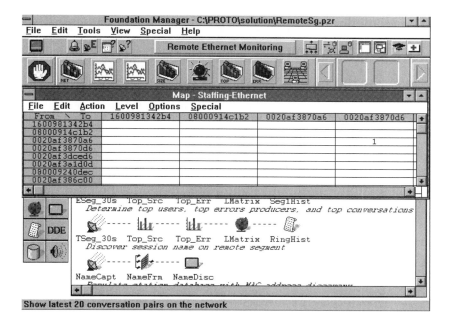

FIGURE 5.5   The ProTool's Foundation Manager Map Display shows the latest 20 conversation pairs on the monitored network.

Through the Alarm window shown in Figure 5.6, you can set alarm conditions as well as view alarms. Table 5.9 lists the Ethernet statistics for which you can set alarms via the use of Foundation Manager, with ProTool's proprietary alarms indicated by asterisks.

ProTools support the setting of alarm thresholds based upon minimum value, maximum value, and interval for actual values or a delta change. The selection of a threshold for an alarm variable is accomplished through a window, and alleviates the necessity to understand the identifiers in the Alarm group, which the program hides from view. Thus, ProTools, as well as other network management platforms, hides from view the complexity of working with object identifiers and global naming tree positions.

To illustrate a more direct use of an Ethernet RMON probe with respect to OBJECT IDENTIFIERs and knowledge of the

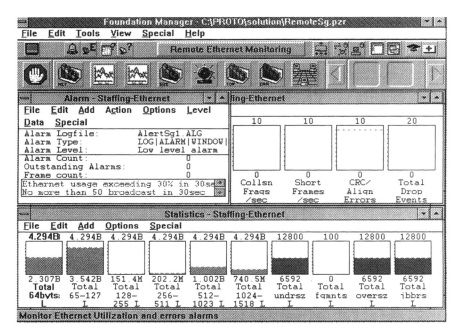

FIGURE 5.6 Through the alarm window, you can set thresholds for alarm generation as well as view alarms.

TABLE 5.9   ProTool's Foundation Manager Ethernet Alarm Variables

---

Byte count

Broadcast frames

Collision fragments

Collisions

CRC/alignment errors

Drop events

Frame counts

Frames 64 bytes

Frames 65-127 bytes

Frames 128-255 bytes

Frames 256-511 bytes

Frames 512-1023 bytes

Frames 1024-1518 bytes

Jabber frames

Multicast frames

Network utilization *

Oversize frames

Total errors *

Undersize frames

---

* ProTool's proprietary statistic

global naming tree, I will use Triticom's SimpleView network manager to query an RMON probe built into a CrossComm router. Doing so will illustrate the use of SimpleView through a series of screen images that will indicate several important concepts concerning the use of an SNMP manager.

Figure 5.7 illustrates the selection of an Ethernet probe at address 198.78.46.41, while Figure 5.8 illustrates the use of the SimpleView Manage menu.

Selecting the Basic entry from the Manage menu shown in Figure 5.8 results in the drop down of a second menu, with the entry System at the top of that menu shown selected. In examining the entries in the second menu, note that in addition to retrieving RMON data from the first menu, the Basic entry in

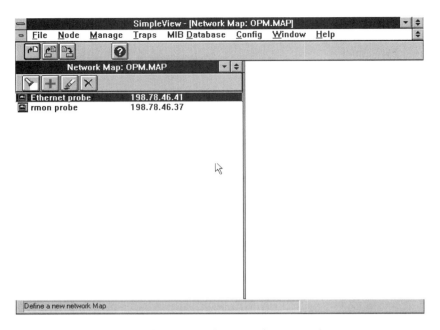

FIGURE 5.7 Using SimpleView to select an Ethernet probe.

the Manage menu provides you with the ability to retrieve basic information concerning mib-2 subtrees 1 through 11, where 1 represents the System Group whose field naming tree identifier is 1.3.6.1.2.1.1, 2 represents the Interface Group whose global naming tree identifier is 1.3.6.1.2.1.2, and so on. Since there is presently no 9 defined and 10, which references the Transmission Group, as previously discussed, is actually a node under which groups that are applicable to different transmission technologies reside, the developers of SimpleView did not include it in their menu. Thus, the last entry in the second menu in Figure 5.8, SNMP, represents location 11 under the mib-2 tree and has the global naming tree address of 1.3.6.1.2.1.11.

Through the selection of the System Group from Figure 5.8, you can retrieve detailed information concerning the managed object, which in this example is an Ethernet probe. Figure 5.9 illustrates a portion of the instances of the OBJECT IDENTIFIERs retrieved by SimpleView. Note that the sysDescr identifier notes that the probe is an XL5 router, and provides

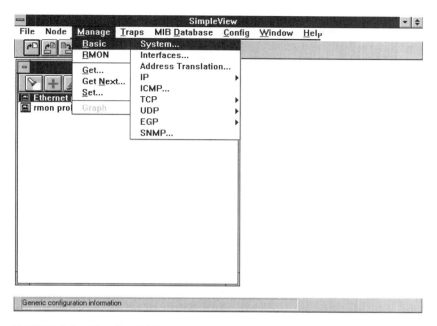

FIGURE 5.8   The SimpleView Manage menu.

information concerning the version and build level of the device. Many times this information can be extremely valuable when attempting to verify your organization has the correct version of a product. The sysObjectID represents the identifier assigned by CrossComm to its product, while the third identifier visible in Figure 5.9, sysUpTime, indicates both the time in hundredths of a second and days, hours, and minutes since the network management portion of the XL5 was last reinitialized. If I scrolled further through Figure 5.9, I would obtain the name of the person responsible for the node, the administratively assigned name of the probe, its physical location, and other information, assuming such data were entered into the probe. Thus, the System Group can be used to obtain a significant amount of information concerning a selected probe.

Another MIB group that can provide valuable information concerning a selected probe is the Interfaces Group. Figure 5.10 illustrates the retrieval of instances from the Interfaces Group, showing the values for six OBJECT IDENTIFIERs for three

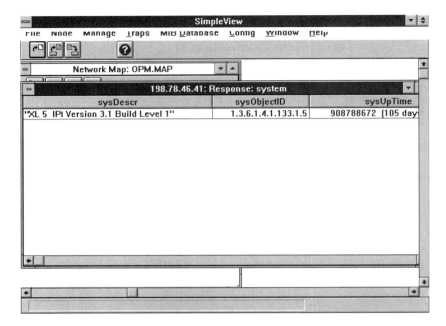

FIGURE 5.9 Using SimpleView to display instances in the System Group of a selected probe.

entries in the Interfaces Table. From Figure 5.10, note that the probe located at 198.78.46.41 has three interfaces, one of which is an Ethernet Card and two Wide Area Network (WAN) cards operating at 56 Kbps. The column labeled ifType contains a numeric identifier of the type of interface, with 6 representing an Ethernet CSMA/CD interface, while 22 represents a proprietary point-to-point serial interface. A description of the types of network interfaces and their numeric identifiers are included in Appendix B.

Although the ifSpeed identifier value for the Ethernet card is indicated to be zero, this means that the value cannot be measured and the nominal value of 10 Mbps is used. The last column shown in Figure 5.10, ifPhysAddress, indicates the physical address of each interface and can be extremely useful to isolate locally administered addressing problems.

In comparing the use of SimpleView to Foundation Manager, the former can be considered to provide a more direct ability to access SNMP identifier instances, while the latter provides a greater indirect capability by, for the most part, hiding most of

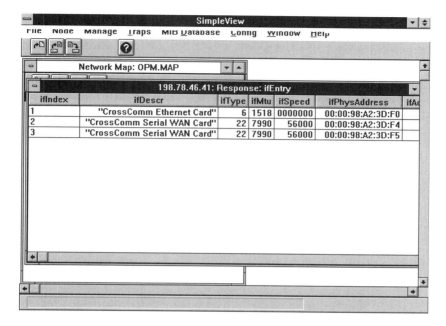

FIGURE 5.10 Using SimpleView to display the Interfaces Group values for a selected RMON probe.

SNMP and RMON from view. For many network managers and administrators, you may wish to consider both types of products, as the use of one can many times complement and supplement the use of the other type of product.

Token-Ring Extensions

As indicated in Chapter 2, a Token-Ring network includes many error-detection facilities within its frame composition, as well as the use of a series of MAC frames that control the configuration of a station and the propagation of station addresses from one neighbor to another, more formally referred to as *neighbor notification*. Recognizing the differences between Ethernet and Token-Ring, RFC 1513, which defined RMON for Token-Ring added media-specific objects applicable to Token-Ring networks that were referred to as Ring Station Statistics in Table 5.7. In actuality, the Ring Station Statistics Group represents an extension of RMON to encompass six areas, while Token-Ring statistics were subdivided into two groups—Token-Ring MAC Layer Statistics and Token-

Ring Promiscuous Statistics. Table 5.10 lists the RFC 1513 RMON extensions as well as provides a brief overview of each extension.

In examining the entries in Table 5.10, I will defer a discussion of the two statistic groups to briefly provide additional information on a few Token-Ring RMON extensions listed in the reference table. Doing so will illustrate their applicability to a unique aspect associated with Token-Ring networks.

The Ring Station Configuration Control extension was developed due to the neighbor notification process associated with Token-Ring networks. As discussed in Chapter 4, that process permits a station to learn the nearest addressable upstream neighbor (NAUN) address. When a beacon occurs to report a

TABLE 5.10 Token-Ring RMON Extensions

Extension	Description
Token-Ring Statistics Group	This extension tracks Token-Ring MAC statistics, diagnostics, and event notifications on the local ring.
Token-Ring Promiscuous Statistics Group	This optional extension tracks non-MAC user data traffic on the local ring.
Ring Station Control	This extension tracks such status information as the ring state, active monitor, hard error beacon fault domain, and number of active stations for each ring being monitored.
Ring Station Table	This extension provides diagnostic and status information, including station MAC address, status, and isolating and nonisolating soft error diagnostics for each station on the ring.
Ring Station Configuration Control	This extension provides a description of the physical configuration of the network.
Ring Station Order	This extension returns a list of stations attached to the monitored ring in logical ring order.
Ring Station Configuration	This extension returns Token-Ring errors that may result from configuration problems.
Source Routing	This extension tracks source routing statistics, which enables the efficiency of source routing to be monitored.

media fault, the fault is reported as a *fault domain* in which the addresses between two adjacent nodes where the problem occurred is reported. Thus, the exact location of the problem can be obtained by referring to a map that a management station can display from data kept by the Ring Station Configuration control extension. To properly position each station on the network map, the Ring Station Order extension tracks the order of each station relative to other stations on the ring. Thus, the Ring Station Configuration Control and Ring Station Order extensions provide a management system with the ability to correctly display a network map indicating the relative location of each station. Now that we have an appreciation for how a network management station can obtain data to indicate where a fault lies on a network map, let's turn to the statistics kept by a Token-Ring RMON MIB.

Table 5.11 lists the collection of MAC layer statistics accumulated by a Token-Ring RMON probe, while Table 5.12 lists the optional promiscuous statistics a probe can accumulate. Included in each referenced table is a group Data Source object that functions in a similar manner to Ethernet Data Source objects, identifying the source of the data that the group is set up to analyze. The Data Source can represent the address of any Token-Ring interface on a probe-connected ring.

As indicated in Table 5.11, Token-Ring RMON Statistics Group provides a measurement of network activity as well as diagnostics and event notifications associated with MAC traffic. In comparison, the Token-Ring RMON Promiscuous Statistics Group tracks non-MAC traffic on the local ring being monitored.

RMON Limitations

One of the problems associated with RMON is the fact that it is limited to tracking packets at layer 2 of the OSI reference model. This means that a pure RMON probe cannot provide information required to provide an application traffic monitoring capability. Recognizing this problem, several vendors have introduced RMON extensions that provide support for application traffic monitoring at layer 7 down through network traffic at layer 3. Through the use of such products as Frontier Soft-

TABLE 5.11 Token-Ring RMON Statistics Group

Object Identifier/Address	Access	Description
tokenRingMLStatsIndex (1.3.6.1.2.1.16.10.2.1.1)	r	Unique identifier of the entry
tokenRingMLStatsDataSource (1.3.6.1.2.1.16.10.2.1.2)	r-w	Source of the data interface
tokenRingMLStatsDropEvents (1.3.6.1.2.1.16.10.2.1.3)	r	Number of times the condition was observed in which packets were dropped by the probe due to a lack of resources
tokenRingMLStatsMacOctets (1.3.6.1.2.1.16.10.2.1.4)	r	Total number of octets of data in good MAC packets received on the network
tokenRingMLStatsMacPkts (1.3.6.1.2.1.16.10.2.1.5)	r	Total number of good MAC packets received
tokenRingMLStatsRingPurgeEvents (1.3.6.1.2.1.16.10.2.1.6)	r	Total number of times the ring enters the ring purge state from the normal ring state
tokenRingMLStatsRingPurgePkts (1.3.6.1.2.1.16.10.2.1.7)	r	Total number of ring purge MAC packets detected
tokenRingMLStatsBeaconEvents (1.3.6.1.2.1.16.10.2.1.8)	r	Total number of times the ring enters a beaconing state
tokenRingMLStatsBeaconTime (1.3.6.1.2.1.16.10.2.1.9)	r	Total amount of time the ring was in the beaconing state
tokenRingMLStatsBeaconPackets (1.3.6.1.2.1.16.10.2.1.10)	r	Total number of beacon MAC packets detected
tokenRingMLStatsClaimTokenEvents (1.3.6.1.2.1.16.10.2.1.11)	r	Total number of times the ring enters the claim token state from the normal state or ring purge state
tokenRingMLStatsClaimTokenPkts (1.3.6.1.2.1.16.10.2.1.12)	r	Claim token state provided in response to a beacon state is not counted
tokenRingMLStatsNAUNChanges (1.3.6.1.2.1.16.10.2.1.13)	r	Total number of claim token MAC packets detected
tokenRingMLStatsLineErrors (1.3.6.1.2.1.16.10.2.1.14)	r	Total number of NAUN changes detected
tokenRingMLStatsInternalErrors (1.3.6.1.2.1.16.10.2.1.15)	r	Total number of line errors reported in detected error reporting packets
tokenRingMLStatsBurstErrors (1.3.6.1.2.1.16.10.2.1.16)	r	Total number of adapter internal errors reported in detected error reporting packets

TABLE 5.11   (*continued*)

Object Identifier/Address	Access	Description
tokenRingMLStatsACErrors (1.3.6.1.2.1.16.10.2.1.17)	r	Total number of burst errors reported in detected error reporting packets
tokenRingMLStatsAbortErrors (1.3.6.1.2.1.16.10.2.1.18)	r	Total number of Address Copied (AC) errors reported in detected error reporting packets
tokenRingMLStatsLostFrameErrors (1.3.6.1.2.1.16.10.2.1.19)	r	Total number of abort delimiters reported in detected error reporting packets
tokenRingMLStatsCongestionErrors (1.3.6.1.2.1.16.10.2.1.20)	r	Total number of lost frame errors reported in detected error reporting packets
tokenRingMLStatsFrameCopiedErrors (1.3.6.1.2.1.16.10.2.1.21)	r	Total number of receive congestion errors reported in detected error reporting packets
tokenRingMLStatsFrequencyErrors (1.3.6.1.2.1.16.10.2.1.22)	r	Total number of frame copied errors reported in detected error reporting packets
tokenRingMLStatsTokenErrors (1.3.6.1.2.1.16.10.2.1.23)	r	Total number of frequency errors reported in detected error reporting packets
tokenRingMLStatsSoftErrorReports (1.3.6.1.2.1.16.10.2.1.24)	r	Total number of token errors reported in detected error reporting packets
tokenRingMLStatsRingPollEvents (1.3.6.1.2.1.16.10.2.1.25)	r	Total number of soft error report frames detected

ware's NETscout Manager, you can monitor Netscape, Notes, ccMail, WordPerfect Office, and similar applications, viewing critical parameters that can be used to resolve network problems and alleviate potential network failures prior to their occurrence.

USING MANAGEMENT PLATFORMS

The ability to use SNMP and one or more RMON probes is dependent upon the use of a management platform. In concluding this chapter covering RMON, I will again use Triticom's SimpleView and ProTool's Foundation Manager SNMP network management platforms.

TABLE 5.12 Token-Ring RMON Promiscuous Statistics Group

Object Identifier	Access	Description
tokenRingPStatsIndex (1.3.6.1.2.1.16.10.3.1.1)	r	Unique identifier of the entry
tokenRingPStatsDataSource (1.3.6.1.2.1.16.10.3.1.2)	r	Source (interface) of the data
tokenRingPStatsDroppedEvents (1.3.6.1.2.1.16.10.3.1.3)		Same as statistics group object
tokenRingPStatsDataOctets (1.3.6.1.2.1.16.10.3.1.4)		Total number of octets of data in good frames received on the network in non-MAC packets
tokenRingPStatsDataPkts (1.3.6.1.2.1.16.10.3.1.5)		Total number of good non-MAC packets received
tokenRingPStatsDataBroadcastPkts (1.3.6.1.2.1.16.10.3.1.6)		Total number of good non-MAC frames received that were directed to an LLC broadcast address
tokenRingPSTatsDataMulticastPkts (1.3.6.1.2.1.16.10.3.1.7)		Total number of good non-MAC frames received that were directed to a local or global multicast or functional address
tokenRingDataPkts 18to630Octets 64to127Octets 128to255Octets 256to511Octets 512to1023Octets 1024to2047Octets 2048to4095Octets 4096to8191Octets 8192to18000Octets GreaterThan18000Octets		Total number of received good non-MAC frames within the indicated length; global naming positions run in sequence from entry 8 through entry 17

Working with SimpleView

Upon occasion the hundreds of identifiers located within Ethernet and Token-Ring RMON MIBs can be intimidating to persons directly working with SNMP, resulting in the development of management stations that hide some, most, or all of the complexities associated with global naming tree locations, SNMP commands, and other functions required to retrieve and display information about the status of a monitored network. As previously discussed, the use of some management products, including SimpleView, require a broader background concerning SNMP knowledge than other products. This section will illustrate the use of SimpleView from its configuration setup to support a newly installed RMON probe to its use to retrieve network information from the probe. The presentation of a series of screen displays provides an indication of the interrelationship and interaction between a management station and a probe, as well as illustrates the operation of a relatively simple management station, including SNMP-related knowledge required to use the station.

Adding a Managed Node

Figure 5.11 illustrates the addition of a Token-Ring RMON probe to SimpleView. In this example, the dialog box was displayed by clicking on the plus (+) icon. Note that the name of the probe *rmonster/tr* references the name of a Triticom Token-Ring software based probe. That probe is located at IP address 198.78. 46.66 on the same network due to the setting of the mask. Thus, in this example the Token-Ring RMON probe, which the program refers to as a node, will be used to provide information concerning the activity of the network to which the management platform operating SimpleView is connected.

Menu Operations

As a GUI-menu based program, SimpleView provides access to each Token-Ring RMON extension via a menu entry. Figure 5.12 illustrates a sequence of SimpleView menu selections from the program's Manage menu. First, RMON was selected, which generated a second drop-down menu containing nine groups and a tenth entry labeled Token-Ring, which when selected generates a new menu consisting of groups under the Token-Ring extension to the RMON MIB. Since the Statistics Group consists of both Mac-Layer and Promiscuous groups, the selection of the Statistics menu entry generates another choice. The three shaded selections indicate that Token-Ring Mac-Layer statistics are to be retrieved from the selected Rmonster/tr probe.

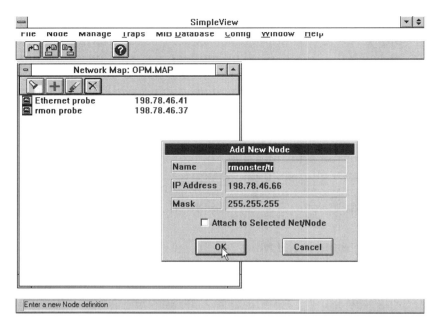

FIGURE 5.11 Using SimpleView to add an RMON probe to its network monitoring station list.

The execution of the selection previously shown in Figure 5.12 results in the retrieval of Token-Ring MAC layer statistics from the selected RMON probe. Figure 5.13 illustrates the results of the retrieval operation performed in Figure 5.12. In examining Figure 5.13 note that since there was one interface on the probe, SimpleView displays MAC layer statistics in one row—true to the concept of SNMP identifiers contained within a table. However, this forces a user to scroll through the row to view the values of different objects. In comparison, other management platforms may summarize the entries in different groups in a manner that is easier to view.

Retrieving Station Order Information

One of the more helpful Token-Ring RMON extension groups is the *Token-Ring Ring Station Order Group*. Through the retrieval of element values from this optional group, you can obtain a list of ring stations that denotes the location of each station with respect to other stations located on the ring. Figure 5.14 illustrates the initial SimpleView display after the Station

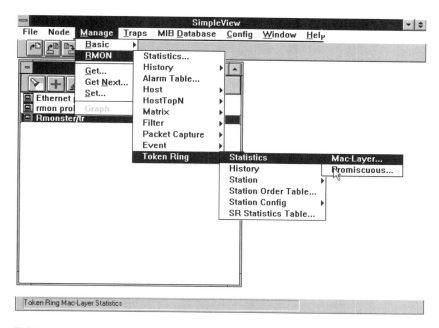

FIGURE 5.12 Using SimpleView to retrieve Mac-Layer statistics from a Token-Ring probe.

Order Table entry was selected from the pull-down menu previously illustrated in Figure 5.12.

In examining Figure 5.14 note that the ring order is displayed to denote the MAC address for each station on the ring. While this data conforms to the manner by which the group's entries are defined (MacAddress syntax), it may be difficult for users to visually note the relationship of MAC addresses to users. Due to this, some management products permit you to associate alphanumeric identifiers with MAC addresses, and extend the capability of responses by performing a table lookup of MAC addresses against predefined names associated with predefined MAC addresses. The result of this operation would be a column extension to the response, which lists names associated with MAC addresses to facilitate the use of the displayed information.

Token-Ring History Group Information Retrieval

In concluding presentation of basic SimpleView functions to illustrate the operation of a management platform, we will focus upon the History Group for which I previously limited my dis-

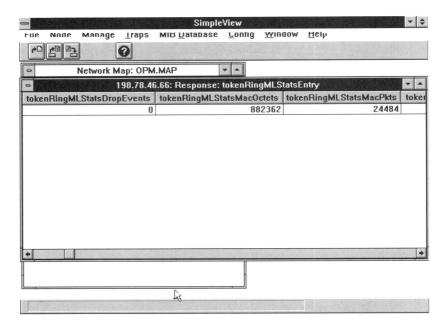

FIGURE 5.13 Using SimpleView to view the Token-Ring MAC-layer statistics captured by a probe.

cussion to providing a summary of its use. The History Group consists of two separate entities—MAC-Layer and Promiscuous identifiers. Table 5.13 provides a summary of the identifiers in each group, while Figure 5.15 illustrates the initial display of Mac-Layer History Group elements. This display results from the initial selection of the History entry from the third menu shown in Figure 5.12, which would display a fourth menu containing Mac-Layer and Promiscuous entries. Selecting Mac-layer would result in the display shown in Figure 5.15.

In examining Figure 5.15, note that only the first three identifiers are displayed in the window. Thus, to view dropped events, MAC packets, or another MAC-Layer historical identifier value, you would have to scroll horizontally through the window. Although I follow this review of SimpleView with an overview of ProTool's Foundation Manager, which provides a more sophisticated identifier viewing capability, I would be remiss if I did not mention that the retail cost of SimpleView is approximately one-

ringStationOrderIfIndex	ringStationOrderOrderIndex	ringStationOrderMacAddress
1	1	00:00:F6:2E:60:D1
1	2	00:00:F6:2E:2D:FE
1	3	40:00:31:72:00:00
1	4	40:00:31:72:00:01
1	5	08:00:5A:32:DB:63
1	6	00:00:F6:2E:2C:65
1	7	10:00:5A:12:E1:E6
1	8	00:00:F6:2E:2D:8D
1	9	00:00:19:C8:42:0D
1	10	00:00:F6:2E:2C:49
1	11	00:00:F6:2E:2B:DE
1	12	10:00:5A:72:65:04
1	13	40:00:31:72:00:02
1	14	00:00:F6:2E:23:D4
1	15	10:00:5A:1C:0C:BA

FIGURE 5.14 Displaying information retrieved from the Token-Ring Ring Station Group.

tenth the cost of Foundation Manager. In addition, SimpleView provides the ability to access any supported MIB identifier, as it supports the entry of global naming tree identifiers and the use of SNMP commands with those identifiers, a feature Foundation Manager lacks. However, if I had to recommend a product I would recommend both, for as previously mentioned, one complements and supplements the use of the other.

Working with Foundation Manager

Since I previously illustrated the retrieval of information from an Ethernet RMON probe using Foundation Manager, in concluding this chapter I will focus upon several features of the manager that were not previously covered. Doing so will illustrate the setting of alarms, the monitoring of errors and determination of the top users of a network, and the examination of MAC layer activity.

TABLE 5.13 Token-Ring History Groups

Identifiers in the Token-Ring MAC-Layer History Group

```
tokenRingMLHistoryIndex
tokenRingMLHistorySampleIndex
tokenRingMLHistoryInterval
tokenRingMLHistoryIntervalStart
tokenRingMLHistoryDropEvents
tokenRingMLHistoryMacOctets
tokenRingMLHistoryMacPkts
tokenRingMLHistoryRingPurgeEvents
tokenRingMLHistoryRingPurgePkts
tokenRingMLHistoryBeaconEvents
tokenRingMLHistoryBeaconTime
tokenRingMLHistoryBeaconPkts
tokenRingMLHistoryClaimTokenEvents
tokenRingMLHistoryClaimTokenPkts
tokenRingMLHistoryNAUNChanges
tokenRingMLHistoryLineErrors
tokenRingMLHistoryInternalErrors
tokenRingMLHistoryBurstErrors
tokenRingMLHistoryACErrors
tokenRingMLHistoryAbortErrors
tokenRingMLHistoryLostFrameErrors
tokenRingMLHistoryCongestionErrors
tokenRingMLHistoryFrameCopiedErrors
tokenRingMLHistoryFrequencyErrors
tokenRingMLHistoryTokenErrors
tokenRingMLHistorySoftErrorReports
tokenRingMLHistoryRingPollEvents
tokenRingMLHistoryActiveStations
```

Identifiers in the Token-Ring Promiscuous History Group

```
tokenRingPHistoryIntervalStart
tokenRingPHistoryDropEvents
tokenRingPHistoryDataOctets
tokenRingPHistoryDataPkts
tokenRingPHistoryDataBroadcastPkts
```

TABLE 5.13 *(continued)*

Identifiers in the Token-Ring MAC-Layer History Group

```
tokenRingPHistoryDataMulticastPkts
tokenRingPHistoryDataPkts18to63Octets
tokenRingPHistoryDataPkts64to127Octets
tokenRingPHistoryDataPkts128to255Octets
tokenRingPHistoryDataPkts256to511Octets
tokenRingPHistoryDataPkts512to1023Octets
tokenRingPHistoryDataPkts1024to2047Octets
tokenRingPHistoryDataPkts2048to4095Octets
tokenRingPHistoryDataPkts4096to8191Octets
tokenRingPHistoryDataPkts8192to18000Octets
tokenRingPHistoryDataPktsGreaterThan18000Octets
```

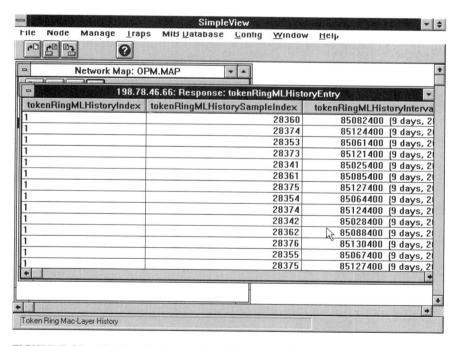

FIGURE 5.15 Viewing the Token-Ring Mac-Layer History Group entries.

Alarm Specification

Figure 5.16 illustrates the display of Foundation Manager's alarm window in the center of the screen. Prior to discussing the manner by which alarms are specified, let me describe some of the icon groups that form the boundaries of the display.

Under the conventional Windows menu bar is a ribbon bar containing icons that, when clicked upon provide quick access to such program options as starting or stopping agent monitoring, viewing outstanding alarms, configuring SNMP communications settings, and performing similar actions. The middle of the ribbon bar, which is shown set to Remote Token-Ring Monitoring, is a pull-down menu you can use to invoke local or remote monitoring of Ethernet and Token-Ring networks, sort traffic, and invoke other program features.

Directly under the ribbon bar is the solution bar, which contains icons that, when pressed enable you to quickly invoke different types of predefined network monitoring operations. The

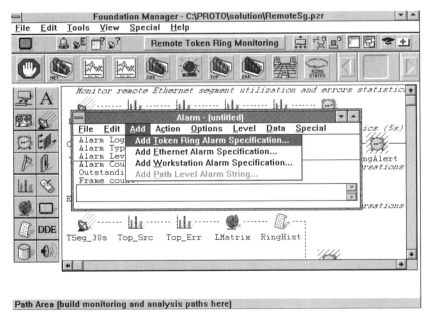

FIGURE 5.16 The Foundation Manager alarm window with its Add menu invoked.

first section of this chapter illustrated the use of several solution bar icons for Remote Ethernet Monitoring.

The vertical column pair of icons are referred to as the *icon panel*. Icons in the icon panel control the construction of paths Foundation Manager uses to analyze a network, including the input of acquired frames into a file, and their playback.

The center of the window, referred to as the *path area*, is where you load solutions or construct paths to perform a specific network analysis. To construct a path, drag an icon from the icon panel to the path area. For example, the top left icon in the icon panel is the Acquire icon. Moving it into the path area results in frames being acquired from the network. Once this occurs you can view and analyze data through the use of an optional protocol decoder module.

The actual enabling of the Alarm window options shown in Figure 5.16 resulted from moving the alarm clock icon located in the first vertical icon column into the path area. Doing so enables

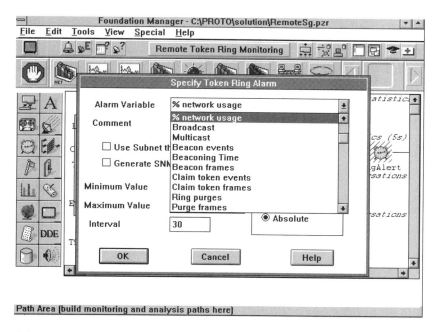

FIGURE 5.17 Foundation Manager permits you to select alarms from a predefined alarm list.

the options in the Alarm window's Add menu, allowing a user to add Token-Ring, Ethernet, or Workstation alarms. Selecting the first option in the Add menu, Add Token-Ring Alarm Specification, results in the display of a new window labeled Specify Token-Ring Alarm.

Figure 5.17 illustrates the Specify Token-Ring Alarm window after the alarm variable option was clicked on to drop a list of predefined alarms from which you can select one. The first alarm variable shown at the top of the list, % network usage, enables you to be alerted when network utilization reaches a predefined level or drops below a predefined level. In fact, once you select an alarm variable, Foundation Manager provides users with several options concerning the generation of a trap as well as the manner by which the resulting alarm condition will be brought to a user's attention.

Figure 5.18 illustrates the setting of a maximum value to the alarm variable % network usage. Note that the calculated value was selected as absolute. Under SNMP, alarm values can

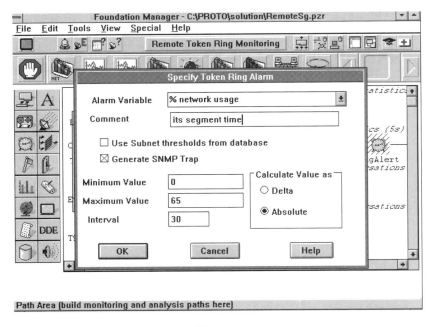

FIGURE 5.18 Setting alarm variable parameters.

be expressed as either a change (delta) or an absolute value. Also note the author entered the comment "its segment time," which will be displayed with the alarm condition.

Once you specify an alarm, Foundation Manager displays a window labeled Alarm notification options, which provides a mechanism to define how you will be informed of the occurrence of the alarm, as well as the alarm level to assign to the alarm. The Alarm notification options window is illustrated in Figure 5.19. Note that the three notification options selected in Figure 5.19 represent the program's default alarm notification options and result in the alarm being displayed in an alarm window, while a flashing icon and an audible alarm indicate something is amiss and you should view the alarm window.

Clicking on the alarm bell icon located under Token in the Remote Token-Ring Monitoring bar entry results in the display of outstanding alarms. Figure 5.20 illustrates the Outstanding Alarms window; however, since network utilization was the only

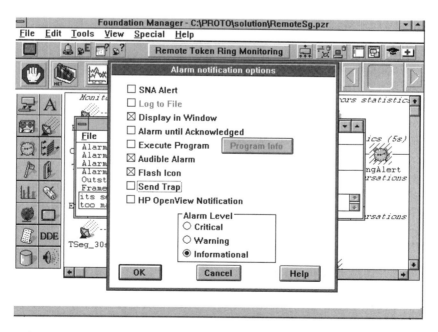

FIGURE 5.19 Foundation Manager's alarm notification options.

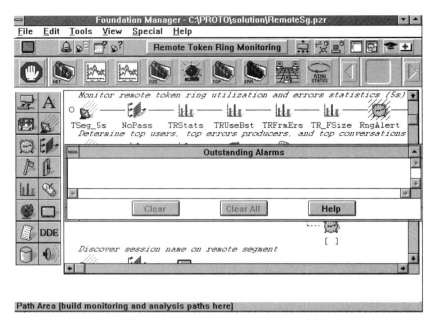

FIGURE 5.20 By clicking on the alarm icon in the solution bar, Foundation Manager's Outstanding Alarms window is opened.

configured alarm and was below a level of 65 percent, no out-standing alarms are displayed in the window.

Multiple Operations

One of the key features of Foundation Manager is its ability to perform multiple operations at the same time. This capability is illustrated in Figure 5.21, which shows the display of three operations resulting from clicking on three solution bar icons.

The window labeled Map, shown across the top of the path area, represents the retrieval of data from the matrix group in the MIB and was discussed earlier in this chapter. By clicking on the icon labeled Top, the bar graph shown in the lower left portion of the path area is displayed. That display summarizes the activity of the top five busiest stations on the network, and is generated by Foundation Manager retrieving data from the MAC-Layer History Group.

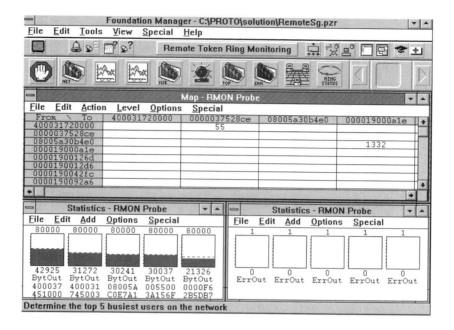

FIGURE 5.21 Foundation Manager supports the retrieval and updating of information from multiple MIB groups.

The third window shown in Figure 5.21, which is labeled Statistics-RMON Probe, resulted from clicking on the bar graph icon labeled ERR. This window would display a bar chart of the five most error-prone nodes on the remote segment; however, no MAC addresses are shown, as there were no errors at the time the window was displayed.

In addition to simultaneously displaying the results of multiple operations that retrieve MIB values, Foundation Manager will poll the probe to continuously update the entries in each window.

Monitoring MAC-Layer Activity

In concluding my overview of Foundation Manager, I will focus upon its MAC-Layer monitoring capability. Figure 5.22 illustrates the program's display window, which summarizes MAC

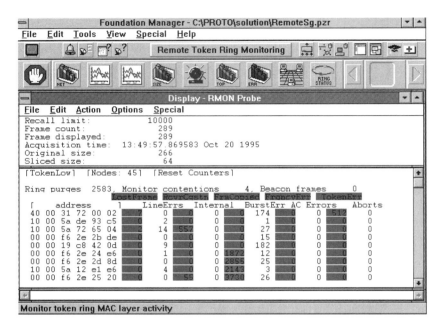

FIGURE 5.22   Viewing MAC Layer activity by MAC address.

layer frame activity, including providing an ordered list of nodes on the network by MAC address and providing a summary of ten error recovery and soft error conditions for each station. This display is generated by clicking on the rightmost active solution bar icon labeled Ring Station.

Through the use of the MAC layer activity display shown in Figure 5.22, you can immediately note error recovery and soft error conditions associated with each station on the monitored network. Thus, this display can be extremely helpful in quickly isolating errors to a workstation, or a lobe routed from a multi-station access unit (MAU) to a workstation.

Managing Bridges and Switching Hubs

The focus of this chapter is upon using SNMP to facilitate the management of *bridges* and *switching hubs*. Since a switching hub functions as a bridge, as you might expect, the bridge MIB is commonly used by manufacturers of switching hubs to provide a nonproprietary SNMP management capability.

This chapter will first review the operation of different types of bridges. Since switching hubs are built upon the operation of bridges, following the review of bridge operations will be an overview of the operation of switching hubs. Although no switching hub MIB had been developed at the time this book was prepared, there are several operational characteristics of this type of communications product that could eventually result in an extension of MIB objects to provide an additional insight into the operation, as well as for the control, of this device.

Following the overview of the operation of bridges and switching hubs, we will turn to the examination of the objects in the bridge MIB. Doing so will explain how to use some of the objects in different bridge MIB groups to facilitate the management of your network.

BRIDGE OPERATIONAL OVERVIEW

A bridge is a communications device that operates at the data link layer, or layer 2, of the OSI reference model. Figure 6.1 illustrates the operation of a generic bridge with respect to the OSI reference model, as well as its use to connect two separate Ethernet local area networks. Since a bridge is designed to operate at the data link layer, it reads and acts upon LAN frames since those frames represent the flow of information at the data link layer. By reading the source address included in each frame, the bridge assembles a table of local addresses for each network. In addition to reading each source address, the bridge also reads the destination address contained in the frame. If the destination address is not contained in the local address table that the bridge constructs, this fact indicates that the frame's destination is not on the current network or network segment. In this situation, the bridge transmits the frame onto the other network or network segment. If the destination address is contained in the local address table, this indicates that the frame should remain on the local network. In this situation the bridge simply repeats the frame without altering its routing.

The previously described method of bridging operation is referred to as *transparent bridging*, and represents one of several types of bridge operations that will be described later in this chapter.

We can summarize the operation of the bridge illustrated in the lower portion of Figure 6.1 as follows:

- Bridge reads all frames transmitted on network A.
- Frames with destination address on network A are repeated back onto that network.
- Frames with destination address on network B are removed from network A and retransmitted onto network B.
- The above process is reversed for traffic on network B.

Filtering and Forwarding

The process of examining each frame is known as *filtering*. The filtering rate of a bridge is directly related to its level of perfor-

OSI Operation

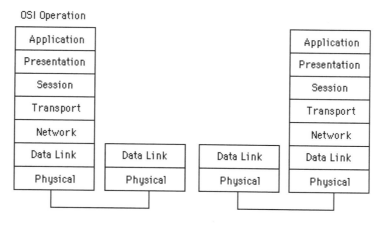

Application Example

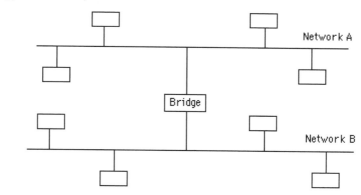

Legend: [   ] = Workstations

FIGURE 6.1 Bridge operation. A bridge connects two logical area networks or network segments at the data link layer.

mance. That is, the higher the filtering rate of a bridge the lower the probability it will become a bottleneck to network performance. A second performance measurement associated with bridges is their *forwarding rate*. The forwarding rate is expressed in frames per second and denotes the maximum capacity of a bridge to transmit traffic from one network to another.

Types of Bridges

There are two general types of bridges—*transparent* and *translating*. Each type of bridge can be obtained as a local or remote device, with a remote device including a wide area network interface as well as the ability to convert frames onto a WAN transmission protocol.

Transparent Bridging

A transparent bridge examines media access control frames to learn the addresses of stations on the network, storing information in internal memory in the form of an address table. Thus, this type of bridge is also known as a *self-learning bridge*. To understand the operation of a transparent bridge in more detail, and some of the limitations associated with the use of this device, consider the simple internet illustrated in Figure 6.2. This internet consists of one Ethernet and two Token-Ring local area networks connected through the use of two self-learning bridges. For simplicity of illustration, only two workstations are shown and labeled on each local area network.

Transparent bridges were originally developed to interconnect Ethernet local area networks. This type of bridge can also be used to connect Ethernet and Token-Ring networks; however, in doing so the bridge must, as a minimum, be capable of performing frame conversion.

Frame Conversion The frame formats used by Ethernet and Token-Ring networks, while similar, are not equal to one another. For example, Ethernet frames are prefixed with a Preamble field that is followed by a Starting Delimiter field. The Ethernet Preamble field is not used in a Token-Ring frame and the Ethernet Starting Delimiter field differs in composition from its Token-Ring equivalent field. Similarly, each Token-Ring frame is prefixed with a Starting Delimiter field that is quite different from the field with that name used on an Ethernet frame. Another significant difference between Ethernet and Token-Ring networks concerns the methods used for bridging. Ethernet networks use transparent bridging employing a spanning tree algorithm. IBM Token-Ring networks support an optional routing method known as *source routing*. If that routing method is not used, an IBM bridge can support transparent bridging. In addition, a standard known as *Source Routing Transparent (SRT)* bridging provides the ability for bridges to support both methods in constructing Ethernet and IBM Token-Ring networks. The spanning tree algorithm used by transparent bridges, the source routing algorithm used by source routing bridges, and the operation of SRT bridges are discussed in detail later in this section.

Address/Routing Table Construction   In examining the construction of bridge address/routing tables for the network illustrated in Figure 6.2, I will assume each bridge operates as a transparent bridge. As frames flow on the Ethernet, bridge 1 examines the source address of each frame. Eventually after both stations A and B have become active, the bridge associates their address as being on port 1 of that device. Any frames with a destination address other than stations A or B are considered to

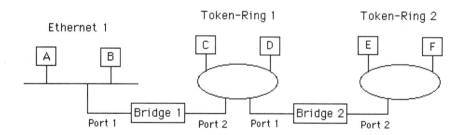

FIGURE 6.2   Transparent bridge operation. A transparent or self-learning bridge examines the source and destination addresses to form addresses or routing tables in memory.

be on another network. Thus, bridge 1 would eventually associate addresses C, D, E, and F with port 2 once it receives frames with those addresses in their destination address fields. Similarly, bridge 2 constructs its address/routing table. Since frames from Ethernet 1 and Token-Ring 1 can have source addresses of A, B, C or D, eventually the address/routing table of bridge 2 associates those addresses with port 1 of that device. Since frames from Ethernet 1 or Token-Ring 1 with a destination address of E or F are not on those local area networks, bridge 2 then associates those addresses with port 2 of that device.

Advantages One of the key advantages of a transparent bridge is that it operates independently of the contents of the information field and is protocol-independent. Since this type of bridge is self-learning, it requires no manual configuration and is essentially a plug-and-play device. Thus, this type of bridge is attractive for connecting a few local area networks together and is commonly sufficient for most small and medium-sized businesses. Unfortunately, its use limits the development of certain interconnection topologies, as we will soon see.

Disadvantages To illustrate the disadvantages associated with transparent bridges, consider Figure 6.3 in which the three Ethernet local area networks are interconnected through the use of three bridges. In this example the internet forms a circular or loop topology. Since a two-port transparent bridge views stations as either being connected to port 1 or port 2, a circular or loop topology will create problems. Those problems can result in an unnecessary duplication of frames, which will not only degrade the overall level of performance of the internet, but also quite possibly confuse end stations.

For example, consider a frame whose source address is A and whose destination address is F. Both bridge 1 and bridge 2 will forward the frame. Although bridge 1 will forward the frame to its appropriate network using the most direct route, the frame will also be forwarded by bridge 3 to Ethernet 2, resulting in a duplicate frame arriving at workstation F. At station F a mechanism would be required to reject duplicate frames. Even if such a mechanism were available, the additional traffic flowing across multiple internet paths would result in an increase in network utilization approaching 100 percent. This in turn would saturate some networks, while significantly reducing the level of performance of other networks. For those reasons transparent bridging is prohibited from creating a loop or circular topology. However, transparent bridging supports concurrently active multiple bridges, using an algorithm known as the *spanning tree* to determine which bridges should forward and which bridges should only filter frames.

Translating Bridge

A *translating bridge* provides a connection capability between two local area networks that employ different protocols at the data link layer. Since networks using different data link layer protocols normally use different media, a translating bridge will also provide support for different physical layer connections.

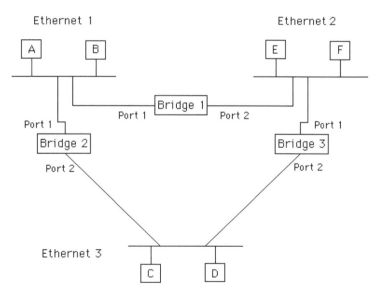

FIGURE 6.3 Transparent bridges do not support network loops. The construction of a circular or loop topology through the use of transparent bridges can result in an unnecessary duplication of frames as well as confusing end stations. To avoid those problems the spanning tree protocol (STP) will open a loop by placing one bridge in a standby mode of operation.

Figure 6.4 illustrates the use of a translating bridge to inter-connect a Token-Ring and an Ethernet local area network. In this example, the bridge functions as an Ethernet node on the Ether-net, and as a Token-Ring node on the Token-Ring. When a frame from one network has a destination on the other network, the bridge will perform a series of operations, including frame and transmission rate conversion. For example, consider an Ethernet frame destined to the Token-Ring network. The bridge will strip the frame's preamble and FCS, then it will convert the frame into a Token-Ring frame format. Once the bridge receives a free token the new frame will be transmitted onto the Token-Ring; however, the transmission rate will be at the Token-Ring network rate and not at the Ethernet rate. For frames going from the Token-Ring to the Ethernet the process would be reversed.

One of the problems associated with the use of a translating

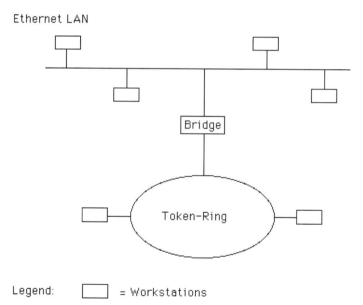

FIGURE 6.4 Translating bridge operation. A translating bridge connects local area networks that employ different protocols at the data link layer. In this example the translating bridge is used to connect an Ethernet local area network to a Token-Ring network.

bridge is the conversion of frames from their format on one network to the format required for use on another network. For example, the information field on an Ethernet frame can vary from 64 to 1500 bytes, while a Token-Ring can have a maximum information field size of 4500 bytes when the ring operates at 4 Mbps, and 18,000 bytes when the ring operates at 16 Mbps. If a station on a Token-Ring network has a frame whose information field exceeds 1500 bytes in length, the bridging of that frame onto an Ethernet network cannot occur. This is because there is no provision within either protocol to inform a station that a frame flowing from one network to another was fragmented and requires reassembly. To effectively use a bridge in this situation requires software on each workstation on each network to be configured to use the smallest maximum frame size of any network to be connected together. In this example, Token-Ring workstations would not be allowed to transmit information fields greater than 1500 bytes.

Spanning Tree Protocol

The problem of active loops was addressed by the IEEE Committee 802 in the 802.1D standard with an intelligent algorithm known as the *spanning tree protocol (STP)*. The STP is based upon graph theory and converts a loop into a tree topology by disabling a link. This action ensures there is a unique path from any node in an internet to every other node. Disabled nodes are then kept in a standby mode of operation until a network failure occurs. At that time, the spanning tree protocol will attempt to construct a new tree using any of the previously disabled links.

Operation

To illustrate the operation of the spanning tree protocol, we must first become familiar with the difference between the physical and active topology of bridged networks. In addition, we should become familiar with a number of terms defined by the protocol and associated with the spanning tree algorithm. Thus, we will also review those terms prior to discussing the operation of the algorithm.

Physical versus Active Topology In transparent bridging, a distinction is made between the *physical* and *active* topology resulting from bridged local area networks. This distinction enables the construction of a network topology in which inactive but physically constructed routes can be placed into operation if a primary route should fail, and in which the inactive and active routes would form an illegal circular path violating the spanning tree algorithm if both routes were active at the same time.

The top of Figure 6.5 illustrates one possible physical topology of bridged networks. The cost (C) assigned to each bridge will be discussed later in this section. The lower portion of Figure 6.4 illustrates a possible active topology for the physical configuration shown at the top of that illustration.

When a bridge is used to construct an active path, it will forward frames through those ports used to form active paths. The ports through which frames are forwarded are said to be in a *forwarding state of operation*. Ports that cannot forward frames due to their operation forming a loop are said to be in a *blocking state of operation*.

Under the spanning tree algorithm, a port in a blocking state can be placed into a forwarding state, and provides a path that becomes part of the active network topology. This new path must not form a closed loop and usually occurs due to the failure of another path, bridge component, or the reconfiguration of interconnected networks.

Spanning Tree Algorithm The basis for the spanning tree algorithm is a tree structure since a tree forms a pattern of connections that has no loops. The term *spanning* is used because the branches of a tree structure span or connect subnetworks.

Root Bridge and Bridge Identifiers

Similar to the root of a tree, one bridge in a spanning tree network will be assigned to a unique position in the network. Known as the *root bridge*, this bridge is assigned as the top of the spanning tree and has the potential to carry the largest amount of internet traffic due to its position.

Since bridges and bridge ports can be active or inactive, a

A. Physical topology

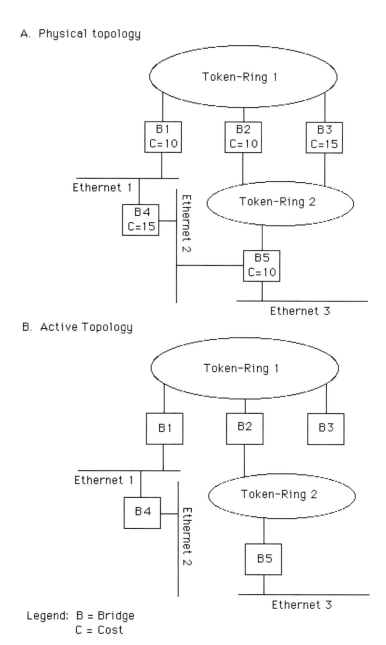

B. Active Topology

Legend: B = Bridge
C = Cost

FIGURE 6.5 Physical versus active topology. When transparent bridges are used, the active topology cannot form a closed loop in the internet.

mechanism is required to identify bridges and bridge ports. Each bridge in a spanning tree network is assigned a *unique bridge identifier*, which is the MAC address on the bridge's lowest port number and a 2-byte bridge priority level. The priority level is defined when a bridge is installed, and functions as a bridge number. Similar to the bridge priority level, each adapter on a bridge that functions as a port has a 2-byte *port identifier*. Thus, the unique bridge identifier and port identifier enables each port on a bridge to be uniquely identified.

Path Cost

Under the spanning tree algorithm, the difference in physical routes between bridges is recognized and a mechanism is provided to indicate the preference for one route over another. That mechanism is accomplished by the ability to assign a *path cost* to each path. Thus, you could assign a low cost to a preferred route, and a high cost to a route you want to be used only in a backup situation.

Once path costs are assigned to each path in an internet, each bridge will have one or more costs associated with different paths to the root bridge. One of those costs is lower than all other path costs. That cost is known as the bridge's *root path cost*, and the port used to provide the least path cost toward the root bridge is known as the *root port*.

Designated Bridge

As previously discussed, the spanning tree algorithm does not permit active loops in an interconnected network. To prevent this situation from occurring, only one bridge linking two networks can be in a forwarding state at any particular time. That bridge is known as the *designated bridge*, while all other bridges linking two networks will not forward frames and will be in a blocking state of operation.

Constructing the Spanning Tree   The spanning tree algorithm employs a three-step process to develop an active topology. First, the root bridge is identified. In Figure 6.5b I will assume bridge 1 was selected as the root bridge. Next, the path cost from each bridge to the root bridge is determined, and the minimum cost from each bridge becomes the root path cost. The port in the direction of the least path cost to the root bridge, known as the root port, is then determined for each bridge. If the root path cost is the same for two or more bridges linking LANs, then the bridge with the highest priority will be selected to furnish the minimum path cost. Once the paths are selected, the designated ports are activated.

In examining Figure 6.5A, let us now use the cost entries assigned to each bridge. Let us assume bridge 1 was selected as the root bridge, as we expect a large amount of traffic to flow between Token-Ring 1 and Ethernet 1 networks. Therefore, bridge 1 will become the designated bridge between Token-Ring 1 and Ethernet 1 networks.

In examining the path costs to the root bridge, note that the path through bridge 2 was assigned a cost of 10, while the path through bridge 3 was assigned a cost of 15. Thus, the path from Token-Ring 2 via bridge 2 to Token-Ring 1 becomes the designated bridge between those two networks. Hence, Figure 6.5B shows bridge 3 inactive by the omission of a connection to the Token-Ring 2 network. Similarly, the path cost for connecting the Ethernet 3 network to the root bridge is lower by routing through the Token-Ring 2 and Token-Ring 1 networks. Thus, bridge 5 becomes the designated bridge for the Ethernet 3 and Token-Ring 2 networks.

Bridge Protocol Data Unit

One question that is probably in readers' minds by now is, How does each bridge know whether to participate in a spanned tree topology? Bridges obtain topology information by the use of *Bridge Protocol Data Unit (BPDU)* frames.

The root bridge is responsible for periodically transmitting a *HELLO* BPDU frame to all networks to which it is connected. According to the spanning tree protocol, HELLO frames must be transmitted every 1 to 10 seconds. The BPDU has the group MAC address 800143000000, which is recognized by each bridge. A designated bridge will then update the path cost and timing information, and forward the frame. A standby bridge will monitor the BPDUs but does not update or forward them.

When a standby bridge is required to assume the role of the

root or designated bridge, as the operational states of other bridges change, the HELLO BPDU will indicate that a standby bridge should become a designated bridge. The process by which bridges determine their role in a spanning tree network is an *iterative* process. As new bridges enter a network they assume a listening state to determine their role in the network. Similarly, when a bridge is removed, another iterative process occurs to reconfigure the remaining bridges.

Although the STP algorithm procedure eliminates duplicate frame and degraded internet performance, it can be a hindrance for situations where multiple active paths between networks are desired. Another disadvantage of the spanning tree protocol is when it is used in remote bridges connecting geographically dispersed networks. For example, returning to Figure 6.3, suppose Ethernet 1 was located in Los Angeles, Ethernet 2 in New York, and Ethernet 3 in Atlanta. If the link between Los Angeles and New York were placed in a standby mode of operation, all frames from Ethernet 2 routed to Ethernet 1 would be routed through Atlanta. Depending upon the traffic between networks, this situation may require an upgrade in the bandwidth of the links connecting each network to accommodate the extra traffic flowing through Atlanta. Since the yearly cost of upgrading a 56- or 64-Kbps circuit to a 128-Kbps fractional T1 link can easily exceed the cost of a bridge or router, one may wish to consider the use of routers to accommodate this networking situation. In comparison, when using local bridges, their higher operating rate in interconnecting local area networks will normally allow an acceptable level of performance to occur when LAN traffic is routed through an intermediate bridge.

Source Routing Protocol

Source routing is a bridging technique developed by IBM for connecting Token-Ring networks. The key to the implementation of source routing is the use of a portion of the information field in the Token-Ring frame to carry routing information and the transmission of *discovery* packets to determine the best route between two networks.

The presence of source routing is indicated by the setting of the first bit position in the source address field of a Token-Ring frame to a binary one. When set, this indicates that the information field is preceded by a *route information field (RIF)* that contains both control and routing information.

RIF Field

Figure 6.6 illustrates the composition of a Token-Ring (RIF). This field is variable in length and is developed during a discovery process described later in this section.

The control field contains information that defines how information will be transferred and interpreted, as well as the size of the remainder of the RIF. The three broadcast bit positions indicate a nonbroadcast, all-routes broadcast, or single-route broadcast situation. A nonbroadcast designator indicates a local or specific route frame. An all-routes broadcast designator indicates that a frame will be transmitted along every route to the destination station. A single-route broadcast designator is used only by designated bridges to relay a frame from one network to another. In examining the broadcast bit settings shown in Figure 6.6, note that the letter *X* indicates a *don't care bit* setting that can be either a 1 or 0.

The length bits identify the length of the RIF in bytes, while the D bit indicates how the field is scanned, left to right or right to left. Since vendors have incorporated different memory in bridges that may limit frame sizes, the LF bits enable different devices to negotiate the size of the frame. Normally a default setting indicates a frame size of 512 bytes. Each bridge can select a number and, if supported by other bridges, that number is then used to represent the negotiated frame size. Otherwise, a smaller number used to represent a smaller frame size is selected and the negotiation process is repeated. Note that a 1500-byte frame is the largest frame size supported by Ethernet IEEE 802.3 networks. Thus, a bridge used to connect Ethernet and Token-Ring networks cannot support the use of Token-Ring frames exceeding 1500 bytes.

Up to eight route number subfields, each consisting of a 12-bit ring number and a 4-bit bridge number, can be contained in the routing information field. This permits two to eight route designators, enabling frames to traverse up to eight rings across

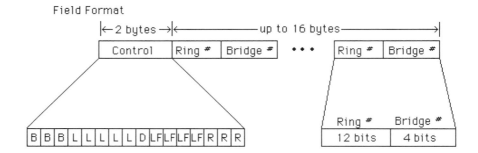

Field Format

B are broadcast bits

Bit Settings	Designator
0XX	Nonbroadcast
10X	All-routes broadcast
11X	Single route broadcast

L are length bits which denote length of the RIF in bytes.
D is direction bit.
LF identifies largest frame.

Bit Settings	Size in Bytes
000	516
001	1500
010	2052
011	4472
100	8191
101	Reserved
110	Reserved
111	Used in all-routes broadcast frame

R are reserved bits.

FIGURE 6.6 Token-Ring information field. The Token-Ring is variable in length.

seven bridges in a given direction. Both ring numbers and bridge numbers are expressed as hexadecimal characters, with three hex characters used to denote the ring number and one hex character used to identify the bridge number.

Operation Example To illustrate the concept behind source routing consider the internet illustrated in Figure 6.7. In this example let us assume two Token-Ring networks are located in Atlanta, and one network is located in New York. Each Token-Ring and every bridge are assigned ring and bridge numbers.

For simplicity, ring numbers R1, R2, and R3 were used; although as previously explained, those numbers are actually represented in hexadecimal. Similarly, for simplicity, bridge numbers are shown as B1, B2, B3, B4, and B5 instead of a hexadecimal character.

When a Token-Ring station wants to originate communications, it is responsible for finding the destination by transmitting a discovery packet to network bridges and other network stations whenever it has a message to transmit to a new destination address. Assuming station A wishes to transmit to station C, it sends a route discovery packet containing an empty route information field and its source address, as indicated in the upper left portion of Figure 6.7. This packet is recognized by each source routing bridge in the network. When received by a source routing bridge, the bridge enters the ring number from which the packet was received and its own bridge identifier in the packet's routing information field. The bridge then trans-

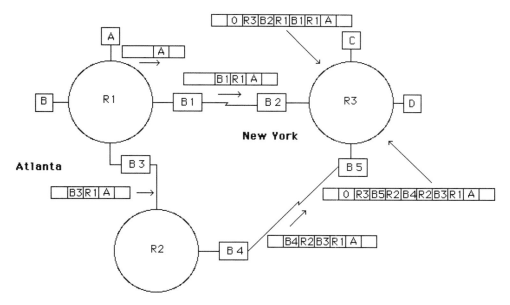

FIGURE 6.7 Source routing discovery operation. The route discovery process results in each bridge entering the originating ring number and its bridge number into the route information field.

mits the packet to all its connections with the exception of the connection on which the packet was received, a process known as *flooding*. Depending upon the topology of the interconnected network, multiple copies of the discovery packet will more than likely reach the recipient. This is illustrated in the upper right corner of Figure 6.7 in which two discovery packets reach station C. Here one packet contains the sequence R1B1R1B2R30, where the zero indicates there is no bridging in the last ring. The second packet contains the route sequence R1B3R2B4R2 B5R30. Station C then picks the best route, based upon either the most direct path or the earliest arriving packet, and transmits a response to the discovery packet originator. The response indicates the specific route to use, and station A then enters that route into memory for the duration of the transmission session.

Under source routing, bridges do not keep routing tables like transparent bridges. Instead, tables are maintained at each Token-Ring station throughout a network. Thus, each station must check its routing table to determine the route frames must traverse to reach their destination station. This routing method results in source routing, using distributed routing tables in comparison to the centralized routing tables used by transparent bridges.

Route Discovery Methods

In actuality, the preceding example represents a simplified explanation of source routing, since there are two types of route discovery frames that can be used as well as two methods by which a source routing bridge can be configured. Both the type of route discovery frame and the configuration of each bridge in a source routing network will determine the flow of data through the network.

Source routing bridges can support *all-routes broadcast* (*ARB*) and *single-route broadcast* (*SRB*) route discovery operations. In addition, a source routing bridge can be configured manually as a single-route broadcast bridge, which is its default setting, or as an all-routes broadcast bridge. As an alternative to manually setting the bridge, its mode of operation can be set to automatic configuration, which enables the bridge to negotiate with other bridges to select an appropriate mode of operation.

Types of Broadcast Frames

An all-routes broadcast frame will traverse all possible routes between source and destination stations. This frame is indicated by the setting of the first 2 bits of the RI field to 10. This value tells each bridge to copy the frame onto all ports other than the port it was received on. In comparison, a single-route broadcast frame is identified by the setting of the first 2 bits of the RI field to a value of 11, and results in the potential for only one route being taken between source and destination stations.

Token-Ring stations can use either an all-routes or a single-route broadcast frame to determine the route to another station on the internet. When an all-routes broadcast route discovery frame is used, that frame is copied by each source routing bridge onto their adjacent rings. This occurs regardless of whether a bridge is set up as a single-route or all-routes broadcast bridge, because both modes of operation forward all-routes broadcast frames. As each bridge copies the frame onto its adjoining ring, it adds into the frame's RIF the ring number into which the frame was copied. The destination station will then receive one frame for each path between the origination and the destination stations. Here the receipt of an all-routes broadcast frame indicates that a station is attempting to locate the destination station. The destination station can respond to the originating station in one of two ways. First, it can respond to each received all-routes broadcast frame. Otherwise, the destination station can reverse the order of the routes placed in each received all-routes broadcast frame, and transmit specifically routed frames to the originating station. That station can then select the shortest route or the first received response.

Bridge Mode of Operation Effect

When a sending station transmits a single-route broadcast frame to determine the best path between that station and its destination, only those bridges configured to pass single-route broadcast frames will copy those frames onto adjacent rings. Depending upon the mode of operations of the bridges, one (if all bridges are set to single-route broadcast) or more frames will reach the destination station. That station can then respond with a single-route, all-routes, or a specifically routed frame.

Table 6.1 summarizes the options that control the route discovery process. The selection of options used in a network is based upon the methods vendors use to implement one or more options, and the degree of control they provide to users in configuring their hardware. Once the route determination process is completed, the originating and destination stations will store a selected route in their route table. This process continues for each station requiring communication with another station, and results in a decentralized approach to routing.

Traffic Considerations

In examining the route options listed in Table 6.1, we can make some general observations about the effect of different options upon internet traffic. As previously discussed, an all-routes broadcast frame will appear on the destination station ring once for each route to that ring. Although this may not appear to be significant, let us examine the flow of an all-routes broadcast frame over a network in which six rings are interconnected through the use of seven bridges. This examination will illustrate the variable effect of an all-routes broadcast frame upon the capacity of different rings formed into a network.

TABLE 6.1 Route Discovery Control Options

A. Bridge frame control

Bridge mode of operation	Frames forwarded
Single-route broadcast	All-routes broadcast Single-route broadcast Specifically routed
All-routes broadcast	All-routes broadcast Specifically routed

B. Source and destination station route options

Originating station options	Destination station options
Single-route broadcast	Single-route broadcast
All-routes broadcast	All-routes broadcast
Data included in route determination frame	Specifically routed

Figure 6.8 illustrates the worst-case scenario in which a station on ring 1 needs to communicate with a station on ring 6. This is a worst-case scenario, since the originating and destination stations are on opposite ends of the internet. In this example, the all-routes broadcast frames would traverse four paths: R1-R2-R3-R6, R1-R2-R5-R6, R1-R4-R5-R6, and R1-R4-R5-R2-R3-R6. As indicated, a different number of all-routes broadcast frames would circulate each ring based upon the paths between ring 1 and ring 6. Since the station on ring 1 will issue one all-routes broadcast frame, that frame flows over ring 1 only once, where it is copied onto rings 2 and 4. The frame on ring 2 is copied onto ring 5, where that ring copies that frame onto rings 2 and 6. When the frame from ring 1 is copied onto frame 2, this results in two copies of the all-routes broadcast frame flowing on ring 2. Next, ring 2 copies the frame received from ring 1 onto rings 5 and 3. This results in ring 5 having two all-routes broadcast frames flowing over that ring. Similarly, the single all-

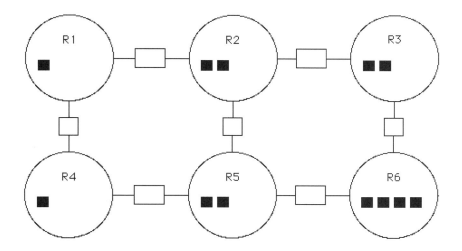

Legend: R = Ring number
■ = 1 copy of all-routes broadcast frame

FIGURE 6.8 All-routes broadcast worst case scenario. An all-routes broadcast frame from a station on R1 to a station on R6 would follow four paths: R1-R2-R3-R6, R1-R2-R5-R6, R1-R4-R5-R6, and R1-R4-R5-R2-R3-R6.

routes broadcast frame occurs twice on ring 3, and four times on ring 6. Note that copies of the single all-routes broadcast frame originated on ring 1 fan out across the internet, requiring a total of 12 frames to be carried by six rings.

Once the destination station on ring 6 receives the all-routes broadcast frame, if set to an all-routes broadcast mode of operation, it responds in a similar but reverse manner. That is, one all-routes broadcast frame generated by a station on ring 6 would result in four such frames being received by a station on ring 1. Thus, a total of 24 frames would be carried by six rings for one station to ascertain the location of another station at the distant end of the internet. When this is multiplied by a large number of network stations becoming active in the morning or after a power outage when stations reattach to network resources, the use of all-routes broadcast frames by the originator and the responding destination stations can flood a network with frames that impair the capacity of rings to convey other information.

Controlling Discovery Frame Flow   One technique to prevent flooding and reduce overhead traffic is obtained by using single-route broadcast frames and single-route operating bridges. A single-route broadcast frame will appear on a destination station ring only as many times as there are single-route broadcast routes to the ring. Thus, the configuration of some bridges to a single-route broadcast mode of operation can be used in conjunction with single-route broadcast frames to create preferred routes for route discovery operations.

In configuring bridges, your goal should be to create a logical network structure in which a single-route is formed to interconnect each ring. Figure 6.9 illustrates a single-route logical network structure for the six rings illustrated in Figure 6.8. This logical configuration is the spanning tree we previously examined in our discussion of transparent bridges.

You can configure bridges to form a single-route through an internet manually, or you can use the automatic feature supported by Token-Ring source routing bridges. The manual method requires you to determine which bridges to set to a single-route broadcast mode of operation to create a logical single network route. In comparison, the automatic method results

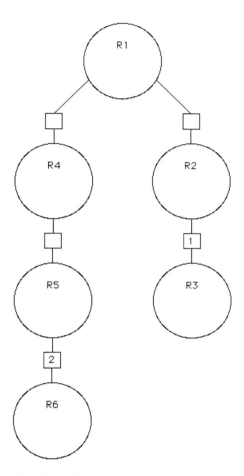

FIGURE 6.9   Single-route logical structure. By placing source routing bridges into a single-route broadcast mode of operation, a logical route structure consisting of a single-route between rings can be formed. This single-route structure represents the physical topology illustrated in Figure 6.6.

in bridges transmitting BPDUs to create a single-route network through the use of the spanning tree protocol. Normally, the automatic method should be used, as bridges placed in this mode will reconfigure themselves automatically when other bridges fail. In comparison, bridges set to a manual mode will require intervention to reconfigure bridges to compensate for failed components in an internet.

Advantages

There are several advantages associated with the use of source routing. One advantage is the ability to construct mesh networks with loops for a fault-tolerant design that cannot be accomplished with the use of transparent bridges. Another advantage is the inclusion of routing information in the information frames.

Through the use of several management products that use the source routing MIB, those products can provide you with information concerning the overhead associated with explorer frames, as well as plot activity over time, which can be helpful when considering the possible upgrade of low-speed WAN connections.

Disadvantages

Although the preceding advantages are considerable, they are not without a price. That price includes a requirement to specifically identify bridges and links, the presence of higher bursts of network activity, and an incompatibility between Token-Ring and Ethernet networks. In addition, due to the structure of the route information field (RIF), which supports a maximum of seven entries, routing of frames is restricted to crossing a maximum of seven bridges.

When using source routing bridges to connect Token-Ring networks, you must configure each bridge with a unique bridge/ring number. In addition, unless you wish to accept the default method by which stations select a frame during the route discovery process, you will have to reconfigure your LAN software. Thus, source routing creates an administrative burden not present when using transparent bridges.

Due to the route discovery process, the flooding of discovery frames occurs in bursts when stations are powered on or after a power outage. Depending upon the complexity of an internet, the discovery process can degrade network performance. Perhaps the biggest problem is for organizations that require the interconnection of Ethernet and Token-Ring networks.

A source routing bridge can be used only to interconnect Token-Ring networks, since it operates on RIF data that is not included in an Ethernet frame. Although transparent bridges can operate in Ethernet, Token-Ring, and mixed environments, their use precludes the ability to construct loop or mesh topologies and inhibits the ability to establish operational redundant paths for load sharing. Another problem associated with bridging Ethernet and Token-Ring networks also involves the RIF in a Token-Ring frame. Unfortunately, different LAN operating systems use the RIF data in different ways. Thus, the use of a transparent bridge to interconnect Ethernet and Token-Ring networks may require the same local area network operating system on each network. To alleviate these problems several vendors have introduced *source routing transparent* (*SRT*) bridges that function in accordance with the IEEE 802.1D standard that was approved during 1992.

Source Routing Transparent Bridges

A source routing transparent bridge supports both IBM's source routing and the IEEE transparent spanning tree protocol operations. This type of bridge can be regarded as two bridges in one, and has been standardized by the IEEE 802.1 committee as the IEEE 802.1D standard.

Operation

Under source routing, the media access control packets contain a status bit in the source field, which identifies whether source routing is to be used for a message. If source routing is indicated, the bridge forwards the frame as a source routing frame. If source routing is not indicated, the bridge determines the destination address and processes the packet using a transparent mode of operation, using routing tables generated by a spanning tree algorithm.

Advantages

There are several advantages associated with the use of source routing transparent bridges. First and perhaps foremost, their use enables different networks to use different local area network operating systems and protocols. This capability enables you to interconnect networks developed independently of one another, and allows organization departments and branches to use LAN operating systems without restriction. Second and also very important, source routing transparent bridges can connect Ethernet and Token-Ring networks while preserving the ability to mesh or loop Token-Ring networks. Thus, their use provides an additional level of flexibility for network construction.

SWITCHING HUBS

The incorporation of microprocessor technology into hubs can be considered the first step in the development of switching hubs. Through additional programming, the microprocessor could examine the destination address of each frame; however, switching capability required the addition of a switching fabric design into the hub. Once this was accomplished, it became possible to use the microprocessor to read the destination address of each frame, and initiate a switching action based upon data stored in the hub's memory that associates destination frame addresses with hub ports.

This section will first examine the rationale for switching hubs by noting the bottlenecks associated with conventional and intelligent hubs as network traffic grows. I will then focus upon the operation and utilization of different types of switching hubs.

Rationale

The earliest types of Ethernet LANs were designed to use coaxial cable configured using a bus topology. The development of the hub-based 10BASE-T local area network offered a number of networking advantages over the use of coaxial cable. Some of those advantages included the use of twisted-pair cable, which is easier to use and less expensive than coaxial cable, and the ability to reconfigure, troubleshoot, and isolate network problems. By simply moving a cable connection from one port to another network, administrators can easily adjust the usage of a hub, or interconnect hubs to form a new network structure. The connection of test equipment to a hub, either to a free port or by temporarily removing an existing network user, could be accomplished much more easily than with a coaxial-based network. Recognizing these advantages, hub manufacturers added microprocessors to their hubs, which resulted in the introduction of a first generation of intelligent Ethernet hubs.

The first generation of intelligent hubs used the capability of a built-in microprocessor to provide a number of network management functions network administrators could use to better control the operation and utilization of their network. Those functions typically include tracking the network utilization level, providing summary statistics concerning the transmission of frames by different workstations, as well as providing the network administrator with the ability to segment the LAN by entering special commands recognized by the hub.

Bottlenecks

Both conventional and first-generation intelligent hubs simply duplicate frames and forward them to all nodes attached to the hub. This restricts the flow of data to one workstation at a time, since collisions occur when two or more workstations attempt to gain access to the media at the same time.

Conventional hubs, including the first generation of intelligent hubs, create network bottlenecks because all network traffic flows through a shared backplane. This results in every workstation connected to the hub competing for a slice of the backplane's bandwidth. For example, consider the hub illustrated in Figure 6.10 in which up to seven workstations and a file server contend for access to the network. Since only one

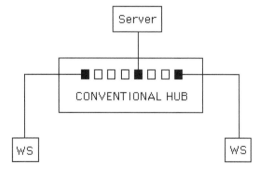

FIGURE 6.10 When using a conventional hub, congestion occurs when several workstations vie for access to a server.

device can transmit at any point in time, the average slice of bandwidth that each device receives is 1.25 Mbps (10 Mbps/8). The actual data transfer capability is less, since attempts by two or more workstations to simultaneously transmit can result in collisions that cause jam signals to be placed on the network, precluding other workstations from transmitting data during the duration of those signals. As more users are added to a network through the interconnection of hubs, network performance will continue to decrease as the potential for congestion increases. Thus, manufacturers of Ethernet products, as well as network administrators, focused their efforts upon developing different tools and techniques to alleviate network congestion, including the manufacture and utilization of switching hubs.

Switching Hub Operations

Switching hubs can be categorized in two main ways—by their method of operation and their support of single or multiple addresses per port. The method of operation is commonly referred to as the *switching technique*, while the address-per-port support is normally referred to as the *switching method*.

Switching Techniques

There are two switching techniques used by switching hubs— *cross-point*, also referred to as cut-through, and *store and forward*.

Cross-Point

A cross-point switch examines the destination address of each packet entering the port. It then searches a predefined table of addresses associated with ports to obtain a port destination. Once the port destination is determined, the switch initiates the cross connection between the incoming port and the outgoing port. Figure 6.11 illustrates cross-point/cut-through switching.

Cross-point switching minimizes the delay or latency associated with placing a packet received on one port onto another port. Since the switching decision is made once the destination address is read, this means the full packet is not examined. Thus, a cross-point switch cannot perform error checking on a packet.

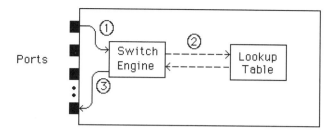

① Packet address examined
② Port destination address obtained
③ Switch to destination port

FIGURE 6.11 Cross-point/cut-through switching.

Store and Forward

A store-and-forward switching hub stores the full incoming packet in a buffer. This enables the switch to perform a CRC check to determine if the received packet is error free. If it is, the switch uses the destination address of the packet to perform a table lookup to obtain the destination port address. Once that address is obtained, the switch performs a cross-connect operation and forwards the packet to its destination.

Figure 6.12 illustrates the operation of a store-and-forward switching hub. Since the packet must first be placed in shared RAM, this results in greater latency than provided by a cross-point switching technique.

Switching Methods

Switching hubs can be classified with respect to their support of single or multiple addresses per port. The support of a single address per port is referred to as *port-based switching*, while the support of multiple addresses per port is referred to as *segment-based switching*.

Port-Based Switching

A port-based switching hub can be considered to operate similar to an n x n matrix switch, reading the destination address of

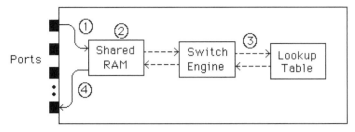

① Packet address read as packet enters RAM

② Full packet enters RAM; CRC computed

③ Destination port obtained

④ Packet forwarded from RAM to destination port

FIGURE 6.12   Store and forward switching.

incoming frames from a single device connected to the port and using that address through a table lookup process to initiate a cross-connect to a destination port.

Figure 6.13 illustrates an example of port-based switching. Since each connected node is isolated from other nodes except when simultaneously contending for access to the same destination port, the resulting network throughput can be considerably higher than a 10BASE-T network. For example, user 1 could communicate with server 1, user 2 with server 2, and so on, all simultaneously. In this best-case example with n users and n servers, the operating rate through the switch becomes $n * 10$ Mbps, or n times the operating rate of a conventional Ethernet network.

Segment-Based Switching

A segment-based switch permits switched connectivity between multiple LAN segments, similar to the manner in which a bridge functions. The key difference between a segment-based switch and a bridge is that the switch is configurable, enabling you to direct packets from each user on a segment to different destination locations. In comparison, most bridges are self-learning and are limited to forwarding packets from one network segment to another based upon source addresses learned to be on the other side of the bridge.

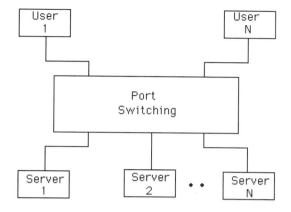

In port-based switching, only a single address per port is
supported, restricting switching to one device per port.

FIGURE 6.13   Port-based switching.

Figure 6.14 illustrates an example of a segment-based
switching hub. Note that ports that support the connection of a
segment must support switching for multiple MAC addresses.
In examining the segment-based switching example illustrated
in Figure 6.14, also note that workstations on each segment contend for access to *n* servers. Since a group of users are connected
to the switching hub via a conventional hub, throughput is limited by the conventional hubs. In this example, two hubs would
limit throughput of the network to 20 Mbps if a user on each
segment accessed a different server. In comparison, a port-based
switching hub can provide a higher throughput, since each network user is directly connected to a port on the switch. The primary advantage of a segment-switching hub is cost, since a few
ports can be used to support network segments containing a
large number of LAN users.

BRIDGE MIB

RFC 1493, which obsoleted RFC 1286, arranged the bridge MIB
into five groups of related objects. Those groups are located

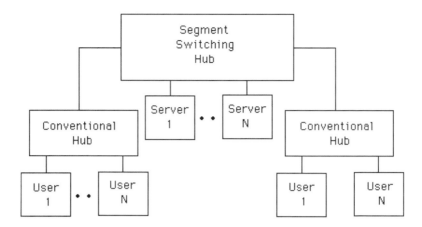

A segment-based switching technique requires each port to support multiple MAC addresses.

FIGURE 6.14 Segment-based switching.

under the dot1dBridge subtree whose address is 1.3.6.1.2.1.17.1 in the global naming tree hierarchy. Table 6.2 lists the bridge MIB groups and provides a description of the objects that reside in each group. In examining the groups contained in Table 6.2, note that the support of certain groups are applicable only to certain types of bridges. Thus, an SNMP-compliant spanning tree bridge would support the dot1dSr Group, while a source routing bridge would not.

Figure 6.15 illustrates the location of the five bridge MIB groups in the global naming tree. The prefix *dot1d* for each of the bridge MIB groups relates to the IEEE 802.1d specification that defined bridge managed objects. Although a large majority of IEEE 802.1d objects are included in the bridge MIB, a number of those objects are not directly included in the MIB. Most of the objects missing from the bridge MIB, such as the bridge name, its up time, and physical address, can be obtained from other groups under the mib-2 node, such as the System group and the Interfaces group. Readers are referred to RFC 1493 for

TABLE 6.2 Bridge MIB Groups

Group	Description
`dot1dBase`	This mandatory group provides hardware configuration and general statistical information.
`dot1dStp`	This group provides configuration, status, and statistical information for bridges supporting the Spanning Tree Protocol.
`dot1dSr`	This group provides configuration, status, and statistical information for bridges supporting Source Route bridging.
`dot1dTp`	This group provides configuration, status, and statistics information for bridges supporting transparent bridging.
`dot1dStatic`	This group provides information about the destination-address filtering state of a bridge.

a list of IEEE 802.1d management objects not included in the bridge MIB, as well as the reason for the exclusion.

dot1dBase Group

The *dot1dBase Group* is mandatory for all SNMP-compliant bridges and can be used to obtain hardware configuration and basic statistical information concerning frames discarded. The address of this group is 1.3.6.1.2.1.17.1. The dot1dBase group consists of three identifiers that provide basic bridge configuration information and a table of generic bridge port information.

Table 6.3 lists the three basic bridge identifiers that provide configuration information and a brief description of each identifier. Each identifier listed in Table 6.3 is restricted to read-only access and is sequentially numbered from 1.3.6.1.2.1.17.1.1.

The Generic Bridge Port Table is used to store generic information about every port associated with the bridge. Table 6.4 lists the identifiers associated with the Generic Bridge Port Table. The address of the first identifier in Table 6.4 is 1.3.6.1.2.1.17.4.1.1, and each of the following identifiers has an incremental address .1 greater than the preceding identifier in the table.

In examining the entries in Table 6.4, the last two, which provide counts of frames discarded for different reasons, can be

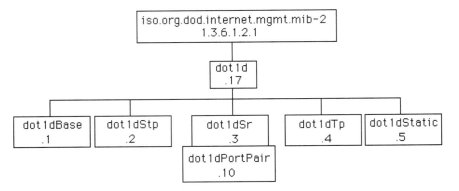

FIGURE 6.15 The location of Bridge MIB groups.

extremely useful in obtaining an insight concerning network operations. Normally, a modern bridge based upon an Intel 486 or higher processor should not discard frames due to the transit delay through the bridge. Instead, a transit delay may indicate the result of speed conversion between different operating LANs, such as a 16-Mbps Token-Ring network and a 10-Mbps Ethernet network. As a series of frames flows from one network to the other via a bridge, they become buffered behind one another for placement onto the lower speed network. Thus, the counter value indicating the number of frames discarded may simply reflect the fact that the bridge interconnects networks with different operating rates. This explanation is also applica-

TABLE 6.3 Bridge Configuration Information

Object Identifier	Access	Description
dot1dBaseBridgeAddress (1.3.6.1.2.1.17.1.1)	r	MAC address used by the bridge.
dot1dBaseNumPorts (1.3.6.1.2.1.17.1.2)	r	Number of ports controlled by the bridge.
dot1dBaseType (1.3.6.1.2.1.17.1.3)	r	Type of bridging performed (unknown (1), transparent-only (2), source-route only (3), srt (4)).

ble for switching hubs that transfer data from a higher-speed port to a lower-speed port.

The last identifier in Table 6.4 can indicate a configuration problem. For example, the maximum Ethernet frame Information field is 1500 bytes, while the maximum Token-Ring Information field length is 4500 bytes at 4 Mbps and 18,000 bytes at 16 Mbps. When bridges are used to connect Token-Ring and Ethernet LANs, Token-Ring workstations requiring access to the Ethernet LAN should be configured to support a maximum Information field length of 1500 bytes. Thus, frames discarded due to excessive size could indicate one or more workstations are improperly configured.

dot1dStp Group

The *dot1dStp Group* provides configuration, status, and statistical information for bridges supporting the Spanning Tree Protocol. Thus, the implementation of this group is optional and is implemented only by SNMP-compliant bridges that support the Spanning Tree Protocol.

TABLE 6.4 Generic Bridge Port Table

Object Identifier	Access	Description
dot1dBasePort (1.3.6.1.2.1.17.1.4.1.1)	r	Port number of the port that provides bridge bridge management information.
dot1dBasePortIfIndex (1.3.6.1.2.1.17.1.4.1.2)	r	The ifIndex object varies for the interface corresponding to the management port.
dot1dBasePortCircuit (1.3.6.1.2.1.17.1.4.1.3)	r	Name of an object instance unique to the management port that differentiates it if it has the same value of dot1dBasePortIfInd ex as another port on the bridge.
dot1dBasePortDelayExceedsDiscards (1.3.6.1.2.1.17.1.4.1.4)	r	Number of frames discarded by this port due to excessive transit delay through the bridge.
dot1dBasePortMtuExceededDiscards (1.3.6.1.2.1.17.1.4.1.5)	r	Number of frames discarded by this port due to an excessive size.

Although the IEEE standardized the Spanning Tree Protocol as its 802.1d standard, there are other versions of the protocol in use. Due to this, the first OBJECT IDENTIFIER in the dot1dStp group is used to identify the version of the Spanning Tree Protocol being run.

The dot1dStp group consists of 14 basic parameters and a Spanning Tree Port Table containing port-specific information for the protocol. Table 6.5 provides a description of the 14 basic Spanning Tree parameters, while Table 6.6 summarizes the OBJECT IDENTIFIERs in the Spanning Tree Port Table.

Although most of the entries in Table 6.5 are self-explanatory, the use of some of those identifiers requires a degree of elaboration. When a bridge moves from a blocking to a forwarding state, it can be configured to do so gracefully by first moving into a listening state. Thus, the forward delay timer, dot1dStpForwardDelay, governs the time until the bridge moves from a forwarding state to a listening state. In addition, once in a listening state, the timer is reset and then governs the time spent learning addresses until the bridge actually moves into its forwarding state. Thus, the value of dot1dStpForwardDelay should actually be doubled when determining the time required for the bridge to move from its blocking to its forwarding state.

In examining the identifiers listed in Table 6.5, their identifiers for the most part can be associated with the operation of the Spanning Tree Protocol previously covered in the first section of this chapter. However, the dot1dSpPriority identifier requires a degree of elaboration. That identifier is used to break ties if there are two or more equivalent cost-effective paths from the bridge to the root.

From the entries in Table 6.6, you can ascertain the current state of the port, its status, and information concerning the Designated Bridge for the segment. Concerning the latter, you can obtain information about the Bridge Identifier of the current route, the path cost, and Port Identifier of the port on the Designated Bridge from the Spanning Tree Port Table. Thus, you can construct the current Spanning Tree topology from the identifiers in the Spanning Tree Port table, which explains how some management platforms perform this action.

TABLE 6.5 Basic Spanning Tree Parameters

Object Identifier	Access	Description
dot1dStpProtocolSpecification (1.3.6.1.2.1.17.2.1)	r	Provides the version of the Spanning Tree Protocol being run (unknown (1), decLb100 (2), ieee8021d (3)).
dot1dStpPriority (1.3.6.1.2.1.17.2.2)	r-w	First two octets of the bridge identifier.
dot1dStpTimeSinceTopologyChange (1.3.6.1.2.1.17.2.3)	r	Time in hundredths of a second since the bridge detected a topology change.
dot1dStpTopChanges (1.3.6.1.2.1.17.2.4)	r	Total number of topology changes detected by the bridge since it was last initialized or reset.
dot1dStpDesignatedRoot (1.3.6.1.2.1.17.2.5)	r	Bridge identifier of the root of the spanning tree.
dot1dStpRootCost (1.3.6.1.2.1.17.2.6)	r	Cost of the best path to the root as seen from the bridge.
dot1dStpRootPort (1.3.6.1.2.1.17.2.7)	r	Port number of the port that has the lowest cost from the bridge to the root bridge.
dot1dStpMaxAge (1.3.6.1.2.1.17.2.8)	r	Maximum age of Spanning Tree Protocol information learned from the network before it is discarded.
dot1dStpHelloTime (1.3.6.1.2.1.17.2.9)	r	Time interval in hundredths of a second that a bridge that is the root or attempting to become the root advertises its presence.
dot1dStpHoldTime (1.3.6.1.2.1.17.2.10)	r	Time interval in hundredths of a second during which no more than two configuration bridge PDUs should be transmitted by this node.
dot1dStpForwardDelay (1.3.6.1.2.1.17.2.11)	r	Time in hundredths of a second that the port stays in its Listening and Learning states while moving toward its Forwarding state.
dot1dStpBridgeMaxAge (1.3.6.1.2.1.17.2.12)	r	Value in seconds that all bridges use for MaxAge when the bridge acts as the root.
dot1dStpBridgeHelloTime (1.3.6.1.2.1.17.2.13)	r	Value in seconds that bridges use for HelloTime when the bridge acts as the root.
dot1dStpBridgeForwardDelay (1.3.6.1.2.1.17.2.14)	r	Value in seconds that all bridges use for ForwardDelay when a bridge acts as the root.

dot1dSr Group

The *dot1dSr Group* differs from the other managed bridge groups in that, although described in RFC 1493, the actual definitions are contained in a different RFC. RFC 1525 contains the definitions of managed objects for Source Routing Bridges, including the dot1dSr group and an optional dot1dPortPair group.

The dot1dSr Group contains objects that describe the state of the source route bridging being performed by a Source Route Bridge, and as such are applicable only to that type of bridge

TABLE 6.6 The Spanning Tree Port Table

Object Identifier	Access	Description
dot1dStpPort (1.3.6.1.2.1.17.2.15.1.1)	r	Port number of the port that contains STP management information.
dot1dStpPortPriority (1.3.6.1.2.1.17.2.15.1.2)	r	Port priority.
dot1dStpPortStatus (1.3.6.1.2.1.17.2.15.1.3)	r	Current state of the port (disabled (1), blocking (2), listening (3), learning (4), forwarding (5), broken (6)).
dot1dStpPortEnable (1.3.6.1.2.1.17.2.15.1.4)	r-w	Status of the port (enabled (1), disabled (2)).
dot1dStpPortPathCost (1.3.6.1.2.1.17.2.15.1.5)	r-w	Contribution of the port to the path cost of paths toward the spanning tree root.
dot1dStpPortDesignatedRoot (1.3.6.1.2.1.17.2.15.1.6)	r	Bridge Identifier of the current route transmitted by the Designated Bridge for the segment.
dot1dStpPortDesignatedCost (1.3.6.1.2.1.17.2.15.1.7)	r	Path cost of the Designated Port of the segment connected to this port.
dot1dStpPortDesignatedBridge (1.3.6.1.2.1.17.2.15.1.8)	r	Bridge Identifier of the bridge that this port considers to be the Designated Bridge for this port's segment.
dot1dStpPortDesignatedPort (1.3.6.1.2.1.17.2.15.1.9)	r	Port Identifier of the port on the Designated Bridge for this port's segment.
dot1dStpPortForwardTransitions (1.3.6.1.2.1.17.2.15.1.10)	r-w	Number of times this port transitioned from the Learning state to the Forwarding state.

and Source Routing Transparent bridges. The optional dot1-dPortPair Group is applicable for multiport bridges that can be configured with port pairings, with each pair corresponding to a unique source to target bridge path. The port-pair multiport model of source route bridging is defined in the IEEE 802.5M SRT Addendum to the IEEE standard 802.1d.

The key to obtaining information concerning the operation of an SNMP managed source routing bridge is the Source Routing Port Table. This table contains information about each port on a Source Routing bridge.

Table 6.7 lists the OBJECT IDENTIFIERs contained in the Source Routing Port Table, their access, and a brief description of each identifier. The address of the Source Routing Port Table is 1.3.6.1.2.1.17.3.1.1, while its entries have the suffix .1 through .18 to that address. In addition to the Source Routing Port Table, the Source Routing Group has one scalar identifier, which is listed at the bottom of Table 6.7.

One of the more important identifiers you can use to verify bridge performance is dot1dSrPortLongestFrame, which defines

TABLE 6.7 The Source Routing Port Table and Scalar Identifier

Object Identifier	Access	Description
dot1dSrPort (1.3.6.1.2.1.17.3.1.1.1)	r	Port number of the port.
dot1dSrPortHopCount (1.3.6.1.2.1.17.3.1.1.2)	r-w	Maximum number of routing descriptors allowed in an All Paths or Spanning Tree Explorer frame.
dot1dSrPortLocalSegment (1.3.6.1.2.1.17.3.1.1.3)	r-w	Segment number the port is connected to. A value of 65535 means nonassigned.
dot1dSrPortBridgeNum (1.3.6.1.2.1.17.3.1.1.4)	r-w	Bridge number; a value of 65535 means nonassigned.
dot1dSrPortTargetSegment (1.3.6.1.2.1.17.3.1.1.5)	r-w	Target segment of the port. A value of 65535 means nonassigned.
dot1dSrPortLargestFrame (1.3.6.1.2.1.17.3.1.1.6)	r-w	Maximum size of the Information field of frames the port can send and receive.
dot1dSrPortSTESpanMode (1.3.6.1.2.1.17.3.1.1.7)	r-w	Defines how the port responds to a Spanning Tree Explorer frame.

TABLE 6.7 (*continued*)

Object Identifier	Access	Description
dot1dSrPortSpecInFrames (1.3.6.1.2.1.17.3.1.1.8)	r	Number of Source Routed Frames received at the port.
dot1dSrPortSpecOutFrames (1.3.6.1.2.1.17.3.1.1.9)	r	Number of Source Routed frames transmitted by the port.
dot1dSrPortApeInFrames (1.3.6.1.2.1.17.3.1.1.10)	r	Number of All Paths Explorer frames received by the port.
dot1dSrPortApeOutFrames (1.3.6.1.2.1.17.3.1.1.11)	r	Number of All Paths Explorer frames transmitted by the port.
dot1dSrPortSteInFrames (1.3.6.1.2.1.17.3.1.1.12)	r	Number of Spanning Tree Explorer frames received by the port.
dot1dSrPortSteOutFrames (1.3.6.1.2.1.17.3.1.1.13)	r	Number of Spanning Tree Explorer frames transmitted by the port.
dot1dSrPortSegmentMismatchedDiscards (1.3.6.1.2.1.17.3.1.1.14)	r	Number of Explorer frames discarded by the port due to an invalid adjacent segment value in the routing descriptor field.
dot1dSrPortDuplicateSegmentDiscards (1.3.6.1.2.1.17.3.1.1.15)	r	Number of frames discarded by the port due to a duplicate segment identifier in the routing descriptor field.
dot1dSrPortHopCountExceededDiscards (1.3.6.1.2.1.17.3.1.1.16)	r	Number of Explorer frames discarded by the port due to the Routing Information Field length exceeding its maximum value.
dot1dSrPortDupLanIdOrTree (1.3.6.1.2.1.17.3.1.1.17)	r	Number of duplicate LAN IDs or Tree errors.
dot1dSrPortLanIdMismatches (1.3.6.1.2.1.17.3.1.1.18)	r	Number of ARE and STE frames discarded due to the last LAN ID in the RIF field not being the LAN ID for the port's partner.

Scalar Identifier

dot1dSrBridgeLfMode (1.3.6.1.2.1.17.3.2)	r-w	Indicates if the bridge operates using older 3-bit length (mode 3 (1)) negotiation fields or the newer 6-bit length (mode 6 (2)) fields in its RIF.

the maximum size of the Information field of frames the port can transmit and receive. This identifier, as well as individual workstation configurations, can be important when attempting to determine, for example, why frames transmitted on one ring fail to arrive on another ring.

Port-Pair Group

The *Port-Pair Group* is optional and is implemented by bridges that support the direct multiport model of the source route bridging mode defined in the IEEE 802.5 SRT Addendum to the 802.1d standard. The first identifier in the Port-Pair Group returns the total number of entries in the Bridge-Port Pair Database. The following identifiers in the group are contained in a Port-Pair table that provides information concerning the port numbers for a pair of ports, the bridge number associated with a path between ports, and the current state for the bridge number. Table 6.8 lists the identifiers in the Port-Pair Group.

dot1dTp Group

The implementation of the *dot1dTp Group* is optional, with implementation by bridges that support transparent or SRT bridging. This group consists of two parameters that indicate

TABLE 6.8 Port-Pair Group Identifiers

Object Identifier	Access	Description
dot1dPortPairTableSize (1.3.6.1.2.1.17.10.1)	r	Total number of entries in the Bridge Port Pair Database.
dot1dPortPairLowPort (1.3.6.1.2.1.17.10.2.1.1)	r-w	Lower number port for the pair.
dot1dPortPairHighPort (1.3.6.1.2.1.17.10.2.1.2)	r-w	Higher number port for the pair.
dot1dPortPairBridgeNum (1.3.6.1.2.1.17.10.2.1.3)	r-w	Bridge number that identifies the path between low- and high-numbered ports.
dot1dPortPairBridgeState (1.3.6.1.2.1.17.10.2.1.4)	r-w	Current state of the bridge (enabled (1), disabled (2), invalid (3), with invalid meaning remove the entry).

the general operational capability of the bridge, a Forwarding Database, and a table that provides port statistics. Table 6.9 provides a description of the two bridge parameters, including their OBJECT IDENTIFIERs and access mode. Note that the value of the first identifier can be useful in determining if a bridge should have its memory expanded.

The Forwarding database for transparent bridges contains entries for individual MAC addresses, as broadcast destinations are automatically recognized and do not require learning. In addition, this database contains the port at which the object was seen and the status of the entry. Table 6.10 summarizes the identifiers in the Forwarding database table.

The third part of the dot1dTp Group is the Transparent Bridge Port table. The identifiers in this table, which are summarized in Table 6.11, provide information about every port associated with the transparent bridge.

dot1dStatic Group

The fifth and last group in the bridge MIB is the *Static (destination-address filtering) Database Group*. This group is optional but can be extremely valuable, as it provides a mechanism to control the flow of frames in a bridged internet. This flow control can be used as a security mechanism or as a method to control the flow of frames to enhance the level of performance on seg-

TABLE 6.9 Transparent Bridge Parameters

Object Identifier	Access	Description
dot1dTpLearnedEntryDiscards (1.3.6.1.2.1.17.4.1)	r	Number of Forwarding Database entries that have been or would have been learned but were discarded due to a lack of space.
dot1dTpAgingTime (1.3.6.1.2.1.17.4.2)	r-w	Time-out period in seconds for aging out dynamically learned forwarding information. Recommended default is 300 seconds.

TABLE 6.10 Transparent Bridge Forwarding Database Table

Object Identifier	Access	Description
dot1dTpFdbAddress (1.3.6.1.2.1.17.4.3.1.1)	r	Tnicast MAC address for which the bridge has forwarding/filtering information.
dot1dTpFdbPort (1.3.6.1.2.1.17.4.3.1.2)	r	Number of the port at which the address was seen.
dot1dTpFdbStatus (1.3.6.1.2.1.17.4.3.1.3)	r	Status of the entry (other (1), invalid (2), learned (3), self (4), mgmt (5)).

TABLE 6.11 Transparent Bridge Port Table

Object Identifier	Access	Description
dot1dTpPort (1.3.6.1.2.1.17.4.4.1.1)	r	Port number of the port that contains transparent bridging management information.
dot1dTpPortMaxInfo (1.3.6.1.2.1.17.4.4.1.2)	r	Maximum size of the Information field the port will transmit or receive.
dot1dTpPortInFrames (1.3.6.1.2.1.17.4.4.1.3)	r	Number of frames received by the port from its segment.
dot1dTpPortOutFrames (1.3.6.1.2.1.17.4.4.1.4)	r	Number of frames transmitted by the port to its segment.
dot1dTpPortInDiscards (1.3.6.1.2.1.17.4.4.1.5)	r	Number of valid frames received that were discarded (filtered) by the Forwarding Process.

ments experiencing congestion or high server utilization. For example, through the use of filtering, you could preclude the ability of selected workstations or groups of stations from being able to access one or more servers located on a different network segment.

The *dot1dStatic Group* consists of a Static Filtering Database Table that contains filtering information configured into the bridge either locally or via a network management console. The filtering entries specify the set of ports to which frames received from specific ports that contain predefined destination addresses are allowed to be forwarded. Thus, addresses not specified are blocked.

The identifiers in the Static Filtering Database Table are summarized in Table 6.12. The dot1dStaticAllowedToGoTo identifier is expressed as a bit map for which a setting of 1 for a port indicates the ability of a frame to exit the port. For example, if the bridge has 16 ports or less and all frames are allowed to exit ports 2, 4, and 12, the bit map construction is as indicated below:

```
Port    1 2 3 4 5 6 7 8 9 10 11 12 13 14 15 16
Bit Map 0 1 0 1 0 0 0 0 0 0  0  1  0  0  0  0
```

One of the limitations of SNMP is that the bridge MIB is limited to layer-2 operations. Some switching hub vendors that provide a store-and-forward operation capability permit users to filter based upon the value of the DSAP and SSAP in the frame, providing filtering based upon the application. Although some switching hub vendors provide an SNMP management capability using the bridge MIB, the effective use of their equipment's additional features is based upon proprietary extensions that differ from one vendor to another.

TABLE 6.12   Static Filtering Database Table

Object Identifier	Access	Description
dot1dStaticAddress (1.3.6.1.2.1.17.5.1.1.1)	r-w	Destination MAC address to which the entry's filtering information is applicable.
dot1dStaticReceivePort (1.3.6.1.2.1.17.5.1.1.2)	r-w	Port number of the port from which a frame must be received for filtering to apply. A value of 0 means filtering applies to all ports.
dot1dStaticAllowedToGoTo (1.3.6.1.2.1.17.5.1.1.3)	r-w	Set of ports, expressed as a bit map, for which forwarding is allowed.
dot1dStaticStatus (1.3.6.1.2.1.17.5.1.1.4)	r-w	Status of the entry (other (1), invalid (2), permanent (3), deleteOnRequest (4), deleteOnTimeout (5)).

Managing
the UPS

7

The LAN manager or administrator must be familiar with the operation and utilization of a number of different types of equipment to effectively and efficiently operate the network. One type of equipment which is extremely important is an uninterruptable power supply or UPS system. Originally designed to provide battery backup in the event primary utility-provided power was lost, today's modern UPS system may perform additional functions, including regulating raw power received from the local utility. Thus, the effective management of a UPS system can involve the consideration of a number of features beyond battery backup time.

This chapter will first focus upon the power protection features incorporated into many modern UPS systems, as well as how the capacity of such systems should be computed to satisfy an operational environment. We will then turn to the UPS MIB, providing a summary of the different groups in the database and how they can be used as a tool for managing this important device.

POWER PROTECTION

If you live in the Northeastern United States during a summer heat wave, you are probably familiar with the effect of the local electric utility company lowering the voltage level during peak electrical consumption periods. The dimming of lights, television and monitor screens, and slightly lower operating rates of motor-driven elevators are but a few of the effects of brownouts. Also referred to as voltage sags, this situation can result from the startup power demands of different types of electrical motors and can adversely affect computer systems, causing electrical devices to fail as a result of repetitive brownouts. Although brownouts and sags are a common problem, they are not the only electrical power problem you can expect to encounter.

Table 7.1 lists five of the most common electrical power problems you may encounter, including the previously discussed brownout or sag power problem. Although most, if not all, readers should be familiar with the term *blackout*, which represents

TABLE 7.1 Common Electrical Power Problems

Power Problem	Typical Cause	Potential Effect
Brownout or sag	Startup power consumption of electrical motors or voltage reduction by electric utility	Reduction in the life of electrical equipment
Blackout	Act of God or accident	Loss of data being processed, possible disk crash
Spike	Lightning or resumption of power after a power failure	Damage to hardware, loss of data
Surge	Completion of an electrical motor cycle, such as an air conditioner	Stress upon equipment's electrical components, resulting in premature failure of a service
Noise	Electromagnetic interference caused by equipment and/or lightning and radio interference	Data corruption

the total loss of electrical utility power, the remaining events may require a degree of elaboration.

A *spike* represents an instantaneous increase in voltage level resulting from lightning or when utility power is restored after an electrical outage. The effect of a voltage spike can literally fry computer equipment, causing the destruction of hardware as well as the loss of data stored on the hardware, both in memory and on disk.

A *power surge* represents a short-term increase in voltage, which over a period of time stresses electrical equipment until a point of failure is reached. The most common cause of a power surge is the cycling of equipment, such as air conditioners, refrigerators, and similar machinery for which motors are turned on and off on a periodic basis. When such equipment is turned off, extra voltage that was flowing to operate the equipment is dissipated through the power lines in the office or home.

The last power problem listed in Table 7.1, *noise*, represents electromagnetic and radio frequency interference (EMI/RFI). Both EMI and RFI results in noise that disturbs the smooth alternating sine wave generated by the electrical power utility. Depending upon the amount of noise, the resulting effect can range in scope from no adverse effect upon equipment and data to the corruption of data when noise reaches a level that precludes equipment from operating correctly.

Now that we have an appreciation for the types of power problems we may encounter, let's focus upon how UPS systems operate. This will provide us with information that can be helpful in understanding the role of the UPS MIB.

UPS Operation

Early UPS systems were developed as a backup power source and simply consisted of a battery charger, battery, and inverter. The inverter converts direct current (DC) to alternating current (AC) and is commonly referred to as a DC to AC converter.

A UPS can be used online without bypass mode of operation, in which it always provides power to equipment, or in a standby mode in which a transfer switch is used to provide UPS power in the event utility power fails. Figure 7.1 illustrates the configuration of UPS systems used in an online without bypass mode of operation, and in a standby online mode of operation.

When used in an online without bypass mode of operation, the UPS accepts raw electric utility power and uses that power to charge its battery. In actuality, the battery illustrated in each example shown in Figure 7.1 represents a bank of batteries whose number and charge capacity vary based upon the amount of electrical power you wish to provide in the event primary power fails, and the duration for which battery backup power

Online without bypass mode of operation

Input utility power

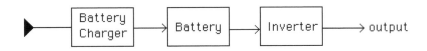

Standby mode of operation

Input utility power

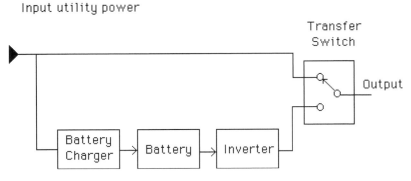

FIGURE 7.1 Basic UPS configurations.

must be furnished during a primary power failure. Since raw electrical power is first used to charge the battery, the effect of any surge, spike, or brownout is isolated from equipment that obtains power from the online UPS system shown in the top portion of Figure 7.1.

In the standby mode of operation illustrated at the bottom of Figure 7.1, note that raw electrical utility power is directly output through the transfer switch to equipment when utility power is present. Only when power fails does the transfer switch sense the loss of power and switch the connection to battery-supplied power. The key problem associated with this UPS configuration is the fact that it does not provide protection to equipment from dirty electric power, either corrupted due to utility company-induced brownouts or from acts of God and acts of people and machinery. Due to this, the standby mode basic UPS configuration illustrated at the bottom of Figure 7.1 was supplemented by the use of separate surge protectors and power line filters. The surge protector is used to block or chop off peak voltage spikes and reduced voltage surges, while the power line filter is used to reshape the power sine wave, eliminating the effect of sags and noise. As you might expect, it was not long before some UPS manufacturers incorporated surge suppression and power line filtering capability into their products. This resulted in the surge suppressor and powerline filter operating upon raw electrical power that will bypass the UPS when electrical utility power is operational. Figure 7.2 illustrates a general-purpose UPS system configuration that protects equipment from utility power irregularities as well as provides a redundant backup power source.

Common Variation

The general-purpose UPS configuration illustrated in Figure 7.2 forms the foundation for all modern UPS equipment. Since batteries used to store electrical power for use in the event primary power fails are both bulky and costly, by itself a typical UPS will be sized to provide no more than 30 minutes to one hour of backup power, typically a sufficient duration to provide an orderly shutdown of a PC- or minicomputer-based server in

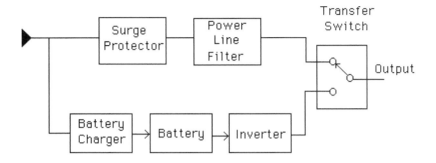

Input utility power

A general-purpose UPS system includes a surge protector and power line filter that regulate raw power received from the utility company.

FIGURE 7.2 General-purpose UPS system configuration.

the event primary power fails. Recognizing that many organizations require the ability to continue computer operations for prolonged periods of time once primary power fails, a common technique used in large organizations that have a data center is to use a diesel generator to supply power to the UPS in the event primary power fails. This can be accomplished by the use of a transfer switch to switch power input to the UPS battery charger between utility company-supplied power and the diesel-generated power. Then, once diesel-generated power flows into the UPS system, the battery backup capability is limited only by the organization's ability to keep the generator operational.

Sizing a UPS

Sizing a UPS is a term used to reference the process by which you determine the battery capacity required to operate equipment for a desired period of time after primary power is lost.

The actual sizing process is based upon the intended use of the UPS. If your intention is to use a relatively small UPS to protect a server and some communications devices, the sizing process will differ from that required to determine the size of a system to protect a data center. For example, if you were considering the protection of a data center, you would first make a list of all equipment used within the data center, as well as lights, air conditioners, and other equipment required for continuity of operations. Next, you would determine the voltage and amperage requirements for each device and other required electrical usage, such as interior lighting that may be on the circuit that UPS will protect.

If you were sizing a UPS to protect a network server of several LAN components, you would restrict your list to the voltage and amperage requirements of those devices. By multiplying voltage times amperage, you would determine the volt amps (VA) requirement for each device. If some types of equipment specify their power consumption in watts (W), you can convert that to VA units by multiplying watts by 1.4. You would then sum the VA requirements for all equipment and other resources requiring power, and select a UPS system with a VA capacity that meets or exceeds your total power requirements.

Since the VA rating references only the power load and does not consider the duration for which battery power at that load level must be supplied, you must determine the period of time during which you will require battery backup power. For many organizations this time period is normally the time required to perform an orderly computer shutdown, plus a small margin of safety time. For example, some servers require ten minutes for an orderly shutdown, resulting in a 20- to 30-minute battery backup at peak load usually being sufficient. Since total power provided by a UPS battery backup is measured in volt-ampere hours (VAH), you would multiply your VA requirements by .5 in this example to determine the VAH capacity for a 30-minute battery backup.

Power Management

Although the operation and utilization of a UPS is relatively straightforward, the rationale for its management may require a degree of elaboration. Thus, in concluding this section, let me explain the advantages associated with obtaining the ability to manage a UPS, as well as focus upon some of the methods by which such systems can be managed.

Rationale

In addition to directly protecting devices from dirty energy and providing a backup power source, a manageable UPS system can provide a variety of important information as well as the potential control of other network devices. For example, a manageable UPS can use traps to provide notification of a power failure, as well as provide power alerts that could inform network users of a potential problem long before it becomes one. As I will soon note from an examination of the UPS MIB, there are a large number of variables that can be used as an early warning and analysis tool. In fact, some vendors, such as American Power Conversion (APC) of West Kingston, RI, market GUI programs that provide a graphical summary of the status of a selected UPS without requiring a user to perform a manual walk through an MIB. The APC software product, known as *PowerNet Manager*, provides users with the ability to reboot locked or frozen network devices, perform an automatic server shutdown during extended power outages and transmit a message about the pending power shutdown to network users, transmit alerts to a designated management console, as well as perform literally hundreds of other functions. Thus, a remote LAN could have its server protected from dirty power, as well as obtain a reboot capability through the use of an APC Smart UPS system, managed either by the firm's PowerNet program or another SNMP manager. Now that we have a general appreciation for the rationale for obtaining a manageable UPS, let's examine some of the methods by which such a system can be managed.

Management Methods

There are two basic methods by which a UPS system can obtain an SNMP management capability—directly or indirectly. Figure 7.3 provides an overview of each method with respect to the connection of the UPS to a local area network.

A. Direct

B. Indirect

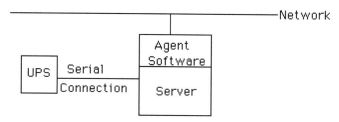

FIGURE 7.3 UPS management methods.

In the *direct method* a UPS either has a built-in LAN adapter or is cabled to a self-contained adapter. This connection method enables the UPS to be directly addressed via the network and permits access to most, if not all, MIB variables, with the amount of access governed by the UPS vendor's implementation of UPS MIB groups and identifiers within each group.

The *indirect method* of access, which is illustrated in the lower portion of Figure 7.3, results in the control of a UPS via agent software operating on a server. The agent software, which might be in the form of a *NetWare Loadable Module* (*NLM*) for a NetWare server, processes queries directed to the server and uses a serial connection to communicate with the UPS. Similarly, traps issued by the UPS would flow to the server, requiring the agent to place the trap onto the network.

UPS MIB

The UPS MIB is specified in RFC 1628, which defines the managed objects for uninterruptible power supplies that are manageable via SNMP. The MIB module that describes uninterruptible power supplies is located at the 33rd node under the mib-2 node and has the address {mib-2 33}, which equates to the global naming tree numeric identifier of 1.3.6.1.2.1.33.

Included within the UPS MIB are nine distinct groups, with each group consisting of related objects. Table 7.2 lists the nine groups and provides a brief description of the objects in each group.

Figure 7.4 illustrates the placement of the UPS MIB groups in the global naming tree. The numeric identifiers for each UPS

TABLE 7.2 SNMP MIB Groups

Group	Description
Device Identification Group	Provides information about the managed device, including manufacturer, model, software version, and agent
Battery Group	Provides information about battery capacity, charge remaining, operation, and time to depletion
Input Group	Provides information about the raw power into the UPS
Output Group	Provides information about the power generated by the UPS
Bypass Group	Provides information about the bypass power
Alarm Group	Provides alarms based upon the occurrence of predefined conditions
Test Group	Provides a mechanism for the initiation of different predefined tests
Control Group	Provides a mechanism to turn off or restart a UPS
Configuration Group	Provides a mechanism to control output from the UPS, its transfer to battery backup, and other parameters.

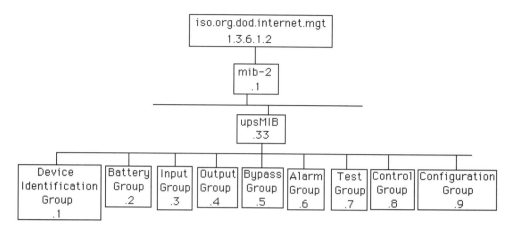

FIGURE 7.4 The UPS MIB structure.

MIB group, which forms a subtree under the UPS node, represent the suffix to the address of the group through the tree. For example, the Device Identification group would be located at 1.3.6.1.2.1.33.1 in the global naming tree hierarchy.

Device Identification Group

Table 7.3 provides a brief description of the six identifiers included in the *Device Identification Group*. In examining the entries in Table 7.3 note that the upsIdentUPSSoftwareVersion and upsIdentAgentSoftwareVersion variables may or may not have the same value, with their settings dependent upon vendor implementation. Although the use of the OBJECT IDENTIFIERs listed in Table 7.3 are fairly self-explanatory, a note of elaboration might be in order for the last one in the table. Since most UPSs provide receptacles to power two or more devices, the upsIdentAttachedDevices variable provides a network administrator with the ability to identify devices connected to the UPS. Thus, an administrator might set the upsIdentName variable to a room number to identify its location, while setting the upsIdentAttachedDevices variable to the names of the devices connected to the system.

TABLE 7.3 Device Identification Group

Object Identifier	Access	Description
upsIdentManufacturer (1.3.6.1.2.1.33.1.1)	r	UPS manufacturer
upsIdentModel (1.3.6.1.2.1.33.1.2)	r	UPS Model designation
upsIdentUPSSoftwareVersion (1.3.6.1.2.1.33.1.3)	r	UPS firmware or software version(s)
upsIdentAgentSoftwareVersion (1.3.6.1.2.1.33.1.4)	r	UPS agent software version
upsIdentName (1.3.6.1.2.1.33.1.5)	r-w	String that identifies the UPS
upsIdentAttachedDevices (1.3.6.1.2.1.33.1.6)	r-w	String that identifies devices powered via the UPS

Battery Group

As its name implies, the *Battery Group* consists of identifiers that provide information concerning battery power information. Table 7.4 provides a brief description of the seven identifiers in the Battery Group.

The first identifier in the Battery Group, upsBatteryStatus, provides a value associated with a configurable variable, upsConfigLowBattTime. That is, a value of batteryNormal for upsBatteryStatus indicates that the remaining runtime is greater than upsConfigLowBattTime, while a value of batteryLow indicates that the remaining battery runtime is less than or equal to upsConfigLowBattTime.

The use of the Battery Group enables power management software programs to provide warnings concerning battery utilization, as well as generate a decreasing bar chart, pie chart, or similar symbol with numerics that indicate the estimated time to battery charge depletion. Thus, this group provides basic but vital information about the capability of the UPS battery.

TABLE 7.4 The Battery Group

Object Identifier	Access	Description
upsBatteryStatus (1.3.6.1.2.1.33.2.1)	r	Remaining capacity of the UPS system's batteries (unknown (1), batteryNormal (2), batteryLow (3), batteryDepleted (4)).
upsSecondsOnBattery (1.3.6.1.2.1.33.2.2)	r	Lower of the elapsed time since the UPS switched to battery power, or the network management subsystem was restarted. Zero if the UPS is not on battery power.
upsEstimatedMinutesRemaining (1.3.6.1.2.1.33.2.3)	r	Estimated time to battery charge depletion under present load conditions.
upsEstimatedChargeRemaining (1.3.6.1.2.1.33.2.4)	r	Estimated remaining battery charge as a percent of full charge.
upsBatteryVoltage (1.3.6.1.2.1.33.2.5)	r	Present battery voltage.
upsBatteryCurrent (1.3.6.1.2.1.33.2.6)	r	Present battery current.
upsBatteryTemperature (1.3.6.1.2.1.33.2.7)	r	Ambient temperature at or near the UPS battery casing.

Input Group

The *Input Group* consists of two scalar variables and a table containing five entries. Table 7.5 lists the OBJECT IDENTIFIERs in the Input Group, including a brief description of each identifier. Although the entries in the referenced table are relatively self-explanatory, a degree of elaboration is warranted concerning the first two entries.

The first entry, upsInputLineBads, represents the number of times the input entered an out-of-tolerance condition as defined by the manufacturer of the device. Thus, the meaning of the resulting count will be dependent upon how a manufacturer

TABLE 7.5 Input Group

Object Identifier	Access	Description
upsInputLineBads (1.3.6.1.2.1.33.3.1)	r	Number of times the input power entered an out-of-tolerance condition
upsInputNumLines (1.3.6.1.2.1.33.3.2)	r	Number of input lines to the UPS
upsInputTable (1.3.6.1.2.1.33.3.3)	n/a	List of input table entries
upsInputEntry (1.3.6.1.2.1.33.3.3.1)	n/a	Entry containing information applicable for a particular input line
upsInputLineIndex (1.3.6.1.2.1.33.3.3.1.1)	n/a	Input line identifier
upsInputFrequency (1.3.6.1.2.1.33.3.3.1.2)	r	Present input frequency in Hz
upsInputVoltage (1.3.6.1.2.1.33.3.3.1.3)	r	Magnitude of the current input voltage in RMS volts
upsInputCurrent (1.3.6.1.2.1.33.3.3.1.4)	r	Magnitude of the current input current in RMS amps
upsInputTruePower (1.3.6.1.2.1.33.3.3.1.5)	r	Magnitude of the current input true power in watts

defined the out-of-tolerance condition. The second entry, upsInputNumLines, indicates the number of power lines into the device. The resulting variable indicates the number of rows contained in the input table, with each row relevant to a specific input line.

Output Group

The *Output Group* is similar to the Input Group in that it consists of several scalars and a table that can contain multiple rows based upon the number of output lines of the device. Table 7.6 provides a brief description of the OBJECT IDENTIFIERs in

TABLE 7.6 The Output Group

Object Identifiers	Access	Description
upsOutputSource (1.3.6.1.2.1.33.4.1)	r	Current source of output power (other (1), none (2), normal (3), bypass (4), battery (5), booster (6), reducer (7))
upsOutputFrequency (1.3.6.1.2.1.33.4.2)	r	Current output frequency
upsOutputNumLines (1.3.6.1.2.1.33.4.3)	r	Number of output lines in the device
upsOutputTable (1.3.6.1.2.1.33.4.3.4)	n/a	List of output table entries, with rows corresponding to output lines
upsOutputEntry (1.3.6.1.2.1.33.4.3.4.1)	n/a	Entry containing information applicable to a particular output line
upsOutputLineIndex (1.3.6.1.2.1.33.4.3.4.1.1)	n/a	Output line identifier
upsOutputVoltage (1.3.6.1.2.1.33.4.3.4.1.2)	r	Current output voltage, in RMS volts
upsOutputCurrent (1.3.6.1.2.1.33.4.3.4.1.3)	r	Present output current, in RMS amps
upsOutputPower (1.3.6.1.2.1.33.4.3.4.1.4)	r	True output power, in watts
upsOutputPercentLoad (1.3.6.1.2.1.33.4.3.4.1.5)	r	Percentage of UPS power capacity being used on the selected output line

the Output Group. Note that the variable upsOutputNumLines not only provides the number of output lines utilized by the managed device, but also indicates the number of rows in the output table.

By accessing each row of the Output Group table, you then obtain the ability to determine the voltage, current, power, and percent load for each output line used to support a device.

Bypass Group

The *Bypass Group* can be used to obtain information concerning the bypass state for each line in the device. To provide this information, the Bypass Group consists of several scalars and a table, with the latter used in a similar fashion to the tables in the preceding groups. That is, the table rows equate to the bypass lines utilized in the device.

Table 7.7 provides a brief description of the OBJECT IDENTIFIERs in the Bypass Group. Note that each row in the Bypass Group table provides information concerning the voltage, current, and power for a bypass line.

Alarm Group

The *Alarm Group* is the sixth group in the UPS MIB. The first identifier in the group provides a count of the present number of

TABLE 7.7 Bypass Group

Object Identifier	Access	Description
upsBypassFrequency (1.3.6.1.2.1.33.5.1)	r	Bypass frequency, in Hz
upsBypassNumLines (1.3.6.1.2.1.33.5.2)	r	Number of bypass lines utilized by the device
upsBypassTable (1.3.6.1.2.1.33.5.3)	n/a	List of bypass table entries
upsBypassEntry (1.3.6.1.2.1.33.5.3.1)	n/a	Entry containing information about a bypass input
upsBypassLineIndex (1.3.6.1.2.1.33.5.3.1.1)	n/a	Bypass line identifier
upsBypassVoltage (1.3.6.1.2.1.33.5.3.1.2)	r	Present bypass voltage, in RMS volts
upsBypassCurrent (1.3.6.1.2.1.33.5.3.1.3)	r	Present bypass current, in RMS amps
upsBypassPower (1.3.6.1.2.1.33.5.3.1.4)	r	Present true power in watts conveyed by the bypass

active alarm conditions. The value of that identifier indicates the number of rows in the alarm table of the Alarm Group.

There are three major subnodes under the Alarm Group. The first is the identifier upsAlarmsPresent, which provides a count of the current number of active alarms, while the second represents the alarm table. Table 7.8 provides a brief description of the identifiers for the first two nodes in the Alarm Group. Note that the first entry in Table 7.8, upsAlarmsPresent, defines the number of rows that will be in the alarm table, as the number of rows will correspond to the number of alarm conditions in effect. The first node contains 24 well-known UPS alarms. Those alarms, including their position in the global naming tree, as well as a description of each alarm, are included in Table 7.9. From the identifiers listed in Tables 7.8 and 7.9, a management system obtains the ability to provide users with the time different alarms occurred, as well as specific information that identifies the alarm condition.

TABLE 7.8 Alarm Group Scalar and Alarm Table

Object Identifier	Access	Description
upsAlarmsPresent (1.3.6.1.2.1.33.6.1)	r	Present number of actual alarm conditions
upsAlarmTable (1.3.6.1.2.1.33.6.2)	n/a	List of alarm table entries with the number of rows corresponding to the number of alarm conditions
upsAlarmEntry (1.3.6.1.2.1.33.6.2.1)	n/a	Entry containing data applicable to a particular alarm
upsAlarmID (1.3.6.1.2.1.33.6.2.1.1)	n/a	Unique identifier for an alarm condition
upsAlarmDesc (1.3.6.1.2.1.33.6.2.1.2)	r	Unique description of the alarm
upsAlarmTime (1.3.6.1.2.1.33.6.2.1.3)	r	Time the alarm condition was detected (a zero value indicates it existed before agent startup)

TABLE 7.9 UPS Well-Known Alarms

Object Identifier	Description
upsAlarmBatteryBad (1.3.6.1.2.1.33.6.3.1)	One or more batteries require replacement.
upsAlarmOnBattery (1.3.6.1.2.1.33.6.3.2)	UPS is drawing power from its batteries.
upsAlarmLowBattery (1.3.6.1.2.1.33.6.3.3)	Remaining battery runtime is less or equal to upsConfigLowBattTime.
upsAlarmDepletedBattery (1.3.6.1.2.1.33.6.3.4)	UPS will not be able to sustain its present load if utility power is lost.
upsAlarmTempBad (1.3.3.1.2.1.33.6.3.5)	UPS temperature is out-of-tolerance.
upsAlarmInputBad (1.3.6.1.2.1.33.6.3.6)	An input condition is out-of-tolerance.
upsAlarmOutputBad (1.3.6.1.2.1.33.6.3.7)	An output condition other than OutputOverload is out-of-tolerance.
upsAlarmOutputOverload (1.3.6.1.2.1.33.6.3.8)	Output load exceeds the UPS output capacity.
upsAlarmOnBypass (1.3.6.1.2.1.33.6.3.9)	Bypass mode is engaged.
upsAlarmBypassBad (1.3.6.1.2.1.33.6.3.10)	Bypass is out-of-tolerance.
upsAlarmOutputOffAsRequested (1.3.6.1.2.1.33.6.3.11)	UPS is shut down as per a prior request.
upsAlarmUpsOffAsRequested (1.3.6.1.2.1.33.6.3.12)	Entire UPS is shut down as per requested.
upsAlarmChargeFailed (1.3.6.1.2.1.33.6.3.13)	An uncorrected problem was detected within the UPS charger system.
upsAlarmUpsOutputOff (1.3.6.1.2.1.33.6.3.14)	Output of the UPS is turned off.
upsAlarmUpsSystemOff (1.3.6.1.2.1.33.6.3.15)	UPS system is in the off state.
upsAlarmFanFailure (1.3.6.1.2.1.33.6.3.16)	One or more UPS fans have failed.
upsAlarmFuseFailure (1.3.6.1.2.1.33.6.3.17)	One or more fuses have failed.

TABLE 7.9 *(continued)*

Object Identifier	Description
upsAlarmGeneralFault (1.3.6.1.2.1.33.6.3.18)	A general fault in the UPS was detected.
upsAlarmDiagnosticTestFailed (1.3.6.1.2.1.33.6.3.19)	Result of the prior diagnostic test indicates a failure occurred.
upsAlarmCommunicationsLost (1.3.6.1.2.1.33.6.3.20)	A problem was encountered in the communications between the agent and the UPS.
upsAlarmAwaitingPower (1.3.6.1.2.1.33.6.3.21)	UPS output is off and the system is awaiting the return of input power.
upsAlarmShutdownPending (1.3.6.1.2.1.33.6.3.22)	A upsShutdownAfterDelay countdown is occurring.
upsAlarmShutdownImminent (1.3.6.1.2.1.33.6.3.23)	UPS will turn off power in less than five seconds.
upsAlarmTestInProgress (1.3.6.1.2.1.33.6.3.24)	A test initiated and indicated by the test group is in progress.

Test Group

The UPS MIB *Test Group* consists of seven subnodes, with the last providing the placement for a series of five well-known tests. Table 7.10 provides a summary of the identifiers and a brief description of the identifiers in the Test Group.

In examining the entries in Table 7.10 note that a *spin lock* represents a procedure that a manager-station performs to make sure that a test is not in progress. Table 7.11 provides a description of the well-known tests defined under the seventh node of this group.

Control Group

The identifiers in the *Control Group* govern the action taken at shutdown, and the ability of a UPS system to restart. The five identifiers in the Control Group and a brief description of each identifier are contained in Table 7.12.

TABLE 7.10 Test Group

Object Identifier	Access	Description
upsTestId (1.3.6.1.2.1.33.7.1)	r-w	Identifies the test.
upsTestSpinLock (1.3.6.1.2.1.33.7.2)	r-w	A spin lock on the test subsystem.
upsTestResultsSummary (1.3.6.1.2.1.33.7.3)	r	Returns the results of the current or last UPS test performed (donePass (1), done-Warning (2), doneError (3), aborted (4), inProgress (5), noTestsInitiated (6)).
upsTestResultsDetailed (1.3.6.1.2.1.33.7.4)	r	Returns a string providing additional information about upsTestResults Summary.
upsTestStartTime (1.3.6.1.2.1.33.7.5)	r	The time the test in progress was initiated. If no test is in progress, the time the previous test was initiated.
upsTestElapsedTime (1.3.6.1.2.1.33.7.6)	r	The amount of time since the test in progress was initiated or, if no test in progress, the amount of time the previous test took to complete.

TABLE 7.11 UPS Well-Known Tests

Object Identifier	Description
upsTestNoTestsInitiated (1.3.6.1.2.1.33.7.7.1)	No test initiated or in progress.
upsTestAbortTestInProgress (1.3.6.1.2.1.33.7.7.2)	Test in progress was or will be aborted.
upsTestGeneralSystemsTest (1.3.6.1.2.1.33.7.7.3)	Manufacturer's standard test.
upsTestQuickBatteryTest (1.3.6.1.2.1.33.7.7.4)	Test to determine if the battery needs replacement.
upsTestDeepBatteryCalibration (1.3.6.1.2.1.33.7.7.5)	Causes the battery to discharge to a level set by the manufacturer, enabling the determination of battery replacement and battery runtime.

Configuration Group

The ninth and last group in the UPS MIB is the *Configuration Group,* which is responsible for defining the input and output power components that have a significant effect upon UPS operations. For example, in the Configuration Group are identifiers that control the transfer of the system to battery backup based upon minimum and maximum line voltages, as well as the number of minutes of battery power remaining to define a low battery condition. Table 7.13 provides a description of the ten identifiers in the UPS Configuration Group.

TABLE 7.12 Configuration Group

Object Identifier	Access	Description
upsShutDownType (1.3.6.1.2.1.33.8.1)	r-w	Action to occur when upsShutdownAfterDelay and upsRebootWithDuration variables reach a zero value (output (1), system (2)).
upsShutDownAfterDelay (1.3.6.1.2.1.33.8.2)	r-w	Turns off either the UPS output or the UPS system based upon the value of the upsShutdownType after the indicated number of seconds.
upsStartupAfterDelay (1.3.6.1.2.1.33.8.3)	r-w	Starts the output after the indicated number of seconds. A value of 0 results in an immediate startup, −1 aborts the countdown.
upsRebootWithDuration (1.3.6.1.2.1.33.8.4)	r-w	Turns off the UPS output or UPS system based upon the value of upsShutdownType for the specified number of seconds, after which the output and, if necessary, UPS are started.
upsAutoRestart (1.3.6.1.2.1.33.8.5)	r-w	Setting to *on* causes the UPS to restart after a power loss caused a shutdown. If set to *off* the UPS will not restart until manual intervention occurs.

TABLE 7.13 Configuration Group

Object Identifier	Access	Description
upsConfigInputVoltage (1.3.6.1.2.1.33.9.1)	r-w	Magnitude of the nominal input voltage, in RMS volts
upsConfigInputFreq (1.3.6.1.2.1.33.9.2)	r-w	Nominal input frequency, in Hz
upsConfigOutputVoltage (1.3.6.1.2.1.33.9.3)	r-w	Magnitude of the nominal output voltage, in RMS volts
upsConfigOutputFreq (1.3.6.1.2.1.33.9.4)	r-w	Nominal output frequency, in Hz
upsConfigOutputVA (1.3.6.1.2.1.33.9.5)	r	Magnitude of the nominal Volt-Amp rating
upsConfigOutputPower (1.3.6.1.2.1.33.9.6)	r	Magnitude of the nominal true power, in watts
upsConfigLowBattTime (1.3.6.1.2.1.33.9.7)	r-w	Value of upsEstimated-MinutesRemaining, at which a lowBattery condition is declared
upsConfigAudibleStatus (1.3.6.1.2.1.33.9.8)	r-w	State of the audible alarm (disabled (1), enabled (2), muted (3))
upsConfigLowVoltageTransferPoint (1.3.6.1.2.1.33.9.9)	r-w	Minimum input line voltage allowed prior to the UPS system transferring to battery backup
upsConfigHighVoltageTransferPoint (1.3.6.1.2.1.33.9.10)	r-w	Maximum line voltage allowed prior to the UPS transferring to battery backup

TABLE 7.14 UPS Traps and Variable Values Returned

Trap	Variables Returned
upsTrapOnBattery	upsEstimatedMinutesRemaining upsSecondsOnBattery upsConfigLowBattTime
upsTrapTestCompleted	upsTestId upsTestSpinLock upsTestResultsSummary upsTestResultsDetail upsTestStartTime upsTestElapsedTime
upsTrapAlarmEntryAdded	upsAlarmId upsAlarmDesc
upsTrapAlarmEntryRemoved	upsAlarmId upsAlarmDesc

Traps

No discussion of a managed UPS is complete without focusing upon the notifications or traps UPS agents can transmit. Thus, in concluding our examination of the UPS MIB, Table 7.14 lists the four defined UPS traps as well as the variable values each trap will return to a management station.

The first trap, upsTrapOnBattery, indicates the UPS is on battery power and is re-sent at one minute intervals until the UPS either turns off or exits its battery mode. The upsTrapTest-Completed is sent upon the completion of a diagnostic test, while upsTrapAlarmEntryAdded is sent each time an alarm is added to the alarm table, with the exception of upsAlarmOnBattery and upsAlarmTestInProgress. The last trap in Table 7.14, upsTrapAlarmEntryRemoved, is sent by the agent each time an alarm is removed from the alarm table, and upon the removal of all alarms except for upsAlarmTestInProgress.

Extending LAN Management Operations

This concluding chapter will focus upon two products and a standards development, which extend the ability of network users to perform LAN management functions. First, I will discuss the operation and utilization of a performance analyzer that interprets statistics collected by RMON probes that are then used to predict potential network bottlenecks as well as provide information concerning the impact of segment modifications. Thus, this product can be considered to represent a proactive performance analyzer. After reviewing the operation and utilization of this proactive performance analyzer, I will turn to a pending extension to RMON, which should be a reality by the time you read this book. In doing so, I will also discuss the use of a currently available product that functions as an extended RMON probe, and the information you can obtain from examining data above the data link layer.

LOGTEL PERFOLYZER

LogTel Systems, a member of the LogTel Computer Communications Ltd. Group of Petach Tikva, Israel, introduced a LAN performance analyzer during late 1995, which provided at that time a unique capability to use RMON statistics for estimation and predictive purposes. This product, marketed under the name PerfoLyzer, not only monitors RMON probe statistics, but can also be operated to use statistics to predict such operations as the effect of the movement of workstations from one network segment to another without requiring you to perform a physical move of equipment and recabling. This capability can significantly increase the ability of network managers and administrators to manage their networks, and examine the potential effect upon their network by performing theoretical moves without having to actually perform those moves. Thus, the PerfoLyzer LAN performance analyzer provides the capability to ask key what-if questions whose answers can provide information that can be used to significantly improve the performance of your network. Although LogTel's PerfoLyzer also performs many additional RMON management functions, this section will focus upon its predictive capability. Since a discussion of that capability is facilitated by illustrating the use of the product, I will do so through a series of screen images that show the operation of the performance analyzer.

Constructing a Profile

PerfoLyzer consists of two applications that operate on a network management station—Profile Builder and Performance Planner. The Profile Builder, as its name implies, is used to develop a database of statistics used by the Performance Planner application. The latter enables a network manager to answer what-if questions concerning the addition, movement, or deletion of hosts from a network segment.

PerfoLyzer runs under HP-UX, SunOS UNIX, and the HP OpenView Network management platform, resulting in a GUI-based application that operates similarly to other windows-type applications. Figure 8.1 illustrates the Profile Building Setup window, which is used to access an RMON probe and retrieve MIB information to form a profile of network activity. In the example illustrated in Figure 8.1, the RMON probe at address 16.1.1.100 will be polled beginning at 9:00 for an eight-hour period, with sampling occurring at 30-minute intervals. Access to the probe will occur using the default *public* community name.

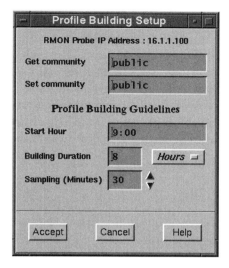

FIGURE 8.1 Profile Building Setup window.

Viewing Segment Performance

Once a database of network information is obtained from a probe, you can use PerfoLyzer to view the performance characteristics of a segment and its hosts. In addition, you can project the effect of altering the composition of a segment by adding, moving, or deleting hosts from a segment. Since it's a logical assumption that most persons will first observe the performance characteristics of a segment and its hosts prior to asking what-if questions to examine the effect of altering a segment, I will continue my examination of the profile portion of PerfoLyzer prior to examining its performance-planning capability.

Figure 8.2 illustrates the Segment Profile View window, which provides a summary of segment activity monitored by the probe and transferred to the PerfoLyzer database for retrieval and display. In examining Figure 8.2, note that the probe at address 16.1.1.100 has six hosts on the monitored segment, with the impact of each host upon the network during the baseline period indicated in the form of a horizontal bar in the lower portion of the window. The network impact should not be confused with the utilization level of the segment shown as a percentage above the chart. The network impact denotes the contribution of the host to the delay on the segment to the overall packet delivery time, and takes into consideration traffic intensity, packet size, and collision intensity. Thus, the network impact provides an indication of throughput delay resulting from the operation of a host on a segment. By focusing upon the network impact chart, you can immediately observe the impact of each host on the segment. Although difficult to observe from the illustration, the segment profile view shown in Figure 8.2 was based upon

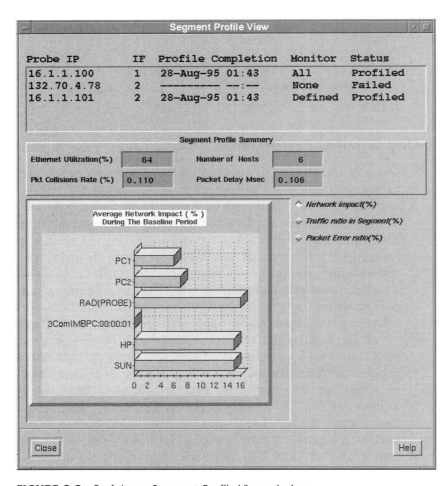

FIGURE 8.2 PerfoLyzer Segment Profile View window.

selecting the *Network impact (%)* button. You can also obtain a segment profile displaying the traffic ratio and packet error ratio by selecting either of those buttons.

From the Segment Profile window, you can focus upon the specific activity of a host during the baseline period. Figure 8.3 illustrates the Host Performance Profile window for the Sun computer attached to the segment that was previously baselined. Note that the Host Performance Profile window provides a summary of the selected host's traffic ratio and packet error ratio as well as its average network impact. By clicking on one of the three time buttons, you can obtain a graph of network impact, traffic ratio, or error ratio vs. time for the baseline period. By selecting the button labeled Peers, you can obtain a display showing the round-trip delays between a selected host and its peers on a segment in the form of a bar chart. Both the graphs and Peers bar chart provide information that can be use-

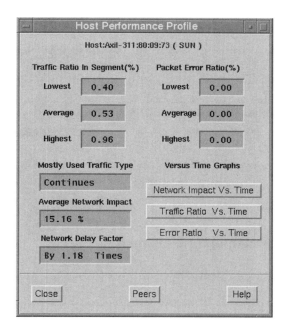

FIGURE 8.3　PerfoLyzer Host Performance Profile window.

ful in determining the effect of specific hosts upon the operation of a network segment; however, the uniqueness of PerfoLyzer is in its ability to examine the effect of changes to a network segment without actually having to physically alter the segment. Since I previously described the use of the Profile Builder application and examined the activity of a segment with six hosts, I will now focus upon the Performance Planner application to indicate the what-if capability of PerfoLyzer.

Using the Performance Planner

As previously discussed, the Performance Planner application of PerfoLyzer provides network managers with the ability to predict the effect upon network segments from the alteration of hosts without having to actually do so. To obtain this capability, Performance Planner provides users with the ability to select hosts to be *moved* from one segment to another. Here the move represents a statistical rather than physical move.

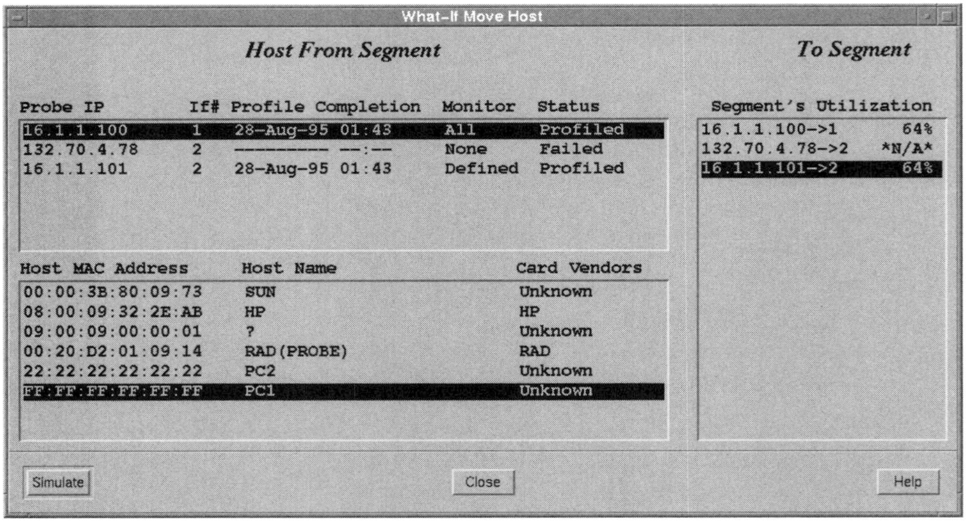

FIGURE 8.4 Through the What-If Move Host window, you can statistically move one or more hosts from one segment to another.

Moving a Host

Figure 8.4 illustrates the PerfoLyzer What-If Move Host window. In this example, the host named PC1 with the MAC address FF:FF:FF:FF:FF:FF was selected to be statistically moved from its current segment location to another network segment. Once you select one or more hosts to be moved, clicking on the Simulate button results in the Performance Planner application statistically simulating the effect of the move.

Figure 8.5 illustrates the Move Host window, which illustrates the before and after effect of each segment after the selected host was statistically moved from one segment to an-

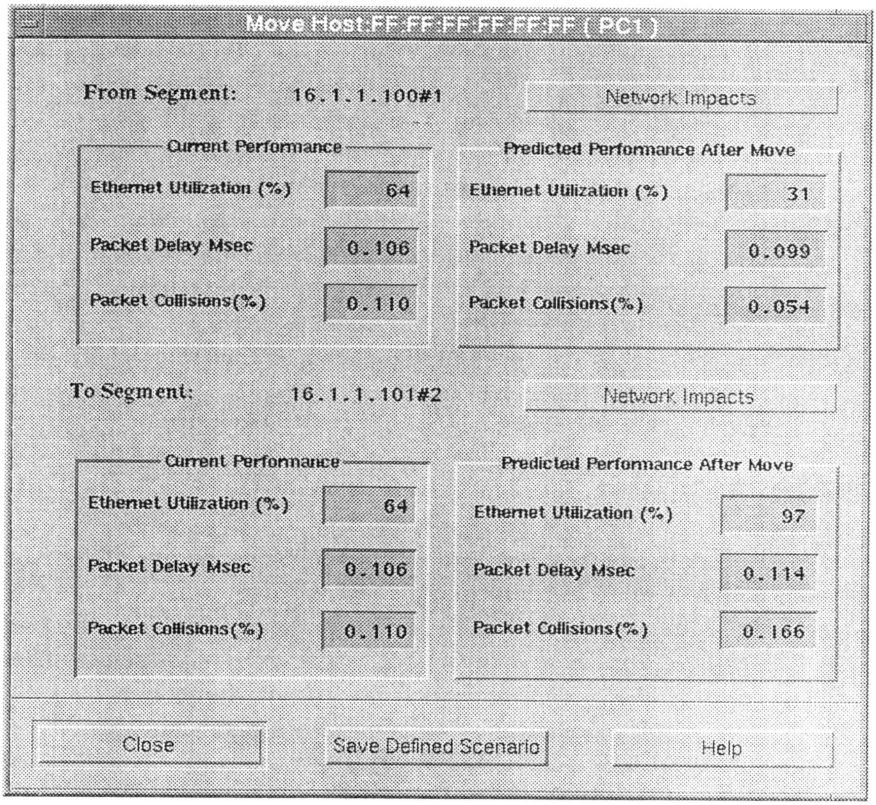

FIGURE 8.5 The Move Host window provides the ability to examine the effect upon segment performance from moving a host from one segment to another.

other segment. Note that the utilization level of the original segment is predicted to decrease from 64 to 31 percent, while the utilization level of the target segment is predicted to increase from 64 to 97 percent. Although this move would enhance the performance of the source segment, it would adversely affect the operation of users of the target segment and you would probably be well advised to consider leaving the host where it is. However, without the use of PerfoLyzer, the ability to determine whether to move one or more hosts, and the effect of their movement, might result in a considerable effort. Through the use of PerfoLyzer you could simply return to the What-If Move Host window and examine the effect of moving other hosts to determine their statistical effect upon network segment operations without having to physically do so. Thus, the predictive network performance capability of this performance analyzer can provide network managers, designers, and analysts with a very productive management tool.

In addition to moving one or more hosts, PerfoLyzer provides users with the ability to examine the effect upon segment performance from the addition and removal of hosts. Both operations result in information concerning segment performance similar to the performance information previously illustrated in Figure 8.5, and provides the ability to examine both current and projected performance based upon the operation performed. Thus, you can use PerfoLyzer to project the effect of the addition, deletion, and movement of hosts to and from different network segments.

RMON EXTENSION

Perhaps the key limitation associated with the use of RMON is the fact that it's currently limited to monitoring frames at the data link layer. At the time this book was prepared, the *Internet Engineering Task Force (IETF)* was in the process of finalizing version 2 of its standard for remote monitoring (RMON). The new standard, which should be published as an RFC by the time you read this book, will provide probe manufacturers and management station developers with a standard for extending the use of probes beyond data link layer statistics for obtaining information concerning the activity on a monitored network segment.

RMON Version 2

Under RMON version 2, monitoring is extended to the network layer. This means that an RMON version 2-compliant management station will be able to provide a breakdown of network traffic by protocol, as well as the ability to trace end-to-end traffic, regardless of the location of the originating and destination nodes.

Similar to the original RMON standard, RMON version 2 consists of defined groups that provide common functions within a group for analyzing traffic on a segment. Table 8.1 lists eight RMON version 2 groups expected to be standardized, and provides a description of the function associated with each group.

TABLE 8.1   RMON Version 2 Groups

Group	Description
Protocol Distribution	Tracks the percentage of traffic by network and application protocol on a segment.
Address Mapping	Identifies traffic-generating hosts by MAC and LAN address, and discovers hub/switch ports to which hosts are connected.
Network-Layer Host Table	Tracks packets, errors, and octets by hosts based upon network-layer protocol.
Network-Layer Matrix Table	Tracks conversations between pairs of hosts by network-layer protocol.
Application-Layer Host Table	Tracks packets, errors, and octets by host according to application.
Application-Layer Matrix Table	Tracks conversations between pairs of hosts by application.
Probe Configuration	Defines a standard method to remotely configure a probe.
History	Provides a mechanism to filter and store statistics based upon user-defined RMON version 2 variables for predefined times.

In examining the entries in Table 8.1, the potential use of two groups requires a degree of elaboration. The application-layer host table can be used to track packets, errors, and octets generated by different hosts on a network segment by application. Applications can include SMTP, telnet, Whois, Finger, ftp, and other applications. RMON version 2 obtains this information from *looking into* the network layer packet to observe the well-known port, socket, or similar field used to denote the application. Similarly, the application-layer matrix table provides statistical information about conversations between pairs of hosts by application. Thus, RMON version 2 extends the ability of RMON to layer 3 of the ISO reference model, and enables network managers to observe the flow of data and error conditions not only by octet count, but also by protocol and application.

Armon OnSite Probes

A current example of the potential of RMON version 2 can be obtained through the use of the Armon OnSite Ethernet and Token-Ring probes in conjunction with that vendor's OnSite manager. Those RMON probes support a proprietary extension of the RMON MIB to provide layer-3 host and matrix information. Although the Armon OnSite level-3 extension represents a proprietary extension to the RMON MIB, by the time RMON version 2 is finalized, it may be fully compliant with the pending standard. For network managers and administrators who require the ability to track data flow by protocol, the use of an Armon OnSite probe provides this capability without having to wait for RMON version 2-compliant products to reach the market.

Through the use of a series of screen images, I will illustrate the use of the Armon OnSite manager in conjunction with the vendor's OnSite probes. Doing so will illustrate some sophisticated management functions that, although applicable to both layer-2 and layer-3 operations, may provide food for thought for readers considering acquiring additional LAN management products.

Figure 8.6 illustrates a display of the Armon OnSite manager Global Statistics application, which enables network managers and administrators to obtain on one display screen a

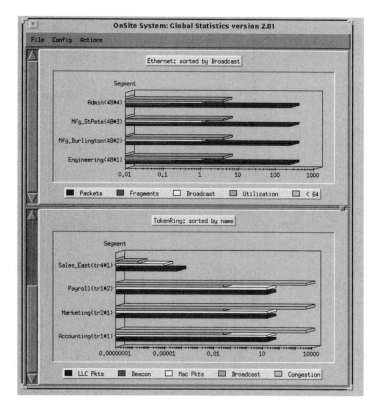

FIGURE 8.6 The Armon OnSite Global Manager provides a display of activity on an enterprise-wide basis.

display of LAN activity for both Ethernet and Token-Ring networks on an enterprise-wide basis. In the Global Manager screen display illustrated in Figure 8.6, five statistics per LAN are displayed for eight networks. In comparison, some management products are restricted to providing a display of two to four statistics, either on an individual network basis or for two to four networks at a time.

Figure 8.7 illustrates a display of the Armon OnSite Manager Host Matrix application. As previously noted, the host matrix application group tracks conversation pairs and the amount of traffic flowing between stations on a network. The OnSite manager uses this information to display a matrix of stations on a seg-

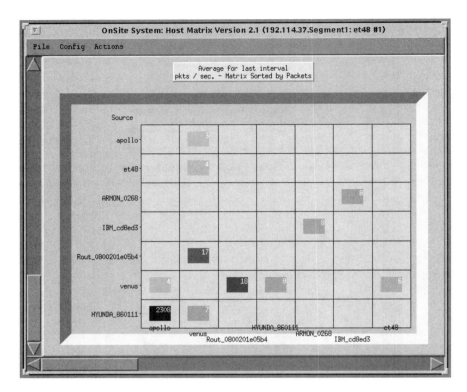

FIGURE 8.7   The Host Matrix application displays the packet-per-second data flow between pairs of stations on a segment.

ment and indicates the data flow in terms of packets per second between pairs of stations. In addition, the manager highlights the higher packet transfers between pairs of stations by displaying the packet-per-second rate in a colored box.

Since OnSite probes have the ability to track data at the network layer, such probes can identify the protocols used on the segment they are monitoring. As you might expect, the Armon OnSite Manager uses network layer data to provide users with different types of protocol distribution information.

Figure 8.8 illustrates the use of the OnSite Manager Protocol Segment application display. Through the use of this application, you can display the protocol distribution for a specific

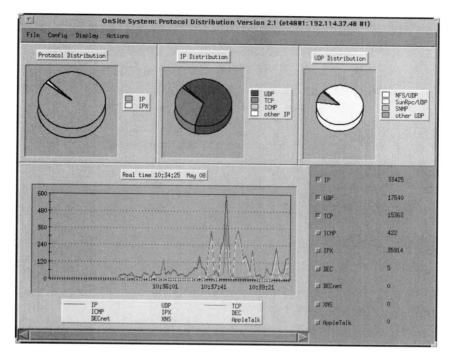

FIGURE 8.8   Through the OnSite Protocol Segment application, you can display the protocol distribution on a specific network segment.

Ethernet or Token-Ring network. The resulting information can be of assistance in determining whether certain types of filtering could be used to enhance network performance, as well as provide managers and administrators with a better insight concerning the use of the monitored network segment.

In addition to providing the ability to observe protocol activity on an individual LAN basis, the OnSite Manager provides users with the ability to display such activity on an enterprise-wide basis. An example of this capability is illustrated in Figure 8.9, where the protocol distribution for every segment that is monitored by an Armon probe is displayed, providing users with the ability to quickly compare activity between monitored network segments.

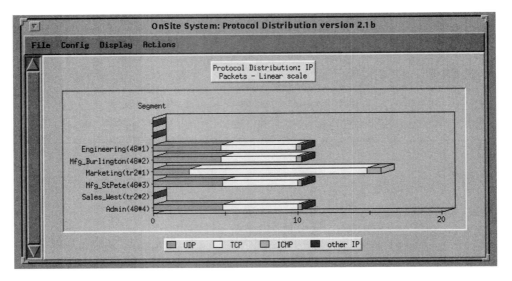

FIGURE 8.9 Through the use of the Armon OnSite manager you can view the protocol distribution on an enterprise-wide basis.

One of the more interesting applications built into the OnSite manager is its *EyeNet* network layer monitor display. EyeNet, as its name implies, provides a visual display of layer-3 (network) conversations between stations. In doing so it also provides an indication of the packet rates between stations on a relative basis.

Figure 8.10 illustrates an example of the Armon OnSite Manager EyeNet application. In an EyeNet display, each bubble is used to represent a subnet, while the lines represent inter- and intrasegment conversations. The thickness of each line is used to indicate the relationship of packet rates between stations. Thus, the EyeNet application provides a visual indication of inter- and intrasegment layer-3 conversations, from which you can rapidly note such activity as well as any conversations that may appear to represent activity that could be the cause of bandwidth problems.

By extending monitoring to layer 3 and providing both segment and enterprise-wide activity display capability, the OnSite

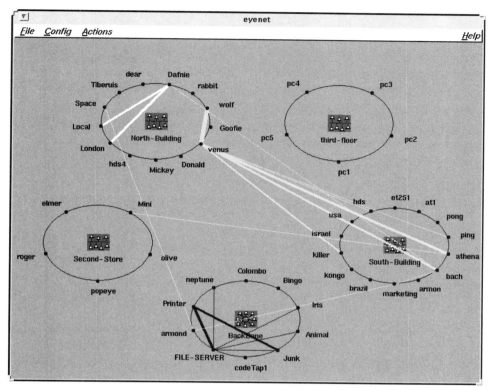

FIGURE 8.10 Through the OnSite EyeNet application, you can obtain a visual indication of layer-3 conversations on an inter- and intrasegment basis.

manager provides visual information that facilitates the rapid observation of potential inter- or intranetwork problems. This in turn can provide network managers and administrators with a tool that can enhance their ability to identify and correct network-related problems.

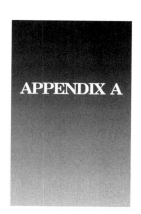

RFC Reference

This appendix contains a listing of RFCs applicable to SNMP, including MIBs, RMON, and the Structure and Identification of Management Information. RFCs are listed in reverse numeric order corresponding to a reverse chronological order. RFC citations included in this appendix are listed using the following format:

RFC number Author(s), "Title of RFC," Issue date. (Pages=nn) (Obsoletes RFC number) (Updates RFC number)

where:

The optional "Obsoletes RFC number" references one or more other RFCs replaced by the indicated one.

The optional "Obsoleted RFC number" references one or more RFCs replaced by the referenced one.

1792 E   T. Sung, "TCP/IPX Connection Mib Specification," 04/18/1995. (Pages=9)

1757 DS   S. Waldbusser, "Remote Network Monitoring Management Information Base," 02/10/1995. (Pages=91) (Obsoletes RFC1271)

1749 PS   K. McCloghrie, F. Baker, E. Decker, "IEEE 802.5 Station Source Routing MIB Using SMIv2," 12/29/1994. (Pages=10) (Updates RFC1748)

1748 DS   K. McCloghrie, E. Decker, "IEEE 802.5 MIB Using SMIv2," 12/29/1994. (Pages=25) (Updated by RFC1749)

1743 DS   K. McCloghrie, E. Decker, "IEEE 802.5 MIB Using SMIv2," 12/27/1994. (Pages=25) (Obsoletes RFC-1231)

1742 PS   S. Waldbusser, K. Frisa, "AppleTalk Management Information Base II," 01/05/1995. (Pages=84) (Obsoletes RFC1243)

1724 DS   G. Malkin, F. Baker, "RIP Version 2 MIB Extension," 11/15/1994. (Pages=18) (Obsoletes RFC1389)

1697 PS   D. Brower, R. Purvy, A. Daniel, M. Sinykin, J. Smith, "Relational Database Management System (RDBMS) Management Information Base (MIB) Using SMIv2," 08/23/1994. (Pages=38)

1696 PS   J. Barnes, L. Brown, R. Royston, S. Waldbusser, "Modem Management Information Base (MIB) Using SMIv2," 08/25/1994. (Pages=31)

1695 PS   M. Ahmed, K. Tesink, "Definitions of Managed Objects for ATM Management Version 8.0 Using SMIv2," 08/25/1994. (Pages=73)

1694 DS   T. Brown, K. Tesink, "Definitions of Managed Objects for SMDS Interfaces Using SMIv2," 08/23/1994. (Pages=35) (Obsoletes RFC1304)

1666 PS   Z. Kielczewski, D. Kostick, K. Shih, "Definitions of Managed Objects for SNA NAUs Using SMIv2," 08/11/1994. (Pages=68)

1665 PS   Z. Kielczewski, D. Kostick, K. Shih, "Definitions of Managed Objects for SNA NAUs Using SMIv2," 07/22/1994. (Pages=67)

1660 DS   B. Stewart, "Definitions of Managed Objects for Parallel-Printer-Like Hardware Devices Using SMIv2," 07/20/1994. (Pages=10) (Obsoletes RFC1318)

1659 DS   B. Stewart, "Definitions of Managed Objects for RS-232-Like Hardware Devices Using SMIv2," 07/20/1994. (Pages=21) (Obsoletes RFC1317)

1658 DS   B. Stewart, "Definitions of Managed Objects for Character Stream Devices Using SMIv2," 07/20/1994. (Pages=18) (Obsoletes RFC1316)

1657 PS   S. Willis, J. Burruss, J. Chu, "Definitions of Managed Objects for the Fourth Version of the Border Gateway Protocol (BGP-4) Using SMIv2," 07/21/1994. (Pages=21)

1650 PS   F. Kastenholz, "Definitions of Managed Objects for the Ethernet-Like Interface Types Using SMIv2," 08/23/1994. (Pages=20)

1643 S   F. Kastenholz, "Definitions of Managed Objects for the Ethernet-Like Interface Types," 07/13/1994. (Pages=19) (Obsoletes RFC1623)

1628 PS   J. Case, "UPS Management Information Base," 05/19/1994. (Pages=45)

1623 S   F. Kastenholz, "Definitions of Managed Objects for Ethernet-Like Interface Types," 05/24/1994. (Pages=23) (Obsoletes RFC1398) (Obsoleted by RFC1643)

1604 PS   T. Brown, "Definitions of Managed Objects for Frame Relay Service," 03/25/1994. (Pages=46) (Obsoletes RFC1596)

1596 PS   T. Brown, "Definitions of Managed Objects for Frame Relay Service," 03/17/1994. (Pages=46) (Obsoleted by RFC1604)

1595 PS   T. Brown, K. Tesink, "Definitions of Managed Objects for the SONET/SDH Interface Type," 03/11/1994. (Pages=59)

1592 E   B. Wijnen, G. Carpenter, K. Curran, A. Sehgal, G. Waters, "Simple Network Management Protocol Distributed Protocol Interface Version 2.0," 03/03/1994. (Pages=54) (Obsoletes RFC1228)

1573 PS   K. McCloghrie, F. Kastenholz, "Evolution of the Interfaces Group of MIB-II," 01/20/1995. (Pages=55) (Obsoletes RFC1229)

1566 PS N. Freed, S. Kille, "Mail Monitoring MIB," 01/11/1994. (Pages=21)

1565 PS N. Freed, S. Kille, "Network Services Monitoring MIB," 01/11/1994. (Pages=18)

1559 DS J. Saperia, "DECnet Phase IV MIB Extensions," 12/27/1993. (Pages=69) (Obsoletes RFC1289)

1525 PS E. Decker, K. McCloghrie, P. Langille, A. Rijsinghani, "Definitions of Managed Objects for Source Routing Bridges," 09/30/1993. (Pages=18) (Obsoletes RFC 1286)

1516 DS D. McMaster, K. McCloghrie, "Definitions of Managed Objects for IEEE 802.3 Repeater Devices," 09/10/1993. (Pages=40) (Obsoletes RFC1368)

1515 PS D. McMaster, K. McCloghrie, S. Roberts, "Definitions of Managed Objects for IEEE 802.3 Medium Attachment Units (MAUs)," 09/10/1993. (Pages=25)

1514 PS P. Grillo, S. Waldbusser, "Host Resources MIB," 09/23/1993. (Pages=33)

1513 PS S. Waldbusser, "Token Ring Extensions to the Remote Network Monitoring MIB," 09/23/1993. (Pages=55) (Updates RFC1271)

1512 PS J. Case, A. Rijsinghani, "FDDI Management Information Base," 09/10/1993. (Pages=51) (Updates RFC1285)

1493 DS E. Decker, P. Langille, A. Rijsinghani, K. McCloghrie, "Definitions of Managed Objects for Bridges," 07/28/1993. (Pages=34) (Obsoletes RFC1286)

1474 PS F. Kastenholz, "The Definitions of Managed Objects for the Bridge Network Control Protocol of the Point-to-Point Protocol," 06/08/1993. (Pages=15)

1473 PS F. Kastenholz, "The Definitions of Managed Objects for the IP Network Control Protocol of the Point-to-Point Protocol," 06/08/1993. (Pages=9)

1472 PS F. Kastenholz, "The Definitions of Managed Objects

for the Security Protocols of the Point-to-Point Protocol," 06/08/1993. (Pages=11)

1471 PS F. Kastenholz, "The Definitions of Managed Objects for the Link Control Protocol of the Point-to-Point Protocol," 06/08/1993. (Pages=25)

1461 PS D. Throop, "SNMP MIB extension for MultiProtocol Interconnect over X.25," 05/27/1993. (Pages=30)

1452 PS J. Case, K. McCloghrie, M. Rose, S. Waldbusser, "Coexistence between Version 1 and Version 2 of the Internet-Standard Network Management Framework," 05/03/1993. (Pages=17)

1451 PS J. Case, K. McCloghrie, M. Rose, S. Waldbusser, "Manager-to-Manager Management Information Base," 05/03/1993. (Pages=36)

1450 PS J. Case, K. McCloghrie, M. Rose, S. Waldbusser, "Management Information Base for Version 2 of the Simple Network Management Protocol (SNMPv2)," 05/03/1993. (Pages=27)

1449 PS J. Case, K. McCloghrie, M. Rose, S. Waldbusser, "Transport Mappings for Version 2 of the Simple Network Management Protocol (SNMPv2)," 05/03/1993. (Pages=24)

1448 PS J. Case, K. McCloghrie, M. Rose, S. Waldbusser, "Protocol Operations for Version 2 of the Simple Network Management Protocol (SNMPv2)," 05/03/1993. (Pages=36)

1447 PS K. McCloghrie, J. Galvin, "Party MIB for Version 2 of the Simple Network Management Protocol (SNMPv2)," 05/03/1993. (Pages=50)

1446 PS J. Galvin, K. McCloghrie, "Security Protocols for Version 2 of the Simple Network Management Protocol (SNMPv2)," 05/03/1993. (Pages=51)

1445 PS J. Davin, K. McCloghrie, "Administrative Model for Version 2 of the Simple Network Management Protocol (SNMPv2)," 05/03/1993. (Pages=47)

1444 PS J. Case, K. McCloghrie, M. Rose, S. Waldbusser,

"Conformance Statements for Version 2 of the Simple Network Management Protocol (SNMPv2)," 05/03/1993. (Pages=33)

1443 PS   J. Case, K. McCloghrie, M. Rose, S. Waldbusser, "Textual Conventions for Version 2 of the Simple Network Management Protocol (SNMPv2)," 05/03/1993. (Pages=31)

1442 PS   J. Case, K. McCloghrie, M. Rose, S. Waldbusser, "Structure of Management Information for Version 2 of the Simple Network Management Protocol (SNMPv2)," 05/03/1993. (Pages=55)

1441 PS   J. Case, K. McCloghrie, M. Rose, S. Waldbusser, "Introduction to Version 2 of the Internet-Standard Network Management Framework," 05/03/1993. (Pages=13)

1420 PS   S. Bostock, "SNMP over IPX," 03/03/1993. (Pages=4) (Obsoletes RFC1298)

1419 PS   G. Minshall, M. Ritter, "SNMP over AppleTalk," 03/03/1993. (Pages=7)

1418 PS   M. Rose, "SNMP over OSI," 03/03/1993. (Pages=4) (Obsoletes RFC1283)

1414 PS   M. St. Johns, M. Rose, "Ident MIB," 02/04/1993. (Pages=13)

1407 PS   T. Cox, K. Tesink, "Definitions of Managed Objects for the DS3/E3 Interface Type," 01/26/1993. (Pages=55) (Obsoletes RFC1233)

1406 PS   F. Baker, J. Watt, "Definitions of Managed Objects for the DS1 and E1 Interface Types," 01/26/1993. (Pages=50) (Obsoletes RFC1232)

1398 DS   F. Kastenholz, "Definitions of Managed Objects for the Ethernet-Like Interface Types," 01/14/1993. (Pages=24) (Obsoletes RFC1284) (Obsoleted by RFC1623)

1389 PS   G. Malkin, F. Baker, "RIP Version 2 MIB Extension," 01/06/1993. (Pages=13) (Obsoleted by RFC1724)

1382 PS   D. Throop, "SNMP MIB Extension for the X.25

Packet Layer," 11/10/1992. (Pages=69)

1381 PS   D. Throop, F. Baker, "SNMP MIB Extension for X.25 LAPB," 11/10/1992. (Pages=33)

1369 I   F. Kastenholz, "Implementation Notes and Experience for the Internet Ethernet MIB," 10/23/1992. (Pages=7)

1368 PS   D. McMaster, K. McCloghrie, "Definitions of Managed Objects for IEEE 802.3 Repeater Devices," 10/26/1992. (Pages=40) (Obsoleted by RFC1516)

1354 PS   F. Baker, "IP Forwarding Table MIB," 07/06/1992. (Pages=12)

1353 H   K. McCloghrie, J. Davin, J. Galvin, "Definitions of Managed Objects for Administration of SNMP Parties," 07/06/1992. (Pages=26)

1352 H   J. Davin, J. Galvin, K. McCloghrie, "SNMP Security Protocols," 07/06/1992. (Pages=41)

1351 H   J. Davin, J. Galvin, K. McCloghrie, "SNMP Administrative Model," 07/06/1992. (Pages=35)

1318 PS   B. Stewart, "Definitions of Managed Objects for Parallel-Printer-Like Hardware Devices," 04/16/1992. (Pages=11) (Obsoleted by RFC1660)

1317 PS   B. Stewart, "Definitions of Managed Objects for RS-232-Like Hardware Devices," 04/16/1992. (Pages=17) (Obsoleted by RFC1659)

1316 PS   B. Stewart, "Definitions of Managed Objects for Character Stream Devices," 04/16/1992. (Pages=17) (Obsoleted by RFC1658)

1315 PS   C. Brown, F. Baker, C. Carvalho, "Management Information Base for Frame Relay DTEs," 04/09/1992. (Pages=19)

1303 I   K. McCloghrie, M. Rose, "A Convention for Describing SNMP-Based Agents," 02/26/1992. (Pages=12)

1298 I   R. Wormley, S. Bostock, "SNMP over IPX," 02/07/1992. (Pages=5) (Obsoleted by RFC1420)

1289 PS   J. Saperia, "DECnet Phase IV MIB Extensions,"
          12/20/1991. (Pages=64) (Obsoleted by RFC1559)

1286 PS   K. McCloghrie, E. Decker, P. Langille, A. Rijsing-
          hani, "Definitions of Managed Objects for Bridges,"
          12/11/1991. (Pages=40) (Obsoleted by RFC1493,
          RFC1525)

1285 PS   J. Case, "FDDI Management Information Base,"
          01/24/1992. (Pages=46) (Updated by RFC1512)

1284 PS   J. Cook, "Definitions of Managed Objects for the Eth-
          ernet-Like Interface Types," 12/04/1991. (Pages=21)
          (Obsoleted by RFC1398)

1283 E   M. Rose, "SNMP over OSI," 12/06/1991. (Pages=8)
          (Obsoletes RFC1161) (Obsoleted by RFC1418)

1271 PS   S. Waldbusser, "Remote Network Monitoring Man-
          agement Information Base," 11/12/1991. (Pages=81)
          (Obsoleted by RFC1757) (Updated by RFC1513)

1270 I   F. Kastenholz, "SNMP Communications Services,"
          10/30/1991. (Pages=11)

1253 PS   F. Baker, R. Coltun, "OSPF Version 2 Management
          Information Base," 08/30/1991. (Pages=42) (Obso-
          letes RFC1252)

1252 PS   F. Baker, R. Coltun, "OSPF Version 2 Management
          Information Base," 08/21/1991. (Pages=42) (Obso-
          letes RFC1248) (Obsoleted by RFC1253)

1248 PS   F. Baker, R. Coltun, "OSPF Version 2 Management
          Information Base," 08/08/1991. (Pages=42) (Obso-
          leted by RFC1252) (Updated by RFC1349)

1239 PS   J. Reynolds, "Reassignment of Experimental MIBs
          to Standard MIBs," 06/25/1991. (Pages=2) (Updates
          RFC1233)

1238 E   G. Satz, "CLNS MIB—For Use with Connectionless
          Network Protocol (ISO 8473) and End System to
          Intermediate System (ISO 9542)," 06/25/1991.
          (Pages=32) (Obsoletes RFC1162)

1233 H   T. Cox, K. Tesink, "Definitions of Managed Objects
          for the DS3 Interface Type," 05/23/1991. (Pages=23)
          (Obsoleted by RFC1407) (Updated by RFC1239)

1232 H   F. Baker, C. Kolb, "Definitions of Managed Objects for the DS1 Interface Type," 05/23/1991. (Pages=28) (Obsoleted by RFC1406)

1231 DS   E. Decker, R. Fox, K. McCloghrie, "IEEE 802.5 Token-Ring MIB," 02/11/1993. (Pages=23) (Obsoleted by RFC1743)

1230 H   R. Fox, K. McCloghrie, "IEEE 802.4 Token Bus MIB," 05/23/1991. (Pages=23)

1229 DS   K. McCloghrie, "Extensions to the Generic-Interface MIB," 08/03/1992. (Pages=16) (Obsoleted by RFC-1573)

1228 E   G. Carpenter, B. Wijnen, "SNMP-DPI—Simple Network Management Protocol Distributed Program Interface," 05/23/1991. (Pages=50) (Obsoleted by RFC1592)

1227 E   M. Rose, "SNMP MUX Protocol and MIB," 05/23/1991. (Pages=13)

1215 I   M. Rose, "A Convention for Defining Traps for Use with the SNMP," 03/27/1991. (Pages=9)

1214 H   L. Labarre, "OSI Internet Management: Management Information Base," 04/05/1991. (Pages=83)

1213 S   K. McCloghrie, M. Rose, "Management Information Base for Network Management of TCP/IP-Based Internets: MIB-II," 03/26/1991. (Pages=70) (Obsoletes RFC1158) (STD 17)

1212 S   K. McCloghrie, M. Rose, "Concise MIB Definitions," 03/26/1991. (Pages=19) (STD 16)

1187 E   J. Davin, K. McCloghrie, M. Rose, "Bulk Table Retrieval with the SNMP," 10/18/1990. (Pages=12)

1180   T. Socolofsky, C. Kale, "A TCP/IP Tutorial," 01/15/1991. (Pages=28)

1161 E   M. Rose, "SNMP over OSI," 06/05/1990. (Pages=8) (Obsoleted by RFC1283)

1158 PS   M. Rose, "Management Information Base for Network Management of TCP/IP-Based Internets: MIB-II," 05/23/1990. (Pages=133) (Obsoletes RFC1156) (Obsoleted by RFC1213)

1157 S   M. Schoffstall, M. Fedor, J. Davin, J. Case, "A Simple Network Management Protocol (SNMP)," 05/10/1990. (Pages=36) (Updates RFC1098)

1156 S   K. McCloghrie, M. Rose, "Management Information Base for Network Management of TCP/IP-Based Internets," 05/10/1990. (Pages=91) (Updates RFC-1066) (Obsoleted by RFC1158)

1155 S   K. McCloghrie, M. Rose, "Structure and Identification of Management Information for TCP/IP-Based Internets," 05/10/1990. (Pages=22) (Updates RFC-1065)

1098   J. Case, C. Davin, M. Fedor, "Simple Network Management Protocol (SNMP)," 04/01/1989. (Pages=34) (Obsoletes RFC1067) (Updated by RFC1157)

1089   M. Schoffstall, C. Davin, M. Fedor, J. Case, "SNMP over Ethernet," 02/01/1989. (Pages=3)

1067   J. Case, M. Fedor, M. Schoffstall, J. Davin, "Simple Network Management Protocol," 08/01/1988. (Pages=33) (Obsoleted by RFC1098)

1066 H   K. McCloghrie, M. Rose, "Management Information Base for Network Management of TCP/IP-Based Internets," 08/01/1988. (Pages=90) (Updated by RFC1156)

1065 H   K. McCloghrie, M. Rose, "Structure and Identification of Management Information for TCP/IP-Based Internets," 08/01/1988. (Pages=21) (Updated by RFC1155)

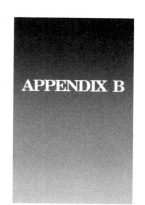

Management Information Base (MIB-II)

This appendix lists the object identifiers included in the ten groups that form the SNMP Management Information Base (MIB-II). Groups included in this appendix are:

System Group
Interfaces Group
Address Translation Group
IP Group
ICMP Group
TCP Group
UDP Group
EGP Group
Transmission Group
SNMP Group

SYSTEM GROUP

Implementation of the System group is mandatory for all systems. If an agent is not configured to have a value for any of these variables, a string of length 0 is returned.

sysDescr OBJECT-TYPE

SYNTAX   DisplayString (SIZE (0..255))
ACCESS   read-only
STATUS   mandatory
DESCRIPTION

> A textual description of the entity. This value should include the full name and version identification of the system's hardware type, software operating-system, and networking software. It is mandatory that this only contain printable ASCII characters."

::= { system 1 }

sysObjectID OBJECT-TYPE

SYNTAX   OBJECT IDENTIFIER
ACCESS   read-only
STATUS   mandatory
DESCRIPTION

> "The vendor's authoritative identification of the network management subsystem contained in the entity. This value is allocated within the SMI enterprises subtree (1.3.6.1.4.1) and provides an easy and unambiguous means for determining 'what kind of box' is being managed. For example, if vendor 'Flintstones, Inc.' was assigned the subtree 1.3.6.1.4.1. 4242, it could assign the identifier 1.3.6.1.4.1.4242.1.1 to its 'Fred Router'."

::= { system 2 }

sysUpTime OBJECT-TYPE

SYNTAX   TimeTicks
ACCESS   read-only
STATUS   mandatory
DESCRIPTION

> "The time (in hundredths of a second) since the network management portion of the system was last re-initialized."

::= { system 3 }

sysContact OBJECT-TYPE

SYNTAX   DisplayString (SIZE (0..255))
ACCESS   read-write
STATUS   mandatory
DESCRIPTION

"The textual identification of the contact person for this managed node, together with information on how to contact this person."

::= { system 4 }

sysName OBJECT-TYPE

SYNTAX   DisplayString (SIZE (0..255))
ACCESS   read-write
STATUS   mandatory
DESCRIPTION

"An administratively-assigned name for this managed node. By convention, this is the node's fully-qualified domain name."

::= { system 5 }

sysLocation OBJECT-TYPE

SYNTAX   DisplayString (SIZE (0..255))
ACCESS   read-write
STATUS   mandatory
DESCRIPTION

"The physical location of this node (e.g., 'telephone closet, 3rd floor')."

::= { system 6 }

sysServices OBJECT-TYPE

SYNTAX   INTEGER (0..127)
ACCESS   read-only
STATUS   mandatory
DESCRIPTION

"A value which indicates the set of services that this entity primarily offers.

The value is a sum. This sum initially takes the value zero, Then, for each layer, L, in the range 1 through 7, that this node performs transactions for, 2 raised to (L - 1) is added to the sum. For example, a node which performs primarily routing functions would have a value of 4 ($2^\wedge(3\text{-}1)$). In contrast, a node which is a host offering application services would have a value of 72 ($2^\wedge(4\text{-}1) + 2^\wedge(7\text{-}1)$). Note that in the context of the Internet suite of protocols, values should be calculated accordingly:

layer functionality

    1 physical (e.g., repeaters)
    2 datalink/subnetwork (e.g., bridges)
    3 internet (e.g., IP gateways)
    4 end-to-end (e.g., IP hosts)
    7 applications (e.g., mail relays)

For systems including OSI protocols, layers 5 and 6 may also be counted."

::= { system 7 }

INTERFACES GROUP

Implementation of the Interfaces group is mandatory for all systems.

ifNumber OBJECT-TYPE

SYNTAX   INTEGER
ACCESS   read-only
STATUS   mandatory
DESCRIPTION

"The number of network interfaces (regardless of their current state) present on this system."

::= { interfaces 1 }

the Interfaces table

The Interfaces table contains information on the entity's interfaces. Each interface is thought of as being attached to a 'subnetwork'. Note that this term should not be confused with 'subnet' which refers to an addressing partitioning scheme used in the Internet suite of protocols.

ifTable OBJECT-TYPE

SYNTAX SEQUENCE OF IfEntry
ACCESS not-accessible
STATUS mandatory
DESCRIPTION

  "A list of interface entries. The number of entries is given by the value of ifNumber."

::= { interfaces 2 }

ifEntry OBJECT-TYPE

SYNTAX IfEntry
ACCESS not-accessible
STATUS mandatory
DESCRIPTION

  "An interface entry containing objects at the subnetwork layer and below for a particular interface."

INDEX { ifIndex }
::= { ifTable 1 }

IfEntry ::=

SEQUENCE {
  ifIndex
   INTEGER,
  ifDescr
   DisplayString,
  ifType
   INTEGER,
  ifMtu
   INTEGER,
  ifSpeed
   Gauge,
  ifPhysAddress
   PhysAddress,

```
                    ifAdminStatus
                        INTEGER,
                    ifOperStatus
                        INTEGER,
                    ifLastChange
                        TimeTicks,
                    ifInOctets
                        Counter,
                    ifInUcastPkts
                        Counter,
                    ifInNUcastPkts
                        Counter,
                    ifInDiscards
                        Counter,
                    ifInErrors
                        Counter,
                    ifInUnknownProtos
                        Counter,
                    ifOutOctets
                        Counter,
                    ifOutUcastPkts
                        Counter,
                    ifOutNUcastPkts
                        Counter,
                    ifOutDiscards
                        Counter,
                    ifOutErrors
                        Counter,
                    ifOutQLen
                        Gauge,
                    ifSpecific
                        OBJECT IDENTIFIER
        }
```

ifIndex OBJECT-TYPE

```
    SYNTAX    INTEGER
    ACCESS    read-only
    STATUS    mandatory
```

DESCRIPTION

"A unique value for each interface. Its value ranges between 1 and the value of ifNumber. The value for each interface must remain constant at least from one re-initialization of the entity's network management system to the next re-initialization."

::= { ifEntry 1 }

ifDescr OBJECT-TYPE

SYNTAX   DisplayString (SIZE (0..255))
ACCESS   read-only
STATUS   mandatory
DESCRIPTION

"A textual string containing information about the interface. This string should include the name of the manufacturer, the product name and the version of the hardware interface."

::= { ifEntry 2 }

ifType OBJECT-TYPE

SYNTAX   INTEGER {
    other(1),   —none of the following
    regular1822(2),
    hdh1822(3),
    ddn-x25(4),
    rfc877-x25(5),
    ethernet-csmacd(6),
    iso88023-csmacd(7),
    iso88024-tokenBus(8),
    iso88025-tokenRing(9),
    iso88026-man(10),
    starLan(11),
    proteon-10Mbit(12),
    proteon-80Mbit(13),
    hyperchannel(14),
    fddi(15),
    lapb(16),

```
            sdlc(17),
            ds1(18),                  —T-1
            e1(19),                   —European equiv. of T-1
            basicISDN(20),
            primaryISDN(21),          —proprietary serial
            propPointToPointSerial(22),
            ppp(23),
            softwareLoopback(24),
            eon(25),                  —CLNP over IP [11]
            ethernet-3Mbit(26)
            nsip(27),                 —XNS over IP
            slip(28),                 —generic SLIP
            ultra(29),                —ULTRA technologies
            ds3(30),                  —T-3
            sip(31),                  —SMDS
            frame-relay(32)
        }
        ACCESS      read-only
        STATUS      mandatory
        DESCRIPTION
```

"The type of interface, distinguished according to the physical/link protocol(s) immediately 'below' the network layer in the protocol stack."

::= { ifEntry 3 }

ifMtu OBJECT-TYPE

```
        SYNTAX      INTEGER
        ACCESS      read-only
        STATUS      mandatory
        DESCRIPTION
```

"The size of the largest datagram which can be sent/received on the interface, specified in octets. For interfaces that are used for transmitting network datagrams, this is the size of the largest network datagram that can be sent on the interface."

::= { ifEntry 4 }

ifSpeed OBJECT-TYPE

SYNTAX Gauge
ACCESS read-only
STATUS mandatory
DESCRIPTION

"An estimate of the interface's current bandwidth in bits per second. For interfaces which do not vary in bandwidth or for those where no accurate estimation can be made, this object should contain the nominal bandwidth."

::= { ifEntry 5 }

ifPhysAddress OBJECT-TYPE

SYNTAX PhysAddress
ACCESS read-only
STATUS mandatory
DESCRIPTION

"The interface's address at the protocol layer immediately 'below' the network layer in the protocol stack. For interfaces which do not have such an address (e.g., a serial line), this object should contain an octet string of zero length."

::= { ifEntry 6 }

ifAdminStatus OBJECT-TYPE

SYNTAX INTEGER {
                up(1),   —ready to pass packets
                down(2),
                testing(3)   —in some test mode
        }
ACCESS read-write
STATUS mandatory
DESCRIPTION

"The desired state of the interface. The testing(3) state indicates that no operational packets can be passed."

::= { ifEntry 7 }

ifOperStatus OBJECT-TYPE

SYNTAX   INTEGER {
           up(1),   —ready to pass packets
           down(2),
           testing(3) —in some test mode
    }
ACCESS   read-only
STATUS   mandatory
DESCRIPTION

    "The current operational state of the interface. The testing(3) state indicates that no operational packets can be passed."

::= { ifEntry 8 }

ifLastChange OBJECT-TYPE

SYNTAX   TimeTicks
ACCESS   read-only
STATUS   mandatory
DESCRIPTION

    "The value of sysUpTime at the time the interface entered its current operational state. If the current state was entered prior to the last re-initialization of the local network management subsystem, then this object contains a zero value."

::= { ifEntry 9 }

ifInOctets OBJECT-TYPE

SYNTAX   Counter
ACCESS   read-only
STATUS   mandatory
DESCRIPTION

    "The total number of octets received on the interface, including framing characters."

::= { ifEntry 10 }

ifInUcastPkts OBJECT-TYPE

SYNTAX   Counter
ACCESS   read-only
STATUS   mandatory
DESCRIPTION

> "The number of subnetwork-unicast packets delivered to a higher-layer protocol."

::= { ifEntry 11 }

ifInNUcastPkts OBJECT-TYPE

SYNTAX   Counter
ACCESS   read-only
STATUS   mandatory
DESCRIPTION

> "The number of non-unicast (i.e., subnetwork-broadcast or subnetwork-multicast) packets delivered to a higher-layer protocol."

::= { ifEntry 12 }

ifInDiscards OBJECT-TYPE

SYNTAX   Counter
ACCESS   read-only
STATUS   mandatory
DESCRIPTION

> "The number of inbound packets which were chosen to be discarded even though no errors had been detected to prevent their being deliverable to a higher-layer protocol. One possible reason for discarding such a packet could be to free up buffer space."

::= { ifEntry 13 }

ifInErrors OBJECT-TYPE

SYNTAX   Counter
ACCESS   read-only
STATUS   mandatory

DESCRIPTION

"The number of inbound packets that contained errors preventing them from being deliverable to a higher-layer protocol."

::= { ifEntry 14 }

ifInUnknownProtos OBJECT-TYPE

SYNTAX   Counter
ACCESS   read-only
STATUS   mandatory
DESCRIPTION

"The number of packets received via the interface which were discarded because of an unknown or unsupported protocol."

::= { ifEntry 15 }

ifOutOctets OBJECT-TYPE

SYNTAX   Counter
ACCESS   read-only
STATUS   mandatory
DESCRIPTION

"The total number of octets transmitted out of the interface, including framing characters."

::= { ifEntry 16 }

ifOutUcastPkts OBJECT-TYPE

SYNTAX   Counter
ACCESS   read-only
STATUS   mandatory
DESCRIPTION

"The total number of packets that higher-level protocols requested be transmitted to a subnetwork-unicast address, including those that were discarded or not sent."

::= { ifEntry 17 }

ifOutNUcastPkts OBJECT-TYPE

SYNTAX   Counter
ACCESS   read-only
STATUS   mandatory
DESCRIPTION

"The total number of packets that higher-level protocols requested be transmitted to a non-unicast (i.e., a subnetwork-broadcast or subnetwork-multicast) address, including those that were discarded or not sent."

::= { ifEntry 18 }

ifOutDiscards OBJECT-TYPE

SYNTAX   Counter
ACCESS   read-only
STATUS   mandatory
DESCRIPTION

"The number of outbound packets which were chosen to be discarded even though no errors had been detected to prevent their being transmitted. One possible reason for discarding such a packet could be to free up buffer space."

::= { ifEntry 19 }

ifOutErrors OBJECT-TYPE

SYNTAX   Counter
ACCESS   read-only
STATUS   mandatory
DESCRIPTION

"The number of outbound packets that could not be transmitted because of errors."

::= { ifEntry 20 }

ifOutQLen OBJECT-TYPE

SYNTAX   Gauge

```
ACCESS      read-only
STATUS      mandatory
DESCRIPTION
```
        "The length of the output packet queue (in packets)."
```
::= { ifEntry 21 }
```

ifSpecific OBJECT-TYPE

```
SYNTAX      OBJECT IDENTIFIER
ACCESS      read-only
STATUS      mandatory
DESCRIPTION
```
        "A reference to MIB definitions specific to the particular media being used to realize the interface. For example, if the interface is realized by an ethernet, then the value of this object refers to a document defining objects specific to ethernet. If this information is not present, its value should be set to the OBJECT IDENTIFIER { 0 0 }, which is a syntatically valid object identifier, and any conformant implementation of ASN.1 and BER must be able to generate and recognize this value."
```
::= { ifEntry 22 }
```

ADDRESS TRANSLATION GROUP

Implementation of the Address Translation group is mandatory for all systems. Note however that this group is deprecated by MIB-II. That is, it is being included solely for compatibility with MIB-I nodes, and will most likely be excluded from MIB-III nodes. From MIB-II an onwards, each network protocol group contains its own address translation tables.

The Address Translation group contains one table which is the union across all interfaces of the translation tables for converting a NetworkAddress (e.g., an IP address) into a subnetwork-specific address. For lack of a better term, this document refers to such a subnetwork-specific address as a 'physical' address.

Examples of such translation tables are: for broadcast media where ARP is in use, the translation table is equivalent to the ARP cache; or, on an X.25 network where non-algorithmic translation to X.121 addresses is required, the translation table contains the NetworkAddress to X.121 address equivalences.

atTable OBJECT-TYPE

SYNTAX   SEQUENCE OF AtEntry
ACCESS   not-accessible
STATUS   deprecated
DESCRIPTION

"The Address Translation tables contain the NetworkAddress to 'physical' address equivalences. Some interfaces do not use translation tables for determining address equivalences (e.g., DDN-X.25 has an algorithmic method); if all interfaces are of this type, then the Address Translation table is empty, i.e., has zero entries."

::= { at 1 }

atEntry OBJECT-TYPE

SYNTAX   AtEntry
ACCESS   not-accessible
STATUS   deprecated
DESCRIPTION

"Each entry contains one NetworkAddress to 'physical' address equivalence."

INDEX   { atIfIndex,
                atNetAddress }
::= { atTable 1 }
AtEntry ::=
    SEQUENCE {
        atIfIndex
            INTEGER,

        atPhysAddress
            PhysAddress,
        atNetAddress
            NetworkAddress
    }

atIfIndex OBJECT-TYPE

SYNTAX   INTEGER
ACCESS   read-write
STATUS   deprecated
DESCRIPTION

"The interface on which this entry's equivalence is effective. The interface identified by a particular value of this index is the same interface as identified by the same value of ifIndex."

::= { atEntry 1 }

atPhysAddress OBJECT-TYPE

SYNTAX   PhysAddress
ACCESS   read-write
STATUS   deprecated
DESCRIPTION

"The media-dependent 'physical' address. Setting this object to a null string (one of zero length) has the effect of invaliding the corresponding entry in the atTable object. That is, it effectively dissasociates the interface identified with said entry from the mapping identified with said entry. It is an implementation-specific matter as to whether the agent removes an invalidated entry from the table. Accordingly, management stations must be prepared to receive tabular information from agents that corresponds to entries not currently in use. Proper interpretation of such entries requires examination of the relevant atPhysAddress object."

::= { atEntry 2 }

atNetAddress OBJECT-TYPE

SYNTAX   NetworkAddress
ACCESS   read-write
STATUS   deprecated
DESCRIPTION

"The NetworkAddress (e.g., the IP address) corresponding to the media-dependent 'physical' address."
::= { atEntry 3 }

IP GROUP

Implementation of the IP group is mandatory for all systems.

ipForwarding OBJECT-TYPE

SYNTAX   INTEGER {
        forwarding(1),   —acting as a gateway
        not-forwarding(2) —NOT acting as a gateway
          }
ACCESS   read-write
STATUS   mandatory
DESCRIPTION

"The indication of whether this entity is acting as an IP gateway in respect to the forwarding of datagrams received by, but not addressed to, this entity. IP gateways forward datagrams. IP hosts do not (except those source-routed via the host).

Note that for some managed nodes, this object may take on only a subset of the values possible. Accordingly, it is appropriate for an agent to return a 'badValue' response if a management station attempts to change this object to an inappropriate value."
::= { ip 1 }

ipDefaultTTL OBJECT-TYPE

SYNTAX   INTEGER
ACCESS   read-write
STATUS   mandatory
DESCRIPTION

"The default value inserted into the Time-To-Live field of the IP header of datagrams originated at this entity, whenever a TTL value is not supplied by the transport layer protocol."

::= { ip 2 }

ipInReceives OBJECT-TYPE

SYNTAX   Counter
ACCESS   read-only
STATUS   mandatory
DESCRIPTION

"The total number of input datagrams received from interfaces, including those received in error."

::= { ip 3 }

ipInHdrErrors OBJECT-TYPE

SYNTAX   Counter
ACCESS   read-only
STATUS   mandatory
DESCRIPTION

"The number of input datagrams discarded due to errors in their IP headers, including bad checksums, version number mismatch, other format errors, time-to-live exceeded, errors discovered in processing their IP options, etc."

::= { ip 4 }

ipInAddrErrors OBJECT-TYPE

SYNTAX   Counter
ACCESS   read-only
STATUS   mandatory
DESCRIPTION

"The number of input datagrams discarded because the IP address in their IP header's destination field was not a valid address to be received at this entity. This count includes invalid addresses (e.g., 0.0.0.0) and addresses of unsupported Classes (e.g., Class E). For entities which are not IP Gateways and therefore do not forward datagrams, this counter includes datagrams discarded because the destination address was not a local address."

::= { ip 5 }

ipForwDatagrams OBJECT-TYPE

SYNTAX   Counter
ACCESS   read-only
STATUS   mandatory
DESCRIPTION

"The number of input datagrams for which this entity was not their final IP destination, as a result of which an attempt was made to find a route to forward them to that final destination. In entities which do not act as IP Gateways, this counter will include only those packets which were Source-Routed via this entity, and the Source-Route option processing was successful."

::= { ip 6 }

ipInUnknownProtos OBJECT-TYPE

SYNTAX   Counter
ACCESS   read-only
STATUS   mandatory
DESCRIPTION

"The number of locally-addressed datagrams received successfully but discarded because of an unknown or unsupported protocol."

::= { ip 7 }

ipInDiscards OBJECT-TYPE

SYNTAX   Counter
ACCESS   read-only
STATUS   mandatory
DESCRIPTION

"The number of input IP datagrams for which no problems were encountered to prevent their continued processing, but which were discarded (e.g., for lack of buffer space). Note that this counter does not include any datagrams discarded while awaiting re-assembly."

::= { ip 8 }

ipInDelivers OBJECT-TYPE

SYNTAX   Counter
ACCESS   read-only
STATUS   mandatory
DESCRIPTION

"The total number of input datagrams successfully delivered to IP user-protocols (including ICMP)."

::= { ip 9 }

ipOutRequests OBJECT-TYPE

SYNTAX   Count
ACCESS   read-only
STATUS   mandatory
DESCRIPTION

"The total number of IP datagrams which local IP user-protocols (including ICMP) supplied to IP in requests for transmission. Note that this counter does not include any datagrams counted in ipForw-Datagrams."

::= { ip 10 }

ipOutDiscards OBJECT-TYPE

SYNTAX   Counter
ACCESS   read-only
STATUS   mandatory
DESCRIPTION

"The number of output IP datagrams for which no problem was encountered to prevent their transmission to their destination, but which were discarded (e.g., for lack of buffer space). Note that this counter would include datagrams counted in ipForwDatagrams if any such packets met this (discretionary) discard criterion."

::= { ip 11 }

ipOutNoRoutes OBJECT-TYPE

SYNTAX   Counter
ACCESS   read-only
STATUS   mandatory
DESCRIPTION

"The number of IP datagrams discarded because no route could be found to transmit them to their destination. Note that this counter includes any packets counted in ipForwDatagrams which meet this 'no-route' criterion. Note that this includes any datagrams which a host cannot route because all of its default gateways are down."

::= { ip 12 }

ipReasmTimeout OBJECT-TYPE

SYNTAX   INTEGER
ACCESS   read-only
STATUS   mandatory
DESCRIPTION

"The maximum number of seconds which received fragments are held while they are awaiting reassembly at this entity."

::= { ip 13 }

ipReasmReqds OBJECT-TYPE

SYNTAX   Counter
ACCESS   read-only
STATUS   mandatory
DESCRIPTION

"The number of IP fragments received which needed to be reassembled at this entity."

::= { ip 14 }

ipReasmOKs OBJECT-TYPE

SYNTAX   Counter
ACCESS   read-only
STATUS   mandatory
DESCRIPTION

"The number of IP datagrams successfully re-assembled."

::= { ip 15 }

ipReasmFails OBJECT-TYPE

SYNTAX   Counter
ACCESS   read-only
STATUS   mandatory
DESCRIPTION

"The number of failures detected by the IP re-assembly algorithm (for whatever reason: timed out, errors, etc). Note that this is not necessarily a count of discarded IP fragments since some algorithms (notably the algorithm in RFC 815) can lose track of the number of fragments by combining them as they are received."

::= { ip 16 }

ipFragOKs OBJECT-TYPE

SYNTAX   Counter
ACCESS   read-only
STATUS   mandatory
DESCRIPTION

"The number of IP datagrams that have been successfully fragmented at this entity."

::= { ip 17 }

ipFragFails OBJECT-TYPE

SYNTAX   Counter
ACCESS   read-only

STATUS   mandatory
DESCRIPTION

> "The number of IP datagrams that have been discarded because they needed to be fragmented at this entity but could not be, e.g., because their Don't Fragment flag was set."

::= { ip 18 }

ipFragCreates OBJECT-TYPE

SYNTAX   Counter
ACCESS   read-only
STATUS   mandatory
DESCRIPTION

> "The number of IP datagram fragments that have been generated as a result of fragmentation at this entity."

::= { ip 19 }

The IP address table

The IP address table contains this entity's IP addressing information.

ipAddrTable OBJECT-TYPE

SYNTAX   SEQUENCE OF IpAddrEntry
ACCESS   not-accessible
STATUS   mandatory
DESCRIPTION

> "The table of addressing information relevant to this entity's IP addresses."

::= { ip 20 }

ipAddrEntry OBJECT-TYPE

SYNTAX   IpAddrEntry
ACCESS   not-accessible
STATUS   mandatory
DESCRIPTION

"The addressing information for one of this entity's IP addresses."

INDEX { ipAdEntAddr }

::= { ipAddrTable 1 }

IpAddrEntry ::=

SEQUENCE {
    ipAdEntAddr
        IpAddress,
    ipAdEntIfIndex
        INTEGER,
    ipAdEntNetMask
        IpAddress,
    ipAdEntBcastAddr
        INTEGER,
    ipAdEntReasmMaxSize
        INTEGER (0..65535)
}

ipAdEntAddr OBJECT-TYPE

SYNTAX   IpAddress
ACCESS   read-only
STATUS   mandatory
DESCRIPTION

"The IP address to which this entry's addressing information pertains."

::= { ipAddrEntry 1 }

ipAdEntIfIndex OBJECT-TYPE

SYNTAX   INTEGER
ACCESS   read-only
STATUS   mandatory
DESCRIPTION

"The index value which uniquely identifies the interface to which this entry is applicable. The interface identified by a particular value of this index is the same interface as identified by the same value of ifIndex."

::= { ipAddrEntry 2 }

ipAdEntNetMask OBJECT-TYPE

SYNTAX   IpAddress
ACCESS   read-only
STATUS   mandatory
DESCRIPTION

"The subnet mask associated with the IP address of this entry. The value of the mask is an IP address with all the network bits set to 1 and all the hosts bits set to 0."

::= { ipAddrEntry 3 }

ipAdEntBcastAddr OBJECT-TYPE

SYNTAX   INTEGER
ACCESS   read-only
STATUS   mandatory
DESCRIPTION

The value of the least-significant bit in the IP Broadcast address used for sending datagrams on the (logical) interface associated with the IP address of this entry. For example, when the Internet standard all-ones broadcast address is used, the value will be 1. This value applies to both the subnet and network broadcasts addresses used by the entity on this (logical) interface."

::= { ipAddrEntry 4 }

ipAdEntReasmMaxSize OBJECT-TYPE

SYNTAX   INTEGER (0..65535)
ACCESS   read-only
STATUS   mandatory
DESCRIPTION

The size of the largest IP datagram which this entity can re-assemble from incoming IP fragmented datagrams received on this interface."

::= { ipAddrEntry 5 }

The IP routing table

The IP routing table contains an entry for each route presently known to this entity.

ipRouteTable OBJECT-TYPE

    SYNTAX   SEQUENCE OF IpRouteEntry
    ACCESS   not-accessible
    STATUS   mandatory
    DESCRIPTION
        "This entity's IP Routing table."
    ::= { ip 21 }

ipRouteEntry OBJECT-TYPE

    SYNTAX   IpRouteEntry
    ACCESS   not-accessible
    STATUS   mandatory
    DESCRIPTION
        "A route to a particular destination."
    INDEX { ipRouteDest }
    ::= { ipRouteTable 1 }

IpRouteEntry ::=

    SEQUENCE {
        ipRouteDest
            IpAddress,
        ipRouteIfIndex
            INTEGER,
        ipRouteMetric1
            INTEGER,
        ipRouteMetric2
            INTEGER,
        ipRouteMetric3
            INTEGER,
        ipRouteMetric4
            INTEGER,

```
            ipRouteNextHop
                IpAddress,
            ipRouteType
                INTEGER,
            ipRouteProto
                INTEGER,
            ipRouteAge
                INTEGER,
            ipRouteMask
                IpAddress,
            ipRouteMetric5
                INTEGER,
            ipRouteInfo
                OBJECT IDENTIFIER
    }
```

ipRouteDest OBJECT-TYPE

SYNTAX   IpAddress
ACCESS   read-write
STATUS   mandatory
DESCRIPTION

"The destination IP address of this route. An entry with a value of 0.0.0.0 is considered a default route. Multiple routes to a single destination can appear in the table, but access to such multiple entries is dependent on the table-access mechanisms defined by the network management protocol in use."

::= { ipRouteEntry 1 }

ipRouteIfIndex OBJECT-TYPE

SYNTAX   INTEGER
ACCESS   read-write
STATUS   mandatory
DESCRIPTION

"The index value which uniquely identifies the local interface through which the next hop of this route should be reached. The interface identified by a particular value of this index is the same interface as identified by the same value of ifIndex."

::= { ipRouteEntry 2 }

ipRouteMetric1 OBJECT-TYPE

SYNTAX   INTEGER
ACCESS   read-write
STATUS   mandatory
DESCRIPTION

"The primary routing metric for this route. The semantics of this metric are determined by the routing-protocol specified in the route's ipRouteProto value. If this metric is not used, its value should be set to -1."

::= { ipRouteEntry 3 }

ipRouteMetric2 OBJECT-TYPE

SYNTAX   INTEGER
ACCESS   read-write
STATUS   mandatory
DESCRIPTION

"An alternate routing metric for this route. The semantics of this metric are determined by the routing-protocol specified in the route's ipRouteProto value. If this metric is not used, its value should be set to -1."

::= { ipRouteEntry 4 }

ipRouteMetric3 OBJECT-TYPE

SYNTAX   INTEGER
ACCESS   read-write
STATUS   mandatory
DESCRIPTION

"An alternate routing metric for this route. The semantics of this metric are determined by the

routing-protocol specified in the route's ipRouteProto value. If this metric is not used, its value should
be set to -1."

::= { ipRouteEntry 5 }

ipRouteMetric4 OBJECT-TYPE

SYNTAX   INTEGER
ACCESS   read-write
STATUS   mandatory
DESCRIPTION

"An alternate routing metric for this route. The semantics of this metric are determined by the routing-
protocol specified in the route's ipRouteProto value. If
this metric is not used, its value should be set to -1."

::= { ipRouteEntry 6 }

ipRouteNextHop OBJECT-TYPE

SYNTAX   IpAddress
ACCESS   read-write
STATUS   mandatory
DESCRIPTION

"The IP address of the next hop of this route. (In the
case of a route bound to an interface which is real-
ized via a broadcast media, the value of this field is
the agent's IP address on that interface.)"

::= { ipRouteEntry 7 }

ipRouteType OBJECT-TYPE

SYNTAX   INTEGER {
    other(1),   none of the following
    invalid(2), an invalidated route
    direct(3),   route to directly
            connected (sub-)network
    indirect(4) route to a non-local
            host/network/sub-network

}
ACCESS   read-write
STATUS   mandatory
DESCRIPTION

"The type of route. Note that the values direct(3) and indirect(4) refer to the notion of direct and indirect routing in the IP architecture.

Setting this object to the value invalid(2) has the effect of invalidating the corresponding entry in the ipRouteTable object. That is, it effectively disassociates the destination identified with said entry from the route identified with said entry. It is an implementation-specific matter as to whether the agent removes an invalidated entry from the table. Accordingly, management stations must be prepared to receive tabular information from agents that corresponds to entries not currently in use. Proper interpretation of such entries requires examination of the relevant ipRouteType object."

::= { ipRouteEntry 8 }

ipRouteProto OBJECT-TYPE

SYNTAX   INTEGER {

other(1),	none of the following
local(2),	non-protocol information, e.g., manually configured entries
netmgmt(3),	set via a network management protocol
icmp(4),	obtained via ICMP, e.g., Redirect the remaining values are all gateway routing protocols
egp(5), ggp(6), hello(7),	

rip(8),
is-is(9),
es-is(10),
ciscoIgrp(11),
bbnSpfIgp(12),
ospf(13),
bgp(14)

}

ACCESS   read-only
STATUS   mandatory
DESCRIPTION

"The routing mechanism via which this route was learned. Inclusion of values for gateway routing protocols is not intended to imply that hosts should support those protocols."

::= { ipRouteEntry 9 }

ipRouteAge OBJECT-TYPE

SYNTAX   INTEGER
ACCESS   read-write
STATUS   mandatory
DESCRIPTION

"The number of seconds since this route was last updated or otherwise determined to be correct. Note that no semantics of 'too old' can be implied except through knowledge of the routing protocol by which the route was learned."

::= { ipRouteEntry 10 }

ipRouteMask OBJECT-TYPE

SYNTAX   IpAddress
ACCESS   read-write
STATUS   mandatory
DESCRIPTION

"Indicate the mask to be logical-ANDed with the destination address before being compared to the value in the ipRouteDest field. For those systems that do not support arbitrary subnet masks, an agent constructs the value of the ipRouteMask by determining whether the value of the correspondent ipRouteDest field belong to a class-A, B, or C network, and then using one of:

mask	network
255.0.0.0	class-A
255.255.0.0	class-B
255.255.255.0	class-C

If the value of the ipRouteDest is 0.0.0.0 (a default route), then the mask value is also 0.0.0.0. It should be noted that all IP routing subsystems implicitly use this mechanism."

::= { ipRouteEntry 11 }

ipRouteMetric5 OBJECT-TYPE

SYNTAX   INTEGER
ACCESS   read-write
STATUS   mandatory
DESCRIPTION

"An alternate routing metric for this route. The semantics of this metric are determined by the routing-protocol specified in the route's ipRouteProto value. If this metric is not used, its value should be set to -1."

::= { ipRouteEntry 12 }

ipRouteInfo OBJECT-TYPE

SYNTAX   OBJECT IDENTIFIER
ACCESS   read-only
STATUS   mandatory
DESCRIPTION

"A reference to MIB definitions specific to the particular routing protocol which is responsible for this route, as determined by the value specified in the route's ipRouteProto value. If this information is not present, its value should be set to the OBJECT IDENTIFIER { 0 0 }, which is a syntatically valid object identifier, and any conformant implementation of ASN.1 and BER must be able to generate and recognize this value."

::= { ipRouteEntry 13 }

The IP Address Translation table

The IP address translation table contain the IpAddress to 'physical' address equivalences. Some interfaces do not use translation tables for determining address equivalences (e.g., DDN-X.25 has an algorithmic method); if all interfaces are of this type, then the Address Translation table is empty, i.e., has zero entries.

ipNetToMediaTable OBJECT-TYPE

SYNTAX   SEQUENCE OF IpNetToMediaEntry
ACCESS   not-accessible
STATUS   mandatory
DESCRIPTION

> "The IP Address Translation table used for mapping from IP addresses to physical addresses."

::= { ip 22 }

ipNetToMediaEntry OBJECT-TYPE

SYNTAX   IpNetToMediaEntry
ACCESS   not-accessible
STATUS   mandatory
DESCRIPTION

> "Each entry contains one IpAddress to 'physical' address equivalence."

INDEX   { ipNetToMediaIfIndex,
              ipNetToMediaNetAddress }
::= { ipNetToMediaTable 1 }

ipNetToMediaEntry ::=

> SEQUENCE {
>> ipNetToMediaIfIndex
>>> INTEGER,
>> ipNetToMediaPhysAddress
>>> PhysAddress,
>> ipNetToMediaNetAddress
>>> IpAddress,
>> ipNetToMediaType
>>> INTEGER
> }

ipNetToMediaIfIndex OBJECT-TYPE

> SYNTAX   INTEGER
> ACCESS   read-write
> STATUS   mandatory
> DESCRIPTION
>> "The interface on which this entry's equivalence is effective. The interface identified by a particular value of this index is the same interface as identified by the same value of ifIndex."
> ::= { ipNetToMediaEntry 1 }

ipNetToMediaPhysAddress OBJECT-TYPE

> SYNTAX   PhysAddress
> ACCESS   read-write
> STATUS   mandatory
> DESCRIPTION
>> "The media-dependent 'physical' address."
> ::= { ipNetToMediaEntry 2 }

ipNetToMediaNetAddress OBJECT-TYPE

> SYNTAX   IpAddress
> ACCESS   read-write
> STATUS   mandatory
> DESCRIPTION

"The IpAddress corresponding to the media- dependent 'physical' address."

::= { ipNetToMediaEntry 3 }

ipNetToMediaType OBJECT-TYPE

SYNTAX   INTEGER {
          other(1),   none of the following
          invalid(2),   an invalidated mapping
          dynamic(3),
          static(4)
     }

ACCESS   read-write
STATUS   mandatory
DESCRIPTION

"The type of mapping.

Setting this object to the value invalid(2) has the effect of invalidating the corresponding entry in the ipNetToMediaTable. That is, it effectively dissasociates the interface identified with said entry from the mapping identified with said entry. It is an implementation-specific matter as to whether the agent removes an invalidated entry from the table. Accordingly, management stations must be prepared to receive tabular information from agents that corresponds to entries not currently in use. Proper interpretation of such entries requires examination of the relevant ipNetToMediaType object."

::= { ipNetToMediaEntry 4 }

Additional IP objects

ipRoutingDiscards OBJECT-TYPE

SYNTAX   Counter
ACCESS   read-only
STATUS   mandatory
DESCRIPTION

"The number of routing entries which were chosen to be discarded even though they are valid. One pos-

> sible reason for discarding such an entry could be to free-up buffer space for other routing entries."

::= { ip 23 }

ICMP GROUP

Implementation of the ICMP group is mandatory for all systems.

icmpInMsgs OBJECT-TYPE

SYNTAX   Counter
ACCESS   read-only
STATUS   mandatory
DESCRIPTION

> "The total number of ICMP messages which the entity received. Note that this counter includes all those counted by icmpInErrors."

::= { icmp 1 }

icmpInErrors OBJECT-TYPE

SYNTAX   Counter
ACCESS   read-only
STATUS   mandatory
DESCRIPTION

> "The number of ICMP messages which the entity received but determined as having ICMP-specific errors (bad ICMP checksums, bad length, etc.)."

::= { icmp 2 }

icmpInDestUnreachs OBJECT-TYPE

SYNTAX   Counter
ACCESS   read-only
STATUS   mandatory
DESCRIPTION

> "The number of ICMP Destination Unreachable messages received."

::= { icmp 3 }

icmpInTimeExcds OBJECT-TYPE

SYNTAX   Counter
ACCESS   read-only
STATUS   mandatory
DESCRIPTION

"The number of ICMP Time Exceeded messages received."

::= { icmp 4 }

icmpInParmProbs OBJECT-TYPE

SYNTAX   Counter
ACCESS   read-only
STATUS   mandatory
DESCRIPTION

"The number of ICMP Parameter Problem messages received."

::= { icmp 5 }

icmpInSrcQuenchs OBJECT-TYPE

SYNTAX   Counter
ACCESS   read-only
STATUS   mandatory
DESCRIPTION

"The number of ICMP Source Quench messages received."

::= { icmp 6 }

icmpInRedirects OBJECT-TYPE

SYNTAX   Counter
ACCESS   read-only
STATUS   mandatory
DESCRIPTION

"The number of ICMP Redirect messages received."

::= { icmp 7 }

icmpInEchos OBJECT-TYPE

SYNTAX   Counter
ACCESS   read-only
STATUS   mandatory
DESCRIPTION

> "The number of ICMP Echo (request) messages received."

::= { icmp 8 }

icmpInEchoReps OBJECT-TYPE

SYNTAX   Counter
ACCESS   read-only
STATUS   mandatory
DESCRIPTION

> "The number of ICMP Echo Reply messages received."

::= { icmp 9 }

icmpInTimestamps OBJECT-TYPE

SYNTAX   Counter
ACCESS   read-only
STATUS   mandatory
DESCRIPTION

> "The number of ICMP Timestamp (request) messages received."

::= { icmp 10 }

icmpInTimestampReps OBJECT-TYPE

SYNTAX   Counter
ACCESS   read-only
STATUS   mandatory
DESCRIPTION2

> "The number of ICMP Timestamp Reply messages received."

::= { icmp 11 }

icmpInAddrMasks OBJECT-TYPE

SYNTAX   Counter
ACCESS   read-only
STATUS   mandatory
DESCRIPTION

"The number of ICMP Address Mask Request messages received."

::= { icmp 12 }

icmpInAddrMaskReps OBJECT-TYPE

SYNTAX   Counter
ACCESS   read-only
STATUS   mandatory
DESCRIPTION

"The number of ICMP Address Mask Reply messages received."

::= { icmp 13 }

icmpOutMsgs OBJECT-TYPE

SYNTAX   Counter
ACCESS   read-only
STATUS   mandatory
DESCRIPTION

"The total number of ICMP messages which this entity attempted to send. Note that this counter includes all those counted by icmpOutErrors."

::= { icmp 14 }

icmpOutErrors OBJECT-TYPE

SYNTAX   Counter
ACCESS   read-only
STATUS   mandatory
DESCRIPTION

"The number of ICMP messages which this entity did not send due to problems discovered within

ICMP such as a lack of buffers. This value should not include errors discovered outside the ICMP layer such as the inability of IP to route the resultant datagram. In some implementations there may be no types of error which contribute to this counter's value."

::= { icmp 15 }

icmpOutDestUnreachs OBJECT-TYPE

SYNTAX   Counter
ACCESS   read-only
STATUS   mandatory
DESCRIPTION

"The number of ICMP Destination Unreachable messages sent."

::= { icmp 16 }

icmpOutTimeExcds OBJECT-TYPE

SYNTAX   Counter
ACCESS   read-only
STATUS   mandatory
DESCRIPTION

"The number of ICMP Time Exceeded messages sent."

::= { icmp 17 }

icmpOutParmProbs OBJECT-TYPE

SYNTAX   Counter
ACCESS   read-only
STATUS   mandatory
DESCRIPTION

"The number of ICMP Parameter Problem messages sent."

::= { icmp 18 }

icmpOutSrcQuenchs OBJECT-TYPE

SYNTAX   Counter
ACCESS   read-only
STATUS   mandatory
DESCRIPTION

"The number of ICMP Source Quench messages sent."

::= { icmp 19 }

icmpOutRedirects OBJECT-TYPE

SYNTAX   Counter
ACCESS   read-only
STATUS   mandatory
DESCRIPTION

"The number of ICMP Redirect messages sent. For a host, this object will always be zero, since hosts do not send redirects."

::= { icmp 20 }

icmpOutEchos OBJECT-TYPE

SYNTAX   Counter
ACCESS   read-only
STATUS   mandatory
DESCRIPTION

"The number of ICMP Echo (request) messages sent."

::= { icmp 21 }

icmpOutEchoReps OBJECT-TYPE

SYNTAX   Counter
ACCESS   read-only
STATUS   mandatory
DESCRIPTION

"The number of ICMP Echo Reply messages sent."

::= { icmp 22 }

icmpOutTimestamps OBJECT-TYPE

SYNTAX   Counter
ACCESS   read-only
STATUS   mandatory
DESCRIPTION

> "The number of ICMP Timestamp (request) messages sent."

::= { icmp 23 }

icmpOutTimestampReps OBJECT-TYPE

SYNTAX   Counter
ACCESS   read-only
STATUS   mandatory
DESCRIPTION

> "The number of ICMP Timestamp Reply messages sent."

::= { icmp 24 }

icmpOutAddrMasks OBJECT-TYPE

SYNTAX   Counter
ACCESS   read-only
STATUS   mandatory
DESCRIPTION

> "The number of ICMP Address Mask Request messages sent."

::= { icmp 25 }

icmpOutAddrMaskReps OBJECT-TYPE

SYNTAX   Counter
ACCESS   read-only
STATUS   mandatory
DESCRIPTION

> "The number of ICMP Address Mask Reply messages sent."

::= { icmp 26 }

TCP GROUP

Implementation of the TCP group is mandatory for all systems that implement the TCP.

Note that instances of object types that represent information about a particular TCP connection are transient; they persist only as long as the connection in question.

tcpRtoAlgorithm OBJECT-TYPE

SYNTAX   INTEGER {

other(1),	none of the following
constant(2),	a constant rto
rsre(3),	MIL-STD-1778, Appendix B
vanj(4)	Van Jacobson's algorithm [10]

}
ACCESS   read-only
STATUS   mandatory
DESCRIPTION

"The algorithm used to determine the timeout value used for retransmitting unacknowledged octets."

::= { tcp 1 }

tcpRtoMin OBJECT-TYPE

SYNTAX   INTEGER
ACCESS   read-only
STATUS   mandatory
DESCRIPTION

"The minimum value permitted by a TCP implementation for the retransmission timeout, measured in milliseconds. More refined semantics for objects of this type depend upon the algorithm used to determine the retransmission timeout. In particular, when the timeout algorithm is rsre(3), an object of this type has the semantics of the LBOUND quantity described in RFC 793."

::= { tcp 2 }

tcpRtoMax OBJECT-TYPE

SYNTAX   INTEGER
ACCESS   read-only
STATUS   mandatory
DESCRIPTION

"The maximum value permitted by a TCP implementation for the retransmission timeout, measured in milliseconds. More refined semantics for objects of this type depend upon the algorithm used to determine the retransmission timeout. In particular, when the timeout algorithm is rsre(3), an object of this type has the semantics of the UBOUND quantity described in RFC 793."

::= { tcp 3 }

tcpMaxConn OBJECT-TYPE

SYNTAX   INTEGER
ACCESS   read-only
STATUS   mandatory
DESCRIPTION

"The limit on the total number of TCP connections the entity can support. In entities where the maximum number of connections is dynamic, this object should contain the value -1."

::= { tcp 4 }

tcpActiveOpens OBJECT-TYPE

SYNTAX   Counter
ACCESS   read-only
STATUS   mandatory
DESCRIPTION

"The number of times TCP connections have made a direct transition to the SYN-SENT state from the CLOSED state."

::= { tcp 5 }

tcpPassiveOpens OBJECT-TYPE

SYNTAX   Counter
ACCESS   read-only
STATUS   mandatory
DESCRIPTION

"The number of times TCP connections have made a direct transition to the SYN-RCVD state from the LISTEN state."

::= { tcp 6 }

tcpAttemptFails OBJECT-TYPE

SYNTAX   Counter
ACCESS   read-only
STATUS   mandatory
DESCRIPTION

"The number of times TCP connections have made a direct transition to the CLOSED state from either the SYN-SENT state or the SYN-RCVD state, plus the number of times TCP connections have made a direct transition to the LISTEN state from the SYN-RCVD state."

::= { tcp 7 }

tcpEstabResets OBJECT-TYPE

SYNTAX   Counter
ACCESS   read-only
STATUS   mandatory
DESCRIPTION

"The number of times TCP connections have made a direct transition to the CLOSED state from either the ESTABLISHED state or the CLOSE-WAIT state."

::= { tcp 8 }

tcpCurrEstab OBJECT-TYPE

SYNTAX   Gauge
ACCESS   read-only
STATUS   mandatory
DESCRIPTION

> "The number of TCP connections for which the current state is either ESTABLISHED or CLOSE-WAIT."

::= { tcp 9 }

tcpInSegs OBJECT-TYPE

SYNTAX   Counter
ACCESS   read-only
STATUS   mandatory
DESCRIPTION

> "The total number of segments received, including those received in error. This count includes segments received on currently established connections."

::= { tcp 10 }

tcpOutSegs OBJECT-TYPE

SYNTAX   Counter
ACCESS   read-only
STATUS   mandatory
DESCRIPTION

> "The total number of segments sent, including those on current connections but excluding those containing only retransmitted octets."

::= { tcp 11 }

tcpRetransSegs OBJECT-TYPE

SYNTAX   Counter
ACCESS   read-only
STATUS   mandatory
DESCRIPTION

> "The total number of segments retransmitted—that is, the number of TCP segments transmitted

containing one or more previously transmitted octets."

::= { tcp 12 }

The TCP Connection table

The TCP connection table contains information about this entity's existing TCP connections.

tcpConnTable OBJECT-TYPE

SYNTAX   SEQUENCE OF TcpConnEntry
ACCESS   not-accessible
STATUS   mandatory
DESCRIPTION

"A table containing TCP connection-specific information."

::= { tcp 13 }

tcpConnEntry OBJECT-TYPE

SYNTAX   TcpConnEntry
ACCESS   not-accessible
STATUS   mandatory
DESCRIPTION

"Information about a particular current TCP connection. An object of this type is transient, in that it ceases to exist when (or soon after) the connection makes the transition to the CLOSED state."

INDEX { tcpConnLocalAddress,
    tcpConnLocalPort,
    tcpConnRemAddress,
    tcpConnRemPort }

::= { tcpConnTable 1 }

tcpConnEntry ::=

SEQUENCE {
    tcpConnState
        INTEGER,
    tcpConnLocalAddress

```
                            IpAddress,
             tcpConnLocalPort
                    INTEGER (0..65535),
             tcpConnRemAddress
                    IpAddress,
             tcpConnRemPort
                    INTEGER (0..65535)
      }
```

tcpConnState OBJECT-TYPE

```
SYNTAX      INTEGER {
                    closed(1),
                    listen(2),
                    synSent(3),
                    synReceived(4),
                    established(5),
                    finWait1(6),
                    finWait2(7),
                    closeWait(8),
                    lastAck(9),
                    closing(10),
                    timeWait(11),
                    deleteTCB(12)
            }
ACCESS      read-write
STATUS      mandatory
DESCRIPTION
```

"The state of this TCP connection.

The only value which may be set by a management station is deleteTCB(12). Accordingly, it is appropriate for an agent to return a 'badValue' response if a management station attempts to set this object to any other value.

If a management station sets this object to the value deleteTCB(12), then this has the effect of deleting the TCB (as defined in RFC 793) of the corresponding connection on the managed node, resulting in immediate termination of the connection.

As an implementation-specific option, a RST segment may be sent from the managed node to the other TCP endpoint (note however that RST segments are not sent reliably)."

::= { tcpConnEntry 1 }

tcpConnLocalAddress OBJECT-TYPE

SYNTAX   IpAddress
ACCESS   read-only
STATUS   mandatory
DESCRIPTION

"The local IP address for this TCP connection. In the case of a connection in the listen state which is willing to accept connections for any IP interface associated with the node, the value 0.0.0.0 is used."

::= { tcpConnEntry 2 }

tcpConnLocalPort OBJECT-TYPE

SYNTAX   INTEGER (0..65535)
ACCESS   read-only
STATUS   mandatory
DESCRIPTION

"The local port number for this TCP connection."

::= { tcpConnEntry 3 }

tcpConnRemAddress OBJECT-TYPE

SYNTAX   IpAddress
ACCESS   read-only
STATUS   mandatory
DESCRIPTION

"The remote IP address for this TCP connection."

::= { tcpConnEntry 4 }

tcpConnRemPort OBJECT-TYPE

SYNTAX   INTEGER (0..65535)
ACCESS   read-only

STATUS   mandatory
DESCRIPTION
            "The remote port number for this TCP connection."
::= { tcpConnEntry 5 }

Additional TCP objects:

tcpInErrs OBJECT-TYPE

SYNTAX   Counter
ACCESS   read-only
STATUS   mandatory
DESCRIPTION
            "The total number of segments received in error
            (e.g., bad TCP checksums)."
::= { tcp 14 }

tcpOutRsts OBJECT-TYPE

SYNTAX   Counter
ACCESS   read-only
STATUS   mandatory
DESCRIPTION
            "The number of TCP segments sent containing the
            RST flag."
::= { tcp 15 }

UDP GROUP

Implementation of the UDP group is mandatory for all systems
which implement the UDP.

udpInDatagrams OBJECT-TYPE

SYNTAX   Counter
ACCESS   read-only
STATUS   mandatory

DESCRIPTION
> "The total number of UDP datagrams delivered to UDP users."

::= { udp 1 }

udpNoPorts OBJECT-TYPE

SYNTAX Counter
ACCESS read-only
STATUS mandatory
DESCRIPTION
> "The total number of received UDP datagrams for which there was no application at the destination port."

::= { udp 2 }

udpInErrors OBJECT-TYPE

SYNTAX Counter
ACCESS read-only
STATUS mandatory
DESCRIPTION
> "The number of received UDP datagrams that could not be delivered for reasons other than the lack of an application at the destination port."

::= { udp 3 }

udpOutDatagrams OBJECT-TYPE

SYNTAX Counter
ACCESS read-only
STATUS mandatory
DESCRIPTION
> "The total number of UDP datagrams sent from this entity."

::= { udp 4 }

The UDP Listener table

The UDP listener table contains information about this entity's UDP end-points on which a local application is currently accepting datagrams.

udpTable OBJECT-TYPE

 SYNTAX SEQUENCE OF UdpEntry
 ACCESS not-accessible
 STATUS mandatory
 DESCRIPTION
   "A table containing UDP listener information."
 ::= { udp 5 }

udpEntry OBJECT-TYPE

 SYNTAX UdpEntry
 ACCESS not-accessible
 STATUS mandatory
 DESCRIPTION
   "Information about a particular current UDP listener."
 INDEX { udpLocalAddress, udpLocalPort }
 ::= { udpTable 1 }

UdpEntry ::=

 SEQUENCE {
 udpLocalAddress
 IpAddress,
 udpLocalPort
 INTEGER (0..65535)
 }

udpLocalAddress OBJECT-TYPE

 SYNTAX IpAddress
 ACCESS read-only
 STATUS mandatory
 DESCRIPTION

"The local IP address for this UDP listener. In the case of a UDP listener which is willing to accept datagrams for any IP interface associated with the node, the value 0.0.0.0 is used."

::= { udpEntry 1 }

udpLocalPort OBJECT-TYPE

SYNTAX   INTEGER (0..65535)
ACCESS   read-only
STATUS   mandatory
DESCRIPTION

"The local port number for this UDP listener."

::= { udpEntry 2 }

EGP GROUP

Implementation of the EGP group is mandatory for all systems which implement the EGP.

egpInMsgs OBJECT-TYPE

SYNTAX   Counter
ACCESS   read-only
STATUS   mandatory
DESCRIPTION

"The number of EGP messages received without error."

::= { egp 1 }

egpInErrors OBJECT-TYPE

SYNTAX   Counter
ACCESS   read-only
STATUS   mandatory
DESCRIPTION

"The number of EGP messages received that proved to be in error."

::= { egp 2 }

egpOutMsgs OBJECT-TYPE

SYNTAX   Counter
ACCESS   read-only
STATUS   mandatory
DESCRIPTION

"The total number of locally generated EGP messages."

::= { egp 3 }

egpOutErrors OBJECT-TYPE

SYNTAX   Counter
ACCESS   read-only
STATUS   mandatory
DESCRIPTION

"The number of locally generated EGP messages not sent due to resource limitations within an EGP entity."

::= { egp 4 }

The EGP Neighbor table

The EGP neighbor table contains information about this entity's EGP neighbors.

egpNeighTable OBJECT-TYPE

SYNTAX   SEQUENCE OF EgpNeighEntry
ACCESS   not-accessible
STATUS   mandatory
DESCRIPTION

"The EGP neighbor table."

::= { egp 5 }

egpNeighEntry OBJECT-TYPE

SYNTAX   EgpNeighEntry
ACCESS   not-accessible
STATUS   mandatory

DESCRIPTION
"Information about this entity's relationship with a particular EGP neighbor."
INDEX { egpNeighAddr }
::= { egpNeighTable 1 }

EgpNeighEntry ::=

SEQUENCE {
    egpNeighState
        INTEGER,
    egpNeighAddr
        IpAddress,
    egpNeighAs
        INTEGER,
    egpNeighInMsgs
        Counter,
    egpNeighInErrs
        Counter,
    egpNeighOutMsgs
        Counter,
    egpNeighOutErrs
        Counter,
    egpNeighInErrMsgs
        Counter,
    egpNeighOutErrMsgs
        Counter,
    egpNeighStateUps
        Counter,
    egpNeighStateDowns
        Counter,
    egpNeighIntervalHello
        INTEGER,
    egpNeighIntervalPoll
        INTEGER,
    egpNeighMode
        INTEGER,
    egpNeighEventTrigger
        INTEGER
}

egpNeighState OBJECT-TYPE

SYNTAX   INTEGER {
        idle(1),
        acquisition(2),
        down(3),
        up(4),
        cease(5)
}
ACCESS   read-only
STATUS   mandatory
DESCRIPTION

"The EGP state of the local system with respect to this entry's EGP neighbor. Each EGP state is represented by a value that is one greater than the numerical value associated with said state in RFC 904."

::= { egpNeighEntry 1 }

egpNeighAddr OBJECT-TYPE

SYNTAX   IpAddress
ACCESS   read-only
STATUS   mandatory
DESCRIPTION

"The IP address of this entry's EGP neighbor."

::= { egpNeighEntry 2 }

egpNeighAs OBJECT-TYPE

SYNTAX   INTEGER
ACCESS   read-only
STATUS   mandatory
DESCRIPTION

"The autonomous system of this EGP peer. Zero should be specified if the autonomous system number of the neighbor is not yet known."

::= { egpNeighEntry 3 }

egpNeighInMsgs OBJECT-TYPE

SYNTAX   Counter
ACCESS   read-only
STATUS   mandatory
DESCRIPTION

"The number of EGP messages received without error from this EGP peer."

::= { egpNeighEntry 4 }

egpNeighInErrs OBJECT-TYPE

SYNTAX   Counter
ACCESS   read-only
STATUS   mandatory
DESCRIPTION

"The number of EGP messages received from this EGP peer that proved to be in error (e.g., bad EGP checksum)."

::= { egpNeighEntry 5 }

egpNeighOutMsgs OBJECT-TYPE

SYNTAX   Counter
ACCESS   read-only
STATUS   mandatory
DESCRIPTION

"The number of locally generated EGP messages to this EGP peer."

::= { egpNeighEntry 6 }

egpNeighOutErrs OBJECT-TYPE

SYNTAX   Counter
ACCESS   read-only
STATUS   mandatory
DESCRIPTION

"The number of locally generated EGP messages not sent to this EGP peer due to resource limitations within an EGP entity."

::= { egpNeighEntry 7 }

egpNeighInErrMsgs OBJECT-TYPE

SYNTAX   Counter
ACCESS   read-only
STATUS   mandatory
DESCRIPTION

      "The number of EGP-defined error messages received from this EGP peer."

::= { egpNeighEntry 8 }

egpNeighOutErrMsgs OBJECT-TYPE

SYNTAX   Counter
ACCESS   read-only
STATUS   mandatory
DESCRIPTION

      "The number of EGP-defined error messages sent to this EGP peer."

::= { egpNeighEntry 9 }

egpNeighStateUps OBJECT-TYPE

SYNTAX   Counter
ACCESS   read-only
STATUS   mandatory
DESCRIPTION

      "The number of EGP state transitions to the UP state with this EGP peer."

::= { egpNeighEntry 10 }

egpNeighStateDowns OBJECT-TYPE

SYNTAX   Counter
ACCESS   read-only
STATUS   mandatory
DESCRIPTION

      "The number of EGP state transitions from the UP state to any other state with this EGP peer."

::= { egpNeighEntry 11 }

egpNeighIntervalHello OBJECT-TYPE

SYNTAX   INTEGER
ACCESS   read-only
STATUS   mandatory
DESCRIPTION

> "The interval between EGP Hello command retransmissions (in hundredths of a second). This represents the t1 timer as defined in RFC 904."

::= { egpNeighEntry 12 }

egpNeighIntervalPoll OBJECT-TYPE

SYNTAX   INTEGER
ACCESS   read-only
STATUS   mandatory
DESCRIPTION

> "The interval between EGP poll command retransmissions (in hundredths of a second). This represents the t3 timer as defined in RFC 904."

::= { egpNeighEntry 13 }

egpNeighMode OBJECT-TYPE

SYNTAX   INTEGER { active(1), passive(2) }
ACCESS   read-only
STATUS   mandatory
DESCRIPTION

> "The polling mode of this EGP entity, either passive or active."

::= { egpNeighEntry 14 }

egpNeighEventTrigger OBJECT-TYPE

SYNTAX   INTEGER { start(1), stop(2) }
ACCESS   read-write
STATUS   mandatory
DESCRIPTION

> "A control variable used to trigger operator-initiated Start and Stop events. When read, this variable

always returns the most recent value that egpNeigh-EventTrigger was set to. If it has not been set since the last initialization of the network management subsystem on the node, it returns a value of 'stop'.

When set, this variable causes a Start or Stop event on the specified neighbor, as specified on pages 8-10 of RFC 904. Briefly, a Start event causes an Idle peer to begin neighbor acquisition and a non-Idle peer to reinitiate neighbor acquisition. A stop event causes a non-Idle peer to return to the Idle state until a Start event occurs, either via egp-NeighEventTrigger or otherwise."

::= { egpNeighEntry 15 }

Additional EGP objects

egpAs OBJECT-TYPE

SYNTAX   INTEGER
ACCESS   read-only
STATUS   mandatory
DESCRIPTION

"The autonomous system number of this EGP entity."

::= { egp 6 }

TRANSMISSION GROUP

Based on the transmission media underlying each interface on a system, the corresponding portion of the Transmission group is mandatory for that system.

When Internet-standard definitions for managing transmission media are defined, the transmission group is used to provide a prefix for the names of those objects.

Typically, such definitions reside in the experimental portion of the MIB until they are "proven", then as a part of the Internet standardization process, the definitions are accordingly elevated and a new object identifier, under the transmission group is defined. By convention, the name assigned is:

type OBJECT IDENTIFIER ::= { transmission number }

where "type" is the symbolic value used for the media in the ifType column of the ifTable object, and "number" is the actual integer value corresponding to the symbol.

SNMP GROUP

Implementation of the SNMP group is mandatory for all systems which support an SNMP protocol entity. Some of the objects defined below will be zero-valued in those SNMP implementations that are optimized to support only those functions specific to either a management agent or a management station. In particular, it should be observed that the objects below refer to an SNMP entity, and there may be several SNMP entities residing on a managed node (e.g., if the node is hosting acting as a management station).

snmpInPkts OBJECT-TYPE

SYNTAX   Counter
ACCESS   read-only
STATUS   mandatory
DESCRIPTION

> "The total number of Messages delivered to the SNMP entity from the transport service."

::= { snmp 1 }

snmpOutPkts OBJECT-TYPE

SYNTAX   Counter
ACCESS   read-only
STATUS   mandatory
DESCRIPTION

> "The total number of SNMP Messages which were passed from the SNMP protocol entity to the transport service."

::= { snmp 2 }

snmpInBadVersions OBJECT-TYPE

SYNTAX   Counter
ACCESS   read-only
STATUS   mandatory
DESCRIPTION

> "The total number of SNMP Messages which were delivered to the SNMP protocol entity and were for an unsupported SNMP version."

::= { snmp 3 }

snmpInBadCommunityNames OBJECT-TYPE

SYNTAX   Counter
ACCESS   read-only
STATUS   mandatory
DESCRIPTION

> "The total number of SNMP Messages delivered to the SNMP protocol entity which used a SNMP community name not known to said entity."

::= { snmp 4 }

snmpInBadCommunityUses OBJECT-TYPE

SYNTAX   Counter
ACCESS   read-only
STATUS   mandatory
DESCRIPTION

> "The total number of SNMP Messages delivered to the SNMP protocol entity which represented an SNMP operation which was not allowed by the SNMP community named in the Message."

::= { snmp 5 }

snmpInASNParseErrs OBJECT-TYPE

SYNTAX   Counter
ACCESS   read-only
STATUS   mandatory

DESCRIPTION

"The total number of ASN.1 or BER errors encountered by the SNMP protocol entity when decoding received SNMP Messages."

::= { snmp 6 }

—{ snmp 7 } is not used

snmpInTooBigs OBJECT-TYPE

SYNTAX   Counter
ACCESS   read-only
STATUS   mandatory
DESCRIPTION

"The total number of SNMP PDUs which were delivered to the SNMP protocol entity and for which the value of the error-status field is 'tooBig'."

::= { snmp 8 }

snmpInNoSuchNames OBJECT-TYPE

SYNTAX   Counter
ACCESS   read-only
STATUS   mandatory
DESCRIPTION

"The total number of SNMP PDUs which were delivered to the SNMP protocol entity and for which the value of the error-status field is 'noSuchName'."

::= { snmp 9 }

snmpInBadValues OBJECT-TYPE

SYNTAX   Counter
ACCESS   read-only
STATUS   mandatory
DESCRIPTION

"The total number of SNMP PDUs which were delivered to the SNMP protocol entity and for which the value of the error-status field is 'badValue'."

::= { snmp 10 }

snmpInReadOnlys OBJECT-TYPE

SYNTAX   Counter
ACCESS   read-only
STATUS   mandatory
DESCRIPTION

"The total number valid SNMP PDUs which were
delivered to the SNMP protocol entity and for which
the value of the error-status field is 'readOnly'. It
should be noted that it is a protocol error to generate
an SNMP PDU which contains the value 'readOnly'
in the error-status field, as such this object is provided as a means of detecting incorrect implementations of the SNMP."

::= { snmp 11 }

snmpInGenErrs OBJECT-TYPE

SYNTAX   Counter
ACCESS   read-only
STATUS   mandatory
DESCRIPTION

"The total number of SNMP PDUs which were delivered to the SNMP protocol entity and for which the
value of the error-status field is 'genErr'."

::= { snmp 12 }

snmpInTotalReqVars OBJECT-TYPE

SYNTAX   Counter
ACCESS   read-only
STATUS   mandatory
DESCRIPTION

"The total number of MIB objects which have been
retrieved successfully by the SNMP protocol entity
as the result of receiving valid SNMP Get-Request
and Get-Next PDUs."

::= { snmp 13 }

snmpInTotalSetVars OBJECT-TYPE

SYNTAX   Counter
ACCESS   read-only
STATUS   mandatory
DESCRIPTION

"The total number of MIB objects which have been altered successfully by the SNMP protocol entity as the result of receiving valid SNMP Set-Request PDUs."

::= { snmp 14 }

snmpInGetRequests OBJECT-TYPE

SYNTAX   Counter
ACCESS   read-only
STATUS   mandatory
DESCRIPTION

"The total number of SNMP Get-Request PDUs which have been accepted and processed by the SNMP protocol entity."

::= { snmp 15 }

snmpInGetNexts OBJECT-TYPE

SYNTAX   Counter
ACCESS   read-only
STATUS   mandatory
DESCRIPTION

"The total number of SNMP Get-Next PDUs which have been accepted and processed by the SNMP protocol entity."

::= { snmp 16 }

snmpInSetRequests OBJECT-TYPE

SYNTAX   Counter
ACCESS   read-only
STATUS   mandatory

DESCRIPTION

"The total number of SNMP Set-Request PDUs which have been accepted and processed by the SNMP protocol entity."

::= { snmp 17 }

snmpInGetResponses OBJECT-TYPE

SYNTAX   Counter
ACCESS   read-only
STATUS   mandatory
DESCRIPTION

"The total number of SNMP Get-Response PDUs which have been accepted and processed by the SNMP protocol entity."

::= { snmp 18 }

snmpInTraps OBJECT-TYPE

SYNTAX   Counter
ACCESS   read-only
STATUS   mandatory
DESCRIPTION

"The total number of SNMP Trap PDUs which have been accepted and processed by the SNMP protocol entity."

::= { snmp 19 }

snmpOutTooBigs OBJECT-TYPE

SYNTAX   Counter
ACCESS   read-only
STATUS   mandatory
DESCRIPTION

"The total number of SNMP PDUs which were generated by the SNMP protocol entity and for which the value of the error-status field is 'tooBig.'"

::= { snmp 20 }

snmpOutNoSuchNames OBJECT-TYPE

SYNTAX   Counter
ACCESS   read-only
STATUS   mandatory
DESCRIPTION

"The total number of SNMP PDUs which were generated by the SNMP protocol entity and for which the value of the error-status is 'noSuchName'."

::= { snmp 21 }

snmpOutBadValues OBJECT-TYPE

SYNTAX   Counter
ACCESS   read-only
STATUS   mandatory
DESCRIPTION

"The total number of SNMP PDUs which were generated by the SNMP protocol entity and for which the value of the error-status field is 'badValue'."

::= { snmp 22 }
—{ snmp 23 } is not used

snmpOutGenErrs OBJECT-TYPE

SYNTAX   Counter
ACCESS   read-only
STATUS   mandatory
DESCRIPTION

"The total number of SNMP PDUs which were generated by the SNMP protocol entity and for which the value of the error-status field is 'genErr'."

::= { snmp 24 }

snmpOutGetRequests OBJECT-TYPE

SYNTAX   Counter
ACCESS   read-only
STATUS   mandatory

DESCRIPTION

"The total number of SNMP Get-Request PDUs
which have been generated by the SNMP protocol
entity."

::= { snmp 25 }

snmpOutGetNexts OBJECT-TYPE

SYNTAX   Counter
ACCESS   read-only
STATUS   mandatory
DESCRIPTION

"The total number of SNMP Get-Next PDUs which
have been generated by the SNMP protocol entity."

::= { snmp 26 }

snmpOutSetRequests OBJECT-TYPE

SYNTAX   Counter
ACCESS   read-only
STATUS   mandatory
DESCRIPTION

The total number of SNMP Set-Request PDUs
which have been generated by the SNMP protocol
entity."

::= { snmp 27 }

snmpOutGetResponses OBJECT-TYPE

SYNTAX   Counter
ACCESS   read-only
STATUS   mandatory
DESCRIPTION

"The total number of SNMP Get-Response PDUs
which have been generated by the SNMP protocol
entity."

::= { snmp 28 }

snmpOutTraps OBJECT-TYPE

SYNTAX   Counter
ACCESS   read-only
STATUS   mandatory
DESCRIPTION

> "The total number of SNMP Trap PDUs which have been generated by the SNMP protocol entity."

::= { snmp 29 }

snmpEnableAuthenTraps OBJECT-TYPE

SYNTAX   INTEGER { enabled(1), disabled(2) }
ACCESS   read-write
STATUS mandatory
DESCRIPTION

> "Indicates whether the SNMP agent process is permitted to generate authentication-failure traps. The value of this object overrides any configuration information; as such, it provides a means whereby all authentication-failure traps may be disabled.
>
> Note that it is strongly recommended that this object be stored in non-volatile memory so that it remains constant between re-initializations of the network management system."

::= { snmp 30 }

Index